PARENTAL RESPONSIBILITY, YOUNG CHILDREN AND HEALTHCARE LAW

This book provides a critical analysis of the law governing the provision of healthcare to young and dependent children, identifying an understanding of the child as vulnerable and in need of protection, including from his or her own parents. The argument is made for a conceptual framework of relational responsibilities which would ensure that consideration is given to the needs of the child as an individual and to the experiences of parents gained as they care for their child, and the wider context, such as attitudes towards disability, public health issues or the support and resources available, is examined. This book will make an important contribution to understanding the law regulating the provision of healthcare to young and dependent children and to the development of a discourse on responsibility.

JO BRIDGEMAN is a Senior Lecturer at the Sussex Law School, University of Sussex. She has published widely in the fields of healthcare law and children.

PARENTAL RESPONSIBILITY, YOUNG CHILDREN AND HEALTHCARE LAW

JO BRIDGEMAN

CAMBRIDGE
UNIVERSITY PRESS

CAMBRIDGE UNIVERSITY PRESS
Cambridge, New York, Melbourne, Madrid, Cape Town, Singapore, São Paulo

Cambridge University Press
The Edinburgh Building, Cambridge CB2 2RU, UK

Published in the United States of America by Cambridge University Press, New York

www.cambridge.org
Information on this title: www.cambridge.org/9780521863124

First published 2007

Printed in the United Kingdom at the University Press, Cambridge

A catalogue record for this publication is available from the British Library

ISBN   978-0-521-86312-4 hardback

To my family

CONTENTS

ACKNOWLEDGEMENTS

This book is the result of the natural development of my research from the law regulating the healthcare of adolescents and women to that governing the health of children which occurred, in part, due to the arrival of George and, a few years later, Arthur. It is also an attempt to develop a sustained analysis of the law from the perspective of the feminist ethic of care which for me continues to provide, intellectually and instinctively, a compelling critique of two central issues of law – the nature of the self and the resolution of dilemmas. It was important to me that I provide an academic argument for recognition of the care taken by the vast majority of parents for their children. It was my own mother, in a conversation about the concepts which defined parenthood, who identified responsibility as the central way of thinking about and experience of parenthood. That the law has defined the relationship of parent to child in terms of responsibility without giving it proper definition left the way open for an examination of the concept of parental responsibility through consideration of parents who take responsibility for meeting the healthcare needs of their child.

There are many people to thank for giving me support in the process of writing this book. Malcolm Ross, as Head of Department at the Sussex Law School, has been an enormous source of support and encouragement throughout as well as providing insightful and extremely useful comments upon an earlier draft of a substantial part of the book. The Child and Family Law Research Group in the department has provided an excellent forum for discussion of the concept of relational responsibility through comparison with other concepts of responsibility in the family. Colleagues have also read drafts of this work at various stages and by their contributions helped me to clarify my argument, for which I thank Craig Barker and Heather Keating.

In a different way, I have received enormous support from my friends. Their interest and their positive reaction to the argument I have presented, whether it was on a summer walk on the Downs or over a winter supper, provided a great source of encouragement. But most of all, I must thank all my family for their interest, support and encouragement: in particular, David, for his practical and emotional support, for understanding and for being there; and George and Arthur, who cannot believe how long it can take to write one book. Tonight, when they return from playing with their friends, and ask as they have now for weeks, 'Have you finished the book yet?' I'll be able to give them the answer they are looking for.

TABLE OF CASES

TABLE OF LEGISLATION AND INTERNATIONAL INSTRUMENTS

1

Parents, young children and healthcare law

Introduction

Being a parent brings with it manifold social, moral and legal responsibilities in relation to the physical, emotional and intellectual growth and development of the child as well as his or her safety, security, happiness and well-being. The purpose of this book is to examine the role of parents in caring for the health and well-being of young and dependent children. In the chapters which follow there is an examination of the range of care undertaken by parents from the everyday management of the health of children, to the demands placed upon parents whose child has a life-threatening illness or long-term disabilities, or whose future survival is uncertain due to disabilities arising from prematurity, complications during birth or accidental injury. In addition to undertaking an examination of the existing legal obligations imposed upon parents, this book makes the argument for a new conceptual framework to govern the role of parents in relation to the health of their children. Rather than argue for a legal framework firmly grounded in the rights of young and dependent children, as many commentators do, this book makes the argument for a legal framework situated within the responsibilities of parents and healthcare professionals for the management of children's health.

This book considers the responsibilities of parents and professionals in relation to the health of children who, by virtue of their age, or mental and physical impairments, are dependent upon others to ensure their health and well-being. Whilst newborn (up to twenty-eight days old) and infant (under the age of one) children are totally dependent upon others to interpret and meet their needs, at a young age – four or five, perhaps younger – children will, to varying extents, contribute to maintenance of their health and well-being. They will be able to take some responsibility for their daily care: for example, washing their hands and cleaning their teeth.

Furthermore, young children can be participants in their healthcare: for example, reporting symptoms, taking medicine, sitting still whilst a wound is tended or immunisation administered by injection. By this age, children will be able to understand explanations given in appropriate language and manner and thus can be involved in decisions about their healthcare before they start school. Each child is different. Indeed, that this should be recognised by the law is a central argument of this book. The extent to which each child wants, and is able, to be actively involved in their healthcare will vary. Whilst we would not expect a child of this age to take responsibility, we can demonstrate respect for each child as an individual person by involving them, consulting them and considering their views on the benefits and harms of what is proposed.[1] The extent to which each child can be involved is not only dependent upon the individual child but upon the appropriateness of the explanations given, the willingness of the caring adults to listen to the child and the circumstances in which such an exchange takes place. The responsibility of parents for the healthcare of their young and dependent child not only involves negotiations with healthcare workers but further involves negotiation with the child and, where the child is unable to express his or her views and feelings, careful consideration of their child's needs.

Whilst for most families care of their children remains a private matter, it was the scandal of the 'Bristol Heart Babies' and the revelations about the widespread retention of organs from deceased children which brought to public attention the neglect of children's healthcare services against the concern of parents to secure the best possible healthcare for their children. The evidence of parents to the Bristol Inquiry highlighted the responsibility taken by parents for securing professional help for their child's condition and for working together with professionals to ensure that their child received the best possible care. The revelations about the inadequate quality of care provided at Bristol left many parents with feelings of guilt arising from a sense that they had failed in their responsibility to their child. The abject horror, the raw distress, of parents who subsequently discovered

---

[1] Jane Fortin emphasises the distinction between children having the right to make decisions and the right to participation and consultation recognised in Article 12(1) of the United Nations Convention on the Rights of the Child, 1989. The latter recognises the importance of involving the child in decisions, even when the child is not considered to be an autonomous individual, without imposing responsibility for the decision upon the child: Jane Fortin, *Children's Rights and the Developing Law*, Reed Elsevier: London, 2003, at pp. 19–20.

that parts of their children's bodies were retained has been widely reported in terms which demonstrate sympathetic appreciation of their plight. That much of the attention has been directed at the retention of organs from children's bodies and less at the widespread common practice of retaining the organs of adults can be better understood in light of the particular value attributed to the child and the intimate relationship between children and those caring for them in our society:[2]

> Indisputably, over the past two, or at most three, decades childhood has moved to the forefront of personal, political and academic agendas and not solely in the West. The moving spirit of this process is extremely complex and can be seen to involve an entanglement of factors such as: a structural re-adjustment to time and mortality in the face of quickening social change; a re-evaluation and a re-positioning of personhood given the disassembly of traditional categories of identity and difference; a search for a moral centre or at least an anchor for trust in response to popular routine cynicism; and an age-old desire to invest in futures now rendered urgent.[3]

The majority of parents will be spared the responsibility of deciding whether a very sick child should undergo life-threatening and potentially life-saving surgery. Most will not be faced with the decision whether their newborn babies should undergo separation surgery offering the chance of survival to one but causing the inevitable death of the other, as did the parents of Jodie and Mary, now known to be Gracie Rosie and Rosie Gracie Attard.[4] Courts have been asked to resolve disputes between parents and professionals concerning the healthcare of children, thereby establishing the legal framework for the respective duties of parents and professionals with regard to the healthcare needs of children. It is the premise of this book that judgments about the health of children need to be informed by a full consideration of the difficult issues confronting parents and professionals as they attempt to fulfil their responsibilities to children such as Jaymee Bowen,[5]

---

[2] Jo Bridgeman, 'When Systems Fail: Parents, Children and the Quality of Healthcare' (2005) 58 *Current Legal Problems*, Jane Holder and Colm O'Cinneide (eds.), Oxford University Press: Oxford, 183–213.

[3] Chris Jenks, 'Sociological Perspectives and Media Representations of Childhood' in Julia Fionda (ed.), *Legal Concepts of Childhood*, Hart: Oxford, 2001, 19–42, at p. 22.

[4] *Re A (Children) (Conjoined Twins: Surgical Separation)* [2001] 2 WLR 480: considered in chapters 4 and 5.

[5] *R v Cambridge District Health Authority, ex parte B* [1995] 1 FLR 1055: considered in chapter 2.

Charlotte Wyatt,[6] David Glass,[7] Luke Winston-Jones[8] and all those children who remain anonymous in order to protect them and those caring for them from, amongst other things, intrusive media attention. This chapter explains the theoretical perspective from which the critique of the law governing the provision of healthcare to babies, infants, young and dependent children is undertaken. It ends with an outline of the chapters which follow to guide the reader through the book and point them to chapters which may be of particular relevance or interest.

The legal construction of the young child

Perspectives on childhood

Although as Eva Kittay reminds us in *Love's Labor* we are all 'a mother's child',[9] when we refer to 'child' we are more commonly referring to a particular type of person – one who is currently at a stage of biological, intellectual and emotional immaturity. But what we mean by 'child' is not simply a known given, rather, it is a cultural, social and legal construction. Contemporary concepts of 'child' within England and Wales are culturally and historically specific understandings of the characteristics, abilities, values and priorities of the child and not those of an individual child at a given time in relation to a specific issue. Current constructions of child within law and policy have been influenced by a history of ideas from a range of disciplines, including philosophy, sociology and psychology.[10]

As philosopher David Archard has pointed out, both the concept of childhood[11] (the understanding that children are different from adults)

---

[6] *Portsmouth NHS Trust v Wyatt and Wyatt, Southampton NHS Trust Intervening* [2004] EWHC 2247 (7 October 2004); *Portsmouth Hospitals NHS Trust v Wyatt and others* [2005] EWHC 117 (Fam) (28 January 2005); Unreported [2005] EWCA Civ 185 (9 February 2005); *Wyatt v Portsmouth NHS Trust and Wyatt (By her Guardian) (No. 3)* [2005] EWHC 693 (Fam) (21 April 2005); *Wyatt and another v Portsmouth Hospital NHS and another* [2005] EWCA Civ 1181 (12 October 2005); *Re Wyatt* [2005] EWHC 2293 (Fam) (21 October 2005); *Re Wyatt* [2006] EWHC 319 (23 February 2006): considered in chapter 5.

[7] *R v Portsmouth Hospitals NHS Trust, ex parte Glass*, 50 BMLR 269 (web.lexis-nexis.com/professional/) and *R v Portsmouth Hospitals NHS Trust, ex parte Glass* [1999] 2 FLR 905; *Glass v United Kingdom* [2004] 1 FLR 1019: considered in chapter 5.

[8] *Re L (Medical Treatment: Benefit)* [2004] EWHC 2713 (Fam): considered in chapter 5.

[9] Eva Feder Kittay, *Love's Labor: Essays on Women, Equality and Dependency*, Routledge: New York, 1999, at p. 23.

[10] Alison Diduck, *Law's Families*, LexisNexis UK: London, 2003, at p. 74.

[11] As David Archard explains, this is not a singular concept, rather multiple, contradictory and inconsistent concepts co-exist: *Children: Rights and Childhood*, Routledge: London, 2004, at pp. 27–9.

and the specific conception of the particular ways in which children differ
from adults take the adult as the point of comparison. Children are not-
adults, 'not-men':[12] dependent in contrast to adult independence; innocent
or ignorant in contrast to the experience of adulthood; irrational and
capricious rather than rational and reasoned. By their difference, their lack,
the child gives definition to the particular characteristics which identify an
individual as an adult.[13]

> The ideal adult is equipped with certain cognitive capacities, is rational,
> physically independent and autonomous, has a sense of identity, and is
> conscious of her beliefs and desires, and thus able to make informed
> free choices for which she can be held personally responsible . . .
>   Childhood is defined as that which lacks the capacities, skills and
> powers of adulthood. To be a child is to be not yet an adult. Adulthood
> is something which is gained, and although there may be losses in
> leaving childhood behind, what is lost tends to be construed as that
> which could never possibly serve the adult in an adult world.[14]

This lack is not permanent. Unlike 'women, animals, madmen,
foreigners, slaves, patients and imbeciles'[15] children have the potential
to develop their capacities: that is, the potential to develop the rationality and reason required of citizens to consent to authority and exercise
their rights.[16] Indeed, the development by children of these capacities is
considered a normal, ordinary, expected and natural process. As Alan
Prout and Allison James explain, in the twentieth century psychological
approaches to child development dominated, with material impact
upon child-rearing practices, educational theory and the law.[17] This
natural developmentalism resulted in a focus within sociology upon the
socialisation of the child,[18] and rendered natural the confinement of
children to the private sphere whilst they develop the capacities and

---

[12] Judith Hughes, 'The Philosopher's Child' in Morwenna Griffiths and Margaret Whitford (eds.),
  Feminist Perspectives in Philosophy, Macmillan: Hampshire 1988, 72–89, at p. 72, 'in contrast
  with which male philosophers have defined and valued themselves'.
[13] *Supra*, n. 11, at p. 29.   [14] *Ibid.*, at p. 39.   [15] *Supra*, n. 12, at p. 72.
[16] Barbara Arneil, 'Becoming versus Being: A Critical Analysis of the Child in Liberal Theory' in
  David Archard and Colin Macleod (eds.), *The Moral and Political Status of Children*, Oxford
  University Press: Oxford, 2002, 70–94, at p. 70.
[17] Alan Prout and Allison James, 'A New Paradigm for the Sociology of Childhood? Provenance,
  Promise and Problems' in Allison James and Alan Prout (eds.), *Constructing and Reconstructing
  Childhood: Contemporary Issues in the Sociological Study of Childhood*, Falmer Press: London,
  1997, at p. 9.   [18] *Ibid.*, at p. 12.

learn the appropriate behaviour of adulthood. Acceptable adulthood is the natural end of a process, whether the child originates from a position of innocence or evil:

> Locke's idea of the child as a blank slate, his empirical developmentalism, can be contrasted with the moral developmentalism of Thomas Hobbes, who theorised children as innately evil and therefore in need of taming and saving on their way to adulthood, or that of Rousseau who thought children were born with a natural goodness, clarity of vision and innocence. These conflicting ideas of 'immanent childhood' remain in modern policy.[19]

Possessed of this potential, the focus of concern has been the protection of the autonomous adult the child will become, with a failure to see children as living, active, contributing persons.

The new sociology of childhood, most notably the work of Chris Jenks, Allison James and Alan Prout,[20] exposes the discursive construction of the concept of 'childhood'. Various constructions of childhood have been identified across academic disciplines and historical periods of study: James, Jenks and Prout identify the evil child, the innocent child, the immanent child, the naturally developing child and the unconscious child.[21] The construction of the child as evil presents the child as 'demonic, harbourers of potentially dark forces which risk being mobilized if, by dereliction or inattention, the adult world allows them to veer away from the "straight and narrow" path that civilization has bequeathed to them'.[22] The innocent child is portrayed as pure and uncorrupted, living according to values which adults would do well to attempt to emulate.[23] The immanent child is understood to embody potential, a future person, 'becoming', but is a blank canvas requiring the right environment for appropriate development.[24] And the naturally developing child hurdles over milestones to the inevitable achievement of adulthood and must along their route be subjected to 'measuring, grading, ranking and assessing', compared against other children and against the 'norm'.[25]

---

[19] *Supra*, n. 10, at p. 75.
[20] Chris Jenks, *Childhood*, Routledge: London, 1996; Allison James and Alan Prout (eds.), *Constructing and Reconstructing Childhood: Contemporary Issues in the Sociological Study of Childhood*, Falmer Press: London, 1997; Allison James, Chris Jenks and Alan Prout, *Theorizing Childhood*, Polity Press: Cambridge, 1998; Allison James and Adrian James, *Constructing Childhood: Theory, Policy and Social Practice*, Palgrave Macmillan, Basingstoke, 2004.   [21] James, Jenks and Prout, *Ibid.*, at pp. 10–21.   [22] *Ibid.*, at pp. 10–13, p. 10.
[23] *Ibid.*, at pp. 13–15.   [24] *Ibid.*, at pp. 15–17.   [25] *Ibid.*, at pp. 17–19, p. 19.

There may be competing and conflicting constructions of the child within any particular discourse – for example, the child as both innocent and inherently evil – or one understanding of the idea of child may come to dominate. Either way, constructions of the child operate to silence alternative understandings of what children are, provided, for example, through the experiences of children themselves or of those involved in caring for them. The discursive construction of child thus influences the way in which children are understood and consequently treated in, for example, law. Constructions of the child as innocent, lacking capacity, as *becoming*, can inhibit awareness of children as agents, as *beings* who are not merely the object of concern but subjects actively participating in life. To understand that ideas of child are constructed by discourses and that these ideas have a material impact upon the treatment of children opens up the opportunity for recognition of children's different experiences and identities. Appreciation of the agency of children has had an impact upon some academic writing about children and the law,[26] and some influence upon the extent to which older children have been recognised as being able to participate in decisions affecting their lives. There has been less readiness within academic writing, case law and policy developments to embrace the agency of younger children.

The young child in healthcare law

Children have been treated within law not as legal subjects but as objects of their parents:

> They have been reified, treated as objects of intervention rather than as legal subjects, labelled as a 'problem population', reduced to being seen as property. They complete a family rather as the standard consumer durables furnish a household.[27]

One of the reasons for this, Katherine O'Donovan has argued, is the perception that the child lacks the capacities of a legal subject:

---

[26] In relation to healthcare, in the work of Priscilla Alderson and Jonathan Montgomery, *Health Care Choices: Making Decisions with Children*, IPPR: London, 1996; Fortin, *supra*, n.1; Alison Diduck, 'Solicitors and Legal Subjects' and Hilary Lim and Jeremy Roche, 'Feminism and Children's Rights' in Jo Bridgeman and Daniel Monk (eds.), *Feminist Perspectives on Child Law*, Cavendish: London, 2000.

[27] Michael D. A. Freeman, 'Taking Children's Rights More Seriously' (1992) 6 *International Journal of Law and the Family* 52–71, at p. 54.

There is a space in legal discourse, an emptiness, where a child's individuality should be. General social conditions of children's vulnerability and dependence largely account for this, but also, perhaps, adult power. There are reasons of legal method also. Consider, for example, the standard legal subject that legal discourse constructs for itself. This subject is rational and reasonable, qualities that law does not attribute to children.[28]

This legal subject has been subjected to scrutiny and analysis by feminists:

> The public subject of Western law was born out of this way of thinking about the self: as one who is sovereign to himself, a self-possessing being, essentially a creature of reason – of the mind – autonomous and self-determining . . . The legally regulated subject of the public realm was, and largely remains, also an impersonal, rationally instrumental being. In the public realm, life is appropriately conducted at a physical and emotional distance and 'individuals secure their agreement through contract', not through trust and affection . . . In the public sphere, legal subjects relate as minds, not as sexed bodies: physical and emotional autonomy and separation are intrinsic to the traditional legal ideal of public life.[29]

This public subject of law stands in opposition to the female subject, confined to the private, theoretically beyond the reach of the law, and existing as non-subject, 'other' to, whilst defining the boundaries of, the public subject of, law.[30] It is my argument, demonstrated in the analysis of the law which follows, that the child is similarly positioned within healthcare law as 'other' to the legal subject. An approach to the legal regulation of the provision of healthcare to children which is based upon this understanding fails to accord with the reality of the lives of young children and leads to an inadequate response within law.

Infants, babies and young children are vulnerable and potential beings, dependent upon others to meet their needs – emotionally, physically and financially – for protection and nurture. This way, children grow and develop physically, intellectually and emotionally. The dependency of young children highlights the relationship which they have with those upon whom they depend for food, water, shelter, support, stimulation and

---

[28] Katherine O'Donovan, *Family Law Matters*, Pluto Press: London, 1993, at p. 90.

[29] Ngaire Naffine, 'Sexing the Subject (of Law)' in M. Thornton (ed.), *Public and Private: Feminist Legal Debates*, Oxford University Press: Australia, 1995, 18–39, at pp. 23–4.

[30] *Ibid.*, at p. 26.

encouragement, and love. As Alison Diduck has argued, by virtue of their dependence, young children challenge traditional ways of understanding the self:

> [A] child becomes the best example of the embodiment of a connected, interdependent subject. Unlike adult subjectivity, this intimate and dependent subjectivity is difficult for liberal notions of justice to accommodate, based as they are on abstracted autonomy, independence and disconnection from other subjects and social conditions.[31]

But it is my argument, developed in the chapters which follow, that young children are understood and treated within healthcare law as nothing more than dependent, vulnerable and in need of protection. In order to protect them, decisions are made according to the welfare or best interests of the child.[32] The welfare principle is the vehicle through which adults can protect the child, giving effect to *their* understanding of what is best for the child.[33] Yet, unless consideration is given to the individual child, to the person they are, their personality, character, feelings of pleasure and pain, and relational interests (relationships with those upon whom they depend), determinations about the best interests of the child are reached according to current ideas about the child and according to adult memories of childhood.

Studies of parents' experiences of caring for their children identify the ways in which parents appreciate their child as a person, as a distinct individual with their own character.[34] The study by Priscilla Alderson, Joanna Hawthorn and Margaret Killen of parents of premature newborn babies in neonatal intensive care identified ways in which the character of their baby differed from others. They note how the babies in their study 'appeared to express hurt, misery, calm, contentment, relief, pleasure and excitement'.[35] They noticed how the babies in neonatal intensive care put a lot of effort, physical and mental, into surviving,[36] and further that parents and

---

[31] Alison Diduck, 'Justice and Childhood: Reflections on Refashioned Boundaries' in Michael King (ed.), *Moral Agendas for Children's Welfare*, Routledge: London 1999, 120–37 at pp. 124–5.

[32] *Supra*, n.28. at p.90.

[33] Ann Oakley, 'Women and Children First and Last: Parallels and Differences between Children's and Women's Studies' in Berry Mayall (ed.), *Children's Childhoods: Observed and Experienced*, Falmer Press: London, 1994, 13–32, at pp. 16, 28.

[34] Berry Mayall and Marie-Claude Foster, *Child Health Care: Living with Children, Working for Children*, Oxford: Heinemann Nursing, 1989, at p. 18.

[35] Priscilla Alderson, Joanna Hawthorn and Margaret Killen, 'The Participation Rights of Premature Babies' (2005) 13 *International Journal of Children's Rights* 31–50, at p. 40.

[36] *Ibid.*, at p. 39.

professionals talked of babies both fighting for life and appearing to have had enough. Babies, they argue, '"speak" in an expressive language of sounds, facial expressions and body movements that can be "read"'.[37]

Appreciation that even premature newborn babies have characters and personalities, different levels of tolerance of pain and of medical interventions and different attitudes to life provides the starting point for the required recognition of the individuality of young children and their needs as determined by the child themselves. What becomes important is that adults who are responsible for caring for them pay attention to the child and learn to interpret their expressed needs. Whilst purporting to assess the best interests of the individual child, there is little reference in reported judgments to the child as an individual. Within judgments given in cases considering the medical treatment of young children the child is present as an ideal rather than as a real child with feelings, preferences, attitudes and needs. A desire to ensure that the child survives can preclude honest assessment of the harm and hurt involved, the pain and distress to which they will be exposed or the ability of the child to cope with their condition or treatment. As Priscilla Alderson has argued: 'the view that all means possible should be pursued in order to preserve life, so that in the future the patient may attain or regain full autonomy, can reinforce medical dominance with legal coercion, preventing individual responses to patients'.[38] A focus upon the future adult the child could become can result in a failure to see the child as a person living their life. Or, conversely, due to limited understanding and prejudiced views, the child may be seen as lacking the potential for adulthood, with inadequate appreciation of the quality of life of a disabled child. And, in cases considering obligations to disabled children, there is no examination of the responsibility taken by parents to meet their child's needs or acknowledgement of the impact upon their ability to care of the resources available to them, environmental obstacles and discriminatory attitudes.

Parents and liberal individualism

Within the discourse of healthcare law, there is a further prevailing understanding: liberal individualism. Within liberal individualism, persons are perceived as primarily separate individuals who can, by free agreement,

---

[37] *Ibid.*, at p. 34.

[38] Priscilla Alderson, 'Consent to Children's Surgery and Intensive Medical Treatment' (1990) 17 *Journal of Law and Society* 52–65, at p. 56.

enter into relationships with others. The principal value of the liberal individual is autonomy to exercise choice and seek fulfilment of one's own desires. The primary concern of separate individuals is to protect their selves from invasion or infringement by others.[39] However, all individuals exercise their autonomy and pursue their own ends within the shadow of the possibility of conflict arising from a clash of interests individually desired. Criminal and civil laws place limits upon the selfish pursuit of individual interest and seek to protect the individual from invasion of the boundaries of their bodies.

The inevitable dependency of young children, noted above, confounds this understanding of the self. Young children rely upon others to meet their needs, being primarily connected to, rather than primarily separate from, parents who care for them. They depend upon others to assess their wishes and to fulfil them. They rely upon others for protection from harm and to determine when to agree to the invasion of their bodily boundaries. Likewise, parents fail to accord with this understanding of the individual in their attentiveness to, concern for and care of their children. Parents do not selfishly pursue their own goals but make sacrifices to meet the needs of their children. Their relationship with their children can be more accurately characterised by concern than conflict.

Liberal individualism, irreconcilable as it is with the reality of the parental role, prevails once issues about the provision of healthcare to children come to court. The combined effect of abstract individualism, which conceives of adults as self-interested, isolated individuals who are first and foremost separate but can choose to enter into relationships, with the legal construction of childhood results in an approach within law to the child as in need of protection from his or her parents. I argue that the understanding of the child as mere potential, a 'becoming', must be replaced with attentiveness to the particular child. And, from an original position of primary connection not primary separation of parent and child, I argue for recognition of the particular interest which a parent has in the well-being of his or her child and of their expertise gained as they care.

Before developing this understanding of the parent/child relationship, it is necessary to consider the moral status of the child as person and the rights of the child.

---

[39] Robin West, 'Jurisprudence and Gender' (1988) 55 *University of Chicago Law Review* 1–72, at pp. 1–12.

Personhood

Liberal moral philosophy has traditionally conceived of personhood in terms of capacity and rationality, with the effect of excluding young children from the moral status of persons and, consequently, from entitlement to enjoyment of moral rights. John Locke, for example, considered that to qualify for personhood, it is necessary to demonstrate the qualities of 'a thinking intelligent being, that has reason and reflection, and can consider itself as itself, the same thinking thing, in different times and places'.[40] Similarly, Peter Singer identifies the characteristics of personhood as rationality, self-awareness and the capacity to see 'itself as existing in different times and places'.[41]

The newborn babies, infants and young children considered in this book will not possess these characteristics nor those which John Harris believes to be necessary for qualification to the moral status of a 'person'. This is because, in his view, what makes us persons is the 'capacity to value life'.[42] He explains that he is referring to a capacity (which does not need to be exercised to count) and that potential (which newborn babies do possess) is not sufficient. What is required is an awareness of life: a person is 'aware of itself as an independent centre of consciousness, existing over time with a future that it was capable of envisaging and wishing to experience . . . For each individual life has unique value and that value is determined by what the individual wants to do with his or her own life.'[43] A conceptualisation of moral personhood around self-knowledge and future-oriented preoccupation does, at least, recognise that individuals may value different things about their lives and that there must be mutual respect for the value each accords to his or her own life. It is, however, a narrow formulation which excludes human beings who are incapacitated by illness, disability or age who would be considered by those around

[40] John Locke, *An Essay Concerning Human Understanding*, P. H. Nidditch (ed.), Oxford University Press: New York, 1987, 1.27.11, quoted in Eva Feder Kittay, 'When Caring is Just and Justice is Caring: Justice and Mental Retardation' in Eva Feder Kittay and Ellen K. Feder (eds.), *The Subject of Care: Feminist Perspectives on Dependency*, Rowman and Littlefield: Lanham, 2002, at p. 262.

[41] Peter Singer, *Rethinking Life and Death: The Collapse of our Traditional Ethics*, Oxford University Press: Oxford, 1995, at p. 210. He concludes that killing a newborn baby (who lacks these characteristics) is not as morally wrong as killing a person and provides justification for giving weight to the wishes of parents as those most closely connected to the child and upon whom the existence of the child has the greatest impact, at p. 212.

[42] John Harris, *The Value of Life: An Introduction to Medical Ethics*, Routledge and Kegan Paul: London, 1985, at p. 17.   [43] *Ibid.*, at pp. 18 and 194.

them to be moral persons. Thus, John Harris considers the ethical justification for the decision that separation of the conjoined twins, Jodie and Mary, was lawful to rest in their lack of personhood.[44] As neither Mary nor Jodie were moral persons, according to John Harris, the court was justified in declaring that the separation surgery was lawful. At the same time, he suggests that the hospital would have been acting lawfully had they respected the refusal of consent of the twins' parents. Yet, the professionals caring for the twins clearly responded to them as two, if physically joined, persons, and the reasons given by the parents for their refusal of consent are based in their appreciation of the personhood of both of their daughters.

It was consideration of her own daughter, who has cerebral palsy and severe mental disabilities, that led philosopher Eva Feder Kittay to reconsider traditional concepts of personhood which, based upon requirements of reason and capacity, exclude the very young, very old and the disabled. She proposed a relational concept of personhood in which personhood is dependent upon connections with others, possession of an individuality recognised by others and the ability to have an impact upon each other's lives:

> I propose that being a person means having the capacity to be in certain relationships with other persons, to sustain contact with other persons, to shape one's own world and the world of others, and to have a life that another person can conceive of as an imaginative possibility for him- or herself ... We do not become a person without the engagement of other persons – their care, as well as their recognition of the uniqueness and the connectedness of our human agency, and the distinctiveness of our particularly human relations to others and of the world we fashion.[45]

This conceptualisation of personhood recognises all children as moral persons, irrespective of their capacities. It resonates much more closely with the views of parents, evidenced for example in the study by Priscilla Alderson et al. noted above, who perceive their newborn child to be a person with a distinct and unique personality and with the impact which a newborn child has upon those around him or her. It recognises the value with which parents hold their child even at the point at which the child

---

[44] John Harris, 'Human Beings, Persons and Conjoined Twins: An Ethical Analysis of the Judgment in *Re A*' (2001) 9 Med Law Rev 221–36, at pp. 235–6.

[45] Kittay, *supra*, n. 40, at p. 266.

lacks awareness of their self as an independent existence and at which the child lacks any concept of the future. In this formulation, lives are valued even when the person lacks the capacity to value their own life. This notion of personhood is consistent with the understanding of the child as a living being situated in relationships with his or her parents; the self in relationship constitutive of responsibility: connected, attached and concerned rather than unattached, unaffected and individualistic.

However, it should be noted that, whilst moral personhood is concerned with how we should treat each other, within law the position is that legal personhood is attained at the moment of a live birth – adopting a biological, scientific model to personhood ascribed at an identifiable biological moment.[46] The newborn is entitled to the same protection of the law as is afforded to others.[47]

The nature and scope of children's rights

This book advocates a conceptual framework of responsibility[48] to underpin the legal regulation of the provision of healthcare to young children: just what I mean by that is considered below. It is first necessary to address the rights of young children to explain why I do not think the issue of the legal regulation of the provision of healthcare to children is best approached through a framework of children's rights.

The nature of the rights of children has been open to much discussion, disagreement and debate. There is the clear distinction between legal and moral rights; the former recognised in law and the latter determined on the basis of moral arguments. The first debate concerns whether children are holders of moral rights. Theories of rights offer us either the will or choice theory of

[46] As Ngaire Naffine identifies, this legal understanding of personhood is thus exposed to biological disputes over the beginning of life and the start of the process of death and to social and cultural understandings of personhood: 'Who are Law's Persons? From Cheshire Cats to Responsible Subjects' (2003) 66 MLR 346–67, at pp. 359–60.

[47] Enabling, at common law, an action to be brought in respect of injuries sustained prior to birth, with legal rights crystallising upon a live birth: *Burton v Islington HA; De Martell v Merton and Sutton HA* [1993] QB 204. Births after 22 July 1976 are covered by the Congenital Disabilities (Civil Liability) Act 1976 which gives a child born alive and surviving for at least forty-eight hours an action in respect of injury or disease caused by negligence prior to birth in circumstances actionable by the child's mother or father. Criminal proceedings may be brought for manslaughter where a child is born alive but subsequently dies from injuries sustained *in utero: Attorney-General's Reference (No. 3 of 1994)* [1998] AC 245.

[48] Mary Urban Walker, *Moral Understandings: A Feminist Study in Ethics*, Routledge: New York, 1998, at p. 78.

rights or the welfare or interest theory of rights.[49] In the former, rights are conceived of as choices which impose duties or obligations upon others and are dependent upon the power to enforce the duty to secure the right or to waive it. The problem of relying upon the will theory for the moral basis of children's rights, particularly young children's rights, is immediately apparent, as babies, infants, young and dependent children lack the capacity to enforce their choices. Consequently, the will theory of children's rights tends to be adopted by those focusing upon the rights of older children whose capacity to express their choices most closely approximates adult reasoning. The alternative, the interest theory, is not dependent upon this enforceability but conceives of rights as arising from interests of such importance that they should be recognised by imposing moral duties upon others to act or refrain from acting. This, however, raises the question of which interests are to give rise to moral rights and, in turn, which moral rights translate into legal rights.[50] Consequently, beyond the question of whether children can be rights-holders is the further question of what rights they have – the content or scope of children's rights.

David Archard explains how, if we wish to distinguish the rights enjoyed by adults from those enjoyed by children, we can follow Feinberg's distinction between rights exclusive to adults, those shared by both adults and children and those exclusive to children. In this formulation, adults alone enjoy liberty rights, dependent as they are upon the capacity to choose, such as the right to vote or to freedom of expression. Welfare rights of all include, for example, the right to healthcare. Children enjoy rights of protection. These include the right to goods they cannot secure for themselves given their dependence upon adults (food, clothing, warmth); the right to protection from harms to which their dependence makes them vulnerable (abuse and neglect) and the right to goods which should be given to children, such as the right to be loved.[51] This latter category is specific to the

[49] David William Archard, *Children, Family and the State*, Ashgate: Hampshire, 2003, at pp. 4–9; Jane Fortin, *Children's Rights and the Developing Law*, Reed Elsevier: London, 2003, at pp. 13–15; Tom D. Campbell, 'The Rights of the Minor: As Person, As Child, As Juvenile, As Future Adult' in Philip Alston, Stephen Parker and John Seymour (eds.), *Children, Rights and the Law*, Clarendon Press: Oxford, 1992, 1–23, at pp. 4–5.

[50] And further the relationship between interest-based rights and welfare: '[t]he interest theory permits us to indulge in the apparently dubious practice of justifying the coercion of individuals by an appeal to their rights on the basis that paternalistic interventions can protect the vital interests of those who are thereby constrained'. Campbell, *ibid.*, at p. 6.

[51] Archard, *supra*, n. 49, at pp. 29–31, considering J. Feinberg, 'The Child's Right to an Open Future' in W. Aiken and H. La Follette (eds.), *Whose Child? Parental Rights, Parental Authority and State Power*, Totowa, NJ: Rowman and Littlefield, 1980, 124–53.

state of childhood. Others have devised different categorisations. Tom Campbell distinguishes between rights arising from children's interests as persons (universal rights such as the right to life), as children (and hence in a particular state of dependency), as juveniles and as future adults (rights concerned with development to adulthood).[52] Barbara Arneil considers the rights of children to provision, protection and autonomy, noting that analysis of children's rights tends to focus upon the latter.[53] John Eekelaar distinguishes between children's basic, developmental and autonomy interests, the last being subject to the others.[54] He recognises that the interests of the young child will be claimed as rights by parents acting as the agent of the child involving an 'imaginative leap and guess what a child might retrospectively have wanted once it reaches a position of maturity. In doing this, values of the adult world and of individual adults will inevitably enter.'[55]

Children have rights which may include the right to food, housing, education and care, to protection from abuse, neglect and danger, and to be loved (or, at least, they have interests in all of these things), which are important assertions, in their abstract, of interests which impose duties upon both their parents and the state. Michael Freeman has argued that we need to take 'children's rights more seriously'[56] in order to improve children's lives through recognition 'of humanity, of integrity, of individuality [and] of personality'.[57] His argument is that recognition of rights, establishing minimum entitlements, is necessary to protect children from abuse and neglect; that to focus upon the responsibilities of parents is to adopt a rose-tinted view of children's lives and parents in a world in which children are neglected and abused. He counters the argument that there are other morally significant values with the response that rights are necessary given the particular vulnerability of children when children live in poverty, with hunger, disease, abuse and exploitation and without the care, love and nurturance of adults.[58] To be a rights-holder is to be recognised as an individual worthy of protection, a person of value entitled to minimum standards. To be a rights-holder is to possess a 'valuable commodity',[59] to

---

[52] *Supra*, n. 49, Campbell, at pp. 16–23.   [53] *Supra*, n. 16, at pp. 75–88.

[54] John Eekelaar, 'The Emergence of Children's Rights' (1986) 6 OxJLS 161–82, acknowledging uncertainty about whether these interests amount to moral or legal rights.

[55] *Ibid.*, at p. 170.   [56] *Supra*, n. 27.   [57] *Ibid.*, at p. 56.   [58] *Ibid.*, at pp. 55–6.

[59] R. Wasserstrom, 'Rights, Human Rights and Racial Discrimination' (1964) 61 *Journal of Philosophy* 628, quoted in Michael Freeman, *The Moral Status of Children: Essays on the Rights of the Child*, Martinus Nijhoff: Netherlands, 1997, at p. 21.

hold the 'trump',[60] to have an entitlement irrespective of the consequences for the maximisation of utility.[61]

Claims to moral rights are politically important: to claim a right is empowering and rhetorically powerful. Rights establish universal minimum entitlements. Rights can be enjoyed without being asserted but possession of rights gives individuals the means by which to redress wrongs and to resolve conflict. Rights, which can either be positive, requiring action by others, or negative, restricting the actions of others, have been an important framework through which legal protections have been secured.[62]

Young and dependent children have a moral right to healthcare given legal effect by s. 1 of the Children and Young Persons Act 1933 and the Children Act 1989. It is, however, notable that, whilst being influential in terms of the way problems have been approached, neither moral nor legal rights have been directly engaged to resolve issues concerning children's healthcare. This could suggest that the argument should be made for resolution through consideration of the rights of children, parent and professional; to, as they say, bring rights home for children's health. It is perhaps with regard to decisions about the healthcare of young and dependent children that arguments have most clearly been made for recognition of children's rights, at least by academic commentators. In the sphere of children's healthcare, it is in this area of the law that the inter-relationship between children's rights, interests and welfare most directly arises. As the legal principle governing decision-making cases is the welfare or best interests of the child, there is inevitably limited 'rights talk' in the case law, with the discourse of rights in the background of welfare determinations.[63] Within academic commentary, rights are frequently invoked to challenge decisions made according to the welfare of the child. For example, in *Re T*, in which the court was asked to consent to the performance of a liver transplant

---

[60] R. Dworkin, *Taking Rights Seriously*, Duckworth: London, 1978, quoted in Freeman, *ibid.*
[61] Freeman, *ibid.*, at p. 31.   [62] *Supra*, n. 16, at p. 76.
[63] Jonathan Herring has noted that 'most leading exponents of children's rights include a powerful element of paternalism or welfarism within their description of such rights': 'Farewell Welfare?' (2005) 27 JSWFL 159–71, at p. 165. He gives as examples, John Eekelaar, 'The Interests of the Child and the Child's Wishes: The Role of Dynamic Self-Determinism' (1994) 8 *International Journal of Law and the Family* 42–63; Michael Freeman, *The Rights and Wrongs of Children*, 1983; and Jane Fortin, *Children's Rights and the Developing Law*, 2003. He suggests that these three commentators have all stressed that rights should be consistent with the protection of children from harm and that in many cases, giving the example of child protection, both a children's rights and a child welfare approach would reach the same conclusion.

operation upon an eighteen-month-old child against the refusal of his mother, Lord Justice Waite opined: 'It is not an occasion – even in an age preoccupied with "rights" – to talk of the rights of a child, or the rights of a parent, or the rights of the court.'[64] In response, Andrew Bainham wrote:

> It would of course be possible to have an interesting academic seminar on the subject of rights, but there would surely be widespread surprise, whatever the jurisprudential arguments, at the conclusion that babies do not have them. Whatever else the notion of rights may mean for children, most family lawyers would be inclined to rely on those interest theories which, fundamentally, require recognition that children have *independent* interests which can clash with those of their parents.[65]

Of course babies should be understood as persons possessed of moral and legal rights. In my reading of his judgment, Waite LJ was not seeking to deny that babies have rights; rather, he was questioning whether all difficult decisions involving the welfare of children are best resolved by invoking their rights. This is an extremely important question to ask.

Confronted with the difficult decision whether it was in Charlotte Wyatt's best interests that she be provided with artificial ventilation in the event of suffering a respiratory arrest or whether this invasive treatment should be withheld, inevitably resulting in her death, Hedley J invoked the ethical principle of sanctity of life and respect for Charlotte's 'right to dignity'.[66] In the context of a child whose life at that point was dependent upon extensive medical intervention but who continued to be alive and, confounding medical expectations, to improve, it is not obvious which course of action was more respectful of her 'right to dignity'. This is not to argue that Charlotte did not enjoy a 'right to dignity'. Rather, it is to question whether the issue of her future treatment is best resolved through analysis of her rights. Andrew Bainham notes that the conjoined twins case was determined, with only passing reference to moral rights and to those set out in the European Convention for the Protection of Human Rights and Fundamental Freedoms, 1950 (ECHR, Articles 2, 3 and 8), by the resolution of the conflicting best interests of the babies but suggests that:

> [I]n one sense this makes little difference. At the heart of the matter was a clash of values, whether those values found expression in the concept

---

[64] *Re T (a Minor) (Wardship: Medical Treatment)* [1997] 1 WLR 242, at p. 253.
[65] Andrew Bainham, 'Do Babies Have Rights?' (1997) 56 CLJ 48–50, at p. 50.
[66] *Portsmouth NHS Trust v Wyatt and Others* [2004] EWHC 2247, para. 22.

of interests or rights. The decision to authorise the procedure was taken, in the final analysis, because the court (which could not just abdicate from making a choice) attached greater weight to the value of saving the life of a child where possible, than to the competing values of freedom of religion and parental autonomy.[67]

In this article, examining the welfare principle and the rights enjoyed by all under the ECHR, Andrew Bainham seeks to determine 'what is the difference (if any) between protecting their welfare, or best interests, and giving effect to their rights?'.[68] He argues that the criticism which has been levelled at the welfare principle, of its indeterminacy, is equally applicable to children's rights: both involve assessment, ultimately by the judiciary, of the weight to be accorded to competing values.[69] Whilst considering both welfare and rights to be indeterminate and value-dependent, Andrew Bainham asserts that the benefit of a rights-based approach is to separate out the rights of all involved, thereby exposing the competing values. It is my argument, as examination of the cases considered in this book will demonstrate, that the values of rights-based approaches – individualism, abstraction and conflict – have dominated assessment of children's welfare, needs and interests in litigated disputes. Framed by individualism and a presumption of conflict, rights-influenced welfare determinations are made in abstraction from the lived reality of parent and child.

It is notable that, to date, legal rights within the ECHR now incorporated into English law by the Human Rights Act 1998 and international rights norms to be found in the United Nations Convention on the Rights of the Child, 1989 have had a minimal impact upon the law governing the provision of healthcare to children. As Jane Fortin details, the latter is of far wider scope, extending beyond political and civil rights to social, economic and cultural rights; whereas the ECHR is restricted to positive rights of respect for autonomy and placing limits upon interference by the state. This difference, she suggests, derives from the ECHR focus upon the rights of adults whilst the UN Convention is child-centred.[70] It is notable that, within the case law concerning the healthcare of children, the Human

---

[67] Andrew Bainham, 'Can We Protect Children and Protect Their Rights?' (2002) 32 *Family Law* 279–89, at p. 287. Bainham suggests that approaching the issue from a rights perspective may have resulted in greater weight being given to the duty to save Jodie's life, at p. 287. All three appeal court judges were of the view that the Human Rights Act 1998, which came into force before the surgery was performed, would not have required a different answer from the court.

[68] *Ibid.*, at p. 279.   [69] *Ibid.*, at p. 288.   [70] Fortin, *Supra*, n. 1, at p. 54.

Rights Act 1998 has resulted in increased reference to both Convention rights and the UN Convention with very little consequence – the preferred view of the judiciary being that English common law is consistent with the Convention. The limited impact of the ECHR in the context of parental decision-making about children's health is perhaps not surprising. As Jane Fortin explains, Article 8 (right to private and family life) is consistent with a policy of non-intervention in ordinary family life which is given legal effect at the domestic level by the Children Act 1989.[71] What is perhaps more surprising is that the impact of Convention rights upon English law is rarely fully examined and more frequently assumed to be inconsequential, particularly where private decision-making raises issues of the right to life or death with dignity. In relation to decision-making, the response of the European Court of Human Rights in the case of David Glass, discussed fully in chapter 5, does nothing to challenge this complacency.[72] Furthermore, there is more obvious scope for examination in relation to resource allocation, as Laws J saw in the case of Jaymee Bowen, and issues of public health such as immunisation, in which the rights of the individual and the interests of others may conflict.

Martha Minow and Mary Lyndon Shanley present an argument for family policy and law to be approached from the perspective of 'relational rights and responsibilities'.[73] They argue that '[o]ne problem with "rights-talk" applied to family policy and law has been the tendency to see familial rights as protections for individual freedom, rather than as rights that create, foster, and protect valued relationships'.[74] Relationships are implicit in rights-based theories given that the assertion of a right by one individual imposes duties to act or refrain from acting upon another. However, as Martha Minow and Mary Lyndon Shanley argue, relationships have been inadequately theorised in rights-based approaches. As they observe, in the context of the family, many rights claims are relational in that they refer to relationships between adults or between adult and child.[75] Recognition of 'relational rights and responsibilities' would, they suggest, lead to a changed understanding of the individual and of the family realm. First, family members would be understood as both individuals and as connected

---

[71] Jane Fortin, 'The HRA's Impact on Litigation involving Children and their Families' (1999) 11 CFLQ 237–55, at p. 254.   [72] *Glass v United Kingdom* [2004] 1 FLR 1019.

[73] Martha Minow and Mary Lyndon Shanley, 'Revisioning the Family: Relational Rights and Responsibilities' in Mary Lyndon Shanley and Uma Narayan (eds.), *Reconstructing Political Theory: Feminist Perspectives*, Polity Press: Cambridge, 1997, 84–108, at p. 85.

[74] *Ibid.*, at p. 95.   [75] *Ibid.*, at pp. 98–9.

to others by relationships. Secondly, there would be recognition that the private family realm is affected by public policy. Informed by a critique of contractarian, communitarian and rights-based theories, their analysis provides the basis for an enriched understanding of rights to be employed in the determination of disputes within the family. What they propose does have the advantage of being developed out of the existing dominant rights discourse of law and policy. For the reasons set out below, I think that in the context of the provision of healthcare to children, the discourse of responsibility identified in their analysis is the one which should be developed.

In a further and different response to children's rights discourse, Onora O'Neill questions whether the interests of children are best protected through moral rights, arguing that positive legal rights for children can more effectively be grounded in ethical obligations.[76] She argues that whilst perfect obligations can be understood as the correlative of rights, with obligations addressing what the actor is required to do and rights identifying what the recipient is entitled to receive, there is no correlation between imperfect obligations and rights. In her account, perfect obligations are those in relation to which it is clear upon whom the obligation is imposed and to whom it is owed. Imperfect obligations are owed to some unspecified children so that in the abstract there is no recipient.[77] Thus, whilst rights claims might be sufficient to secure the minimum entitlements of children, beyond the minimum what children require, for example a loving attitude and attentiveness, may be better approached in terms of obligations imposed upon those caring. This is an interesting proposition but one which retains the individualism and conflict of rights discourse.

I do not mean to, and do not need to, deny that children have rights, but I do agree with Katharine Bartlett that not all problems are best addressed through abstract, objective determination and prioritisation of conflicting rights of the individuals involved.[78] Rights have to be used strategically, and in some situations invoking rights can result in abstract calculations which fail to examine the complex realities of the situation.[79] As Vanessa Munro has argued:

---

[76] Onora O'Neill, 'Children's Rights and Children's Lives' (1988) 98 *Ethics* 445–63.
[77] Her arguments have been countered by Michael Freeman: *supra*, n. 27, at pp. 56–9.
[78] Katharine Bartlett, 'Re-Expressing Parenthood' (1988) 98 *Yale Law Journal* 293–340, at pp. 295–6.
[79] Elizabeth Kingdom, *What's Wrong with Rights? Problems for Feminist Politics of Law*, Edinburgh University Press, 1991.

The rhetorical value of rights discourse must not be underestimated. However, the unquestioning assumption employed by the courts that the attribution of individualistic rights represents the most fulfilling way to deal with all complex issues arising within a liberal framework remains highly problematic. In particular, we must question the legitimacy of such attribution in cases where the nature of the relationships and context involved strongly contraindicates the exclusive legitimacy of such radical individualism and conflict.[80]

It is my assertion that issues concerning the provision of healthcare to young and dependent children may not be best determined by prioritisation of the abstract rights of the child in conflict with the rights of his or her parents or healthcare professionals. Carol Gilligan, in her studies of psychological development, identified an alternative way of reasoning to the abstract, objective application of rules. Counterpoised against this was reasoning through contextual determination of conflicting responsibilities arising out of relationships.[81] The two approaches have different starting points. The first, based upon abstract application of rules, assumes separation from where connections with others are made. The second assumes connection to others from which separation occurs. An understanding of individuals as primarily separate or as primarily connected results in different understandings of the self and of relationships.[82] Primary separation brings concern with invasion – the self and others affected by each other through violation or aggression which needs to be restrained. Primary connection involves responsibility to others and the self.[83] This is not to suggest that responsibilities rather than rights should be considered in all situations. It is to suggest that it is necessary to decide whether the particular issue is best approached through a framework of rights or a framework of responsibilities. In the context of the intimate relationships of parent and healthcare professional with the child, consideration of responsibilities rather than rights provides the more appropriate starting point:

> The experiences of inequality and interconnection, inherent in the relation of parent and child, then give rise to the ethics of justice and care, the ideals of human relationship – the vision that self and other will be treated

---

[80] Vanessa Munro, 'Square Pegs in Round Holes: The Dilemma of Conjoined Twins and Individual Rights' (2001) 10 *Social and Legal Studies* 459–82, at p. 463.

[81] Carol Gilligan, *In a Different Voice: Psychological Theory and Women's Development*, Harvard University Press: Cambridge, MA, 1982, at p. 19.   [82] *Ibid.*, at pp. 37–8.

[83] *Ibid.*, at pp. 37–8.

as of equal worth, that despite differences in power, things will be fair; the vision that everyone will be responded to and included, that no one will be left alone or hurt. These disparate visions in their tension reflect the paradoxical truths of human experience – that we know ourselves as separate only insofar as we live in connection with others, and that we experience relationship only insofar as we differentiate other from self.[84]

Children's rights are important but they 'do not exhaust the moral domain'; what parents ought to do to take care of their children goes beyond the rights their children can assert against them.[85] As Michael Freeman argued, considered above, recognition of children's rights is of fundamental importance in the protection of children from neglect, violence and abuse. But rights should not be invoked inevitably and indiscriminately. It is my argument that the legal regulation of the provision of healthcare to children is better approached through a framework of moral and legal responsibilities. My aim is to explore what difference it makes for determination of the provision of healthcare to young children if the starting point is that of moral responsibilities to children rather than children's rights. The next section outlines a conceptual framework of responsibilities which I argue should provide the grounding for the legal responsibilities of parents and professionals in relation to the healthcare of young children.

Parental responsibility

Parental rights

In his closing submission, the father of C said: 'Whatever the outcome of this case, we would have lost if we had not stood up for our rights.'[86] Wilson J admonished him with the response that the case was not about the rights of parents, that the rights of the child were not subsumed within those of her parents but that '[t]his baby has rights of her own'.[87] Reflecting debates about children's rights, there has been a shift in understanding of the rights of parents. Historically, within law, the (legitimate) child was treated as the property of the father. Laws safeguarded the interest which the father had in his child, protecting those interests from infringement by others. The sole rights of custody and control were vested in the father. The

---

[84] *Ibid.,* at pp. 62–3.   [85] Archard, *supra,* n. 49, at p. 8.
[86] *In re C (a Child) (HIV Testing)* [2000] 2 WLR 270, at 282. This case is analysed in chapter 4.
[87] *Ibid.,* at p. 282.

mother had no rights as she had no independent legal status herself. Consequently, fathers exercised 'almost absolute authority' over their children until they reached the age of majority.[88] The Children Act 1989 abolished the father's status as natural guardian of legitimate children.[89] Shortly before this, in 1985, when the House of Lords gave judgment in the *Gillick* case, the view of the child as property of the father was considered to be 'so out of line with present-day views' that it should be considered 'a historical curiosity'.[90] In Lord Fraser's opinion, the current view was that:

> parental rights to control a child do not exist for the benefit of the parent. They exist for the benefit of the child and they are justified only in so far as they enable the parent to perform his duties to the child, and towards other children in the family.[91]

A similar position was adopted by Lord Scarman, who stressed that parental rights are derived from parental duties:

> Parental rights clearly do exist, and they do not wholly disappear until the age of majority. Parental rights relate to both the person and the property of the child – custody, care, and control of the person and guardianship of the property of the child. But the common law has never treated such rights as sovereign or beyond review and control. Nor has our law ever treated the child as other than a person with capacities and rights recognised by law. The principle of the law . . . is that parental rights are derived from parental duty and exist only so long as they are needed for the protection of the person and property of the child.[92]

Jonathan Montgomery argues that, as a consequence of *Gillick*, the model is no longer one of the father as the head of the household with children as his property but one of the family as a realm for the protection of vulnerable persons.[93] In relation to medical treatment, he explains that parents have the power to give consent to a doctor to provide medical treatment to their child where the child lacks capacity to exercise it in order to relieve the doctor of the duty of non-interference with bodily integrity arising from the right of the child. Consequently, parents have the power to protect their child's right not the right to control the child.[94]

---

[88] *Gillick v West Norfolk and Wisbech AHA and another* [1985] 3 WLR 830, at p. 842 (Lord Fraser).
[89] Children Act 1989, s. 2(4).   [90] *Supra*, n. 88, at p. 843 (Lord Fraser).   [91] *Ibid.*, at p. 841.
[92] *Ibid.*, at p. 853.
[93] Jonathan Montgomery, 'Children as Property' (1988) 51 MLR 323–42, at pp. 329–30, 334.
[94] *Ibid.*, at p. 341.

In its Working Paper on Guardianship, the Law Commission took the view that, as the paramount consideration in relation to the child's upbringing is the welfare of the child, it would be more accurate to refer to 'parental powers, authority or responsibilities' than to parental rights.[95] Parents may still be considered to be possessed of parental rights, derived from parental duties, to enable them to fulfil their caring obligations to their child, although the Children Act 1989 re-expressed the parent–child relationship in terms of the legal responsibilities of parents.

Responsibility

The concept of responsibility can be understood as providing nothing more than the 'moral correlative' of rights, that is, that the possession of a right by one person imposes responsibilities upon others to respect or enable fulfilment of that right. Liberal theories of responsibility focus upon responsibility *for* the actions of an individual (and liberal legal ones, their relationship with criminal and civil liability). Consequently, these theories examine the circumstances in which the individual can be held responsible for their freely chosen actions to the state in the case of criminal conduct and the individual harmed in civil proceedings.[96] In relation to children, the questions posed by liberal theories of responsibility include the capacity of children from which follows accountability for their actions and, in the absence of capacity, questions about the allocation of blame to parents for the conduct of their children. In the context of the healthcare of children, the focus has been upon the circumstances in which children gain the capacity to take responsibility for their own health and healthcare decisions, as indeed is shown in the approach of the courts to cases concerning teenage children, from *Gillick* in 1985[97] to *Axon* twenty-one years

---

[95] Law Commission Working Paper No. 91, *Family Law, Review of Child Law: Guardianship* (1985), at para. 1.11.

[96] H. L. A. Hart, *Punishment and Responsibility: Essays in the Philosophy of Law*, Clarendon Press: Oxford, 1968; H. Morris (ed.), *Freedom and Responsibility: Readings in Philosophy and Law*, Stanford University Press, 1961; R. G. Frey and Christopher Morris (eds.), *Liability and Responsibility: Essays in Law and Morals*, Cambridge University Press, 1991; Antony Honoré, *Responsibility and Fault*, Hart: Oxford, 1999.

[97] *Supra*, n. 88. It was described by Michael Freeman as 'a watershed decision: it recognised the personality of children; it undercut their dependence; it defined their decision making abilities. It was a liberating judgment'. 'Feminism and Child Law' in Jo Bridgeman and Daniel Monk (eds.), *Feminist Perspectives on Child Law*, Cavendish: London, 2000, at p. 36.

later.[98] My aim in this book is to develop a conceptual framework of responsibility (concerned with what parents and professionals ought to do in relation to the health of the children in their care) and to argue that that conceptualisation should underpin the legal framework of responsibilities for children's healthcare. This challenges and presents an alternative to the current assumptions of the abstract, individualistic, rights-influenced approach to parents and the vulnerable, dependent, child. I agree with Mary Urban Walker who:

> prefer[s] the more capacious language of responsibility (than 'care') as a conceptual framework for ethics: it invites us to follow the trails of people's diverse responsibilities through different domains . . . Being held responsible in certain ways, or being exempted or excluded from responsibility of certain types or for certain people, forms individuals' own senses, as well as others' expectations, of to whom and for what they have to account.[99]

Rather than responsibility in a liberal contractual sense, the concept of responsibility employed in this book is a post-liberal concept based upon feminist theories of care. There has been extensive consideration of care by feminists from a range of disciplines, including sociology,[100] philosophy,[101] political theory,[102] psychology[103] and law.[104] Feminist theories of care lead us to question the dominant thinking of the western liberal tradition, presenting a challenge to the assumptions upon which liberal

---

[98] *R (on the application of Axon) v Secretary of State for Health* [2006] EWHC 37. Cases in the intervening years suggested a 'retreat from *Gillick*', given enduring reluctance to follow the spirit of *Gillick* and respect the decisions of teenage children to refuse consent to treatment considered by healthcare professionals to be necessary to avoid a severe risk to health or life: Gillian Douglas, 'The Retreat from *Gillick*' (1992) 55 MLR 569–76. Silber J characterised the case of *Axon* as requiring resolution of the tension between the autonomy and confidentiality of the competent child and the responsibility of parents for their child's health, welfare and moral development within the context of a 'change in the landscape of family matters' in which the rights of children have gained in prominence: para. 80 and again para. 115.   [99] *Supra*, n. 48, at p. 78.

[100] Janet Finch and Jennifer Mason, *Negotiating Family Responsibilities*, Routledge: London, 1992.

[101] Kittay, *supra*, n. 9; Grace Clement, *Care, Autonomy and Justice: Feminism and the Ethic of Care*, Westview Press: Boulder, 1996.

[102] Joan Tronto, *Moral Boundaries: The Political Argument for an Ethic of Care*, Routledge: New York, 1993; Selma Sevenhuijsen, *Citizenship and the Ethics of Care: Feminist Considerations on Justice, Morality and Politics*, Routledge: London, 1998.   [103] *Supra*, n. 81.

[104] Carol Smart and Bren Neale, *Family Fragments?* Polity Press: Cambridge, 1999 (considered in chapter 7); Carrie Menkel-Meadow, 'Portia in a Different Voice: Speculating on Women's Lawyering Process' (1987) 1 Berkeley Women's LJ 39.

theories are based. At the heart is a critique of the nature of the subject and the employment of abstract universal principles to resolve conflict, dilemmas and problems. Central to these theories is an understanding of persons taking responsibility for others arising out of their relationships rather than accepting the responsibilities imposed upon them by another's rights or by the state. This is not merely about the willingness or the conscientiousness with which an individual approaches their responsibilities but is premised upon a fundamentally different understanding of the nature of persons and their relationships with each other. Rather than understanding persons to be primarily separate, self-interested, rational individuals whose principal concern is to protect themselves from invasion by others but who form relations by agreement and resolve conflict through the application of abstract, universal principles, feminist theories of care and responsibility understand individuals to be primarily connected through relationships and concerned to maintain relationships with others.

This approach can be developed through consideration of the work of feminists on the 'ethic of care' which is at the root of the feminist theory of responsibility. Joan Tronto has explored the concept of care, arguing that giving and receiving care are important aspects of our lives but that what is meant by reference to the 'ethic of care' is often not examined.[105] Her analysis distinguishes between caring about, taking care of, care giving and receiving care. Each addresses a different stage in the practice of caring from identifying the need, taking on the responsibility for caring, providing the care and responding as the recipient of care.[106] Each stage combines an attitude, or mental disposition, with the physical labour of care: 'feeling concern for, and taking charge of the well-being of others'; both 'love and labour' are required.[107] At each stage there are different levels of caring activity and caring attitude dependent upon the relationship between the carer and the one cared for. The values of care as identified by Joan Tronto are attentiveness (in order to recognise the needs of the other), responsibility, competence (resources) and responsiveness.[108]

In this analysis, moral responsibilities arise out of relationships. We have, of course, responsibilities to numerous others arising from our

---

[105] Tronto, *supra*, n. 102, at p. 125.   [106] *Ibid.*, at pp. 105–7.

[107] Hilary Graham, 'Caring: A Labour of Love' in Janet Finch and Dulcie Groves (eds.), *A Labour of Love: Women, Work and Caring*, Routledge and Kegan Paul, London, 1983, 13–30, at p. 13.

[108] Tronto, *supra*, n. 102, at pp. 127–36.

relationships with them. Perhaps in the weakest sense and generally imposed are responsibilities to our neighbours or communities, with increasing substance the closer the relationship. We have moral responsibilities to spouses, partners, lovers, friends and colleagues, in each case given content by the context of the relationship:

> [A]s the connections among persons not only contribute to persons' sense of who they are, but are themselves the ground of many moral obligations, interpersonal relationships too must be valued. The ways in which persons become connected to one another are diverse and only some are freely chosen, but regardless of how the relationship comes about, if it is allowed to grow it creates responsibilities. These responsibilities become constitutive of the relationship, as well as having arisen from it.[109]

As responsibilities arise out of relationships, the individual is inevitably situated within a web of responsibilities. Parents will have responsibilities not only to their child, or children, but also to each other, to their parents, siblings and friends. Others will have responsibilities to the child, arising from both personal and professional relationships. With differing responsibilities arising out of relationships comes the difficult task of balancing responsibilities to maintain relationships.

Parents, Joan Tronto argues, have obligations to their children by virtue of having them. But, she argues, as responsibilities arise out of relationships not promises, 'we are better served by focusing on a flexible notion of responsibility than we are by continuing to use obligation as the basis for understanding what people should do for each other'.[110] By virtue of the parent–child relationship in which the child is dependent upon the parent to meet their needs, responsibilities arise. She suggests that: 'The moral question an ethic of care takes as central is not – What, if anything, do I (we) owe to others? But rather – How can I (we) best meet my (our) caring responsibilities?'[111] This requires examination of general caring responsibilities arising from the relationship and particular responsibilities arising from the needs of the individual. Rather than the abstraction of rights, theories of responsibility require attention to be paid to the context for resolution of a moral dilemma.

---

[109] Hilde Lindemann Nelson, 'Always Connect: Towards a Parental Ethics of Divorce' in Julia E. Hanigsberg and Sara Ruddick (eds.), *Mother Troubles: Rethinking Contemporary Maternal Dilemmas*, Beacon Press: Boston, 1999, 117–35, at p. 120.

[110] Tronto, *supra*, n. 102, at p. 133.   [111] *Ibid.*, at p. 137.

> From the perspective of caring, what is important is not arriving at the fair decision, understood as how the abstract individual in this situation would want to be treated, but at meeting the needs of particular others or preserving the relationships of care that exist. In this way, moral theory becomes much more closely connected to the concrete needs of others.[112]

What individuals ought to do for another depends upon the nature of the relationship between them (in this context parent/child, doctor/patient, nurse/patient) and their particular needs. The responsibilities of a parent caring for a healthy two-year-old child are different from those of that same parent caring for that same child but who has become seriously ill.

Further, as Katharine Bartlett has argued, ideal roles for every relationship are not only dependent upon the individuals in the relationship but are also in part socially determined.[113] Thus, the responsibilities of parent to child arising from the relationship between them are determined by existing social expectations, the personal interpretation of parent and child and, furthermore, by the particular needs of both parent and child.

To focus upon relationships is not to seek to retain dichotomous thinking with a shift in the allocation of power from professionals to parents. Rather, it is to argue for a focus upon partnership in which parents and professionals work together in the interests of the child. The primary relationship of young children will often be with their parents (or those providing their daily care) but children have relationships with others from which responsibilities arise. The child is situated in a relationship not merely with his or her parents but also with professionals involved in his or her care who, depending on the circumstances, may include midwife, general practitioner, health visitor, teachers, a range of community health, education and social welfare service providers, hospital doctors and nurses. Each of these has a relationship with the child, different from the one the child has with their parents and central to which is their professional responsibility focusing upon the particular aspect of the child within their professional expertise. As Joan Tronto identifies, doctors *take care of* their patients but they do so at a distance, with nurses, or mothers, doing the majority of the *caring for* the child, the hands-on work. Parents and professionals ought to,

---

[112] Joan Tronto, 'Woman and Caring: What Can Feminists Learn about Morality from Caring?' in Alison M. Jaggar and Susan R. Bordo (eds.), *Gender/Body/Knowledge: Feminist Reconstructions of Being and Knowing*, Rutgers University Press: New Brunswick, 1989, 172–87, at p. 176.
[113] *Supra*, n. 78, at p. 299.

and generally do, work together, each making a contribution according to their expertise to the well-being of the child. However, a focus upon context and the particular role of the adult in caring for the child helps us to appreciate that there are different roles, all of which need to be respected and their distinct contributions acknowledged. As both parents and professionals have responsibilities to children, determined by their relationship with them, questions arise about the responsibilities of parents and professionals to each other. In general terms, these take the form of the responsibility to work together, respecting the contribution of the other, in the shared endeavour of caring for the child. I suggest that a conceptual framework of responsibilities and development of a discourse of responsibility[114] would assist the process of change to child-centred care delivered through a partnership between parent and professional. At the same time, the different functions, roles and expertise of the parent and professional in the partnership will become apparent, highlighting the extent to which parents are dependent upon professionals to take proper care of their child.

A post-liberal approach to responsibility can be found within communitarian approaches to the individual and the state. In communitarian theory, responsibility is no longer considered in terms of capacity and free choice (as in the liberal paradigm) but is conceived of as responsible process and responsible attitudes. Individual conformity with community norms is secured by the threat of exposure backed by legal measures. In her analysis of the family policy of the New Labour Government, Val Gillies argues that communitarian thought is evident in policies which seek to 'support' parents by 'encouraging parents to live up to their ethical obligations to their families and communities'.[115] She argues that within family policy the state is portrayed as 'facilitator and enabler', supporting parents through 'empowerment' rather than through more tangible benefits:

> [T]he government constructs the worthy citizen as a self-determining, agentic individual who accepts their obligation to act morally. For parents this entails ethical self-management within the moral parameters of normative definitions of 'successful parenting'. Reasonable, rational, moral citizens, by New Labour definition, seek to do the best for their children, and according to policy doctrine, government should play an active role in guiding and supporting them to do so.[116]

[114] Smart and Neale, *supra*, n. 104, at p. 171.
[115] Val Gillies, 'Meeting Parents' Needs? Discourses of "Support" and "Inclusion" in Family Policy' (2005) 25 *Critical Social Policy* 70–90, at p. 75.   [116] *Ibid.*, at p. 77.

Supporting parents thus becomes ensuring that parents are aware of the expectations of them and surrounded, within their communities, by sources of advice and information from which they can learn to be good parents:

> 'Good' parents are constructed as resourceful, agentic and ethically responsible, able to recognize or learn what is best for their children and tailor their behaviour accordingly. Such self-sufficient and self-governing parents require only access to sources of information and advice, which they utilize to govern and guide their conduct.[117]

In 'From Parental Responsibility to Parenting Responsibly',[118] Helen Reece explores legislative developments in criminal justice and in post-separation contact, detecting within them a shift from parental authority to parental accountability. The Crime and Disorder Act 1998 introduced, and the Anti-social Behaviour Act 2003 extended the scope of, parenting orders making parents take responsibility for the anti-social behaviour of their children. Her analysis of developments in policy and law with respect to the relationship between parent and child is consistent with her earlier analysis of Part II of the Family Law Act 1996.[119] In relation to both, Helen Reece adopts a post-liberal conceptualisation of responsibility which is informed by communitarianism. Her argument is that responsibility has come to be understood as a process which is dependent upon the correct attitude: 'In the context of parenting, this means that to a large extent there is no longer a right way to parent: good parenting is now an attitude, and an important part of that attitude is being prepared to learn.'[120] Responsible parents, she suggests, are expected to seek advice about parenting from the sources of information and advice which are increasingly available to them. However, she contends that the help and information available is not provided in order to empower parents to be authoritative in their parenting but, rather, to 'direct decision-making' towards conformity with norms of 'good' parenting.[121]

At the root of developments in policy and law imposing responsibility

---

[117] *Ibid.*, at p. 85.
[118] Helen Reece, 'From Parental Responsibility to Parenting Responsibly' in Michael Freeman (ed.), *Law and Sociology, Current Legal Issues 2005*, Oxford University Press: Oxford, 2006, 459–83.   [119] Helen Reece, *Divorcing Responsibly*, Hart: Oxford, 2003.
[120] *Supra*, n. 118, at p. 470.   [121] *Ibid.*, at p. 472.

upon parents for the anti-social behaviour of their children are ideas about the ability of parents to instil good moral values and behaviour into their children. Different factors have driven changes to the policy on children's healthcare services, found in the *Every Child Matters* agenda and the *National Service Framework for Children, Young People and Maternity Services*, most directly the failings revealed by the Bristol Royal Infirmary Inquiry and the Laming Inquiry into the death of Victoria Climbié. Inevitably, there are some parallels, such as in the supposition that successful parenting requires knowledge. Parents are thus supported through education and making available to them sources of advice and information. Secondly, universal support to be made available to all families can be understood as a mechanism for imposing normative standards of good parenting upon all. Thirdly, it can be argued that the stated aim of providing universal support for children and families merely masks the reality of a focus upon targeted support for vulnerable, or 'failing', parents which increases the moral pressure upon them to conform to norms of good parenting. However, as identified in *Supporting Families*,[122] responsibility for the health and well-being of children rests with their parents, working together with healthcare professionals to meet the needs of the child. As acknowledged in the consultation document, government should support parents by making available advice, information and guidance and providing health, education and social services. With the exception of extreme circumstances, it is up to parents to decide whether they wish to take advantage of the available advice, information and guidance. In contrast to anti-social behaviour and family breakdown, in this context, the role of the state is to support parents to fulfil their responsibility and to create the institutions, including the law, which foster the partnership between parent and professional in the shared endeavour of meeting the healthcare needs of the child.

In contrast to assertions of rights – right to healthcare, right to life, right to dignity – which are abstract claims, responsibilities require consideration of the particular situation in a given social, cultural and political context. A focus upon responsibilities rather than rights does not make the finding of solutions to difficult decisions easier: on the contrary, it requires greater attention to the particular situation, highlighting its complexities. It involves a shift in focus to address previously unexamined questions and

---

[122] Home Office, *Supporting Families: A Consultation Document*, 1998, at pp. 4–6.

issues. A focus upon responsibility is a focus upon a set of questions which have to be asked to determine how responsibility can best be discharged in the prevailing circumstances. It shifts from the abstract to the particular to respond to needs: 'genuine moral dilemmas arise because the chief concern of moral deliberation is to respond appropriately to the persons with whom we are connected in various ways'.[123] Andrew Bainham in his response to the case of conjoined twins, Mary and Jodie, whilst acknowledging that the Human Rights Act 1998 would probably have made no difference to the legal decision, maintained that: '[T]here is also a *moral* dimension to human rights which surely requires us to continue to ask difficult and uncomfortable questions on behalf of vulnerable, in this case helpless, children.'[124] It is my contention that *responsibilities*, rather than rights, demand examination of the difficult questions arising in relation to caring for the health of children.

Furthermore, as the care of children does not occur in isolation, consideration must be given to the practical resources available to carers and to the prevailing social, cultural and political circumstances in which care is delivered. The healthcare provided to children depends upon the state of medical knowledge and whether the necessary human, technical and material resources are available. The abilities of parents to meet the needs of their child are affected not only by the support offered to them through primary or community healthcare services but also by financial, practical, and importantly, emotional support. Children need to be cared for and seriously ill children or children with severe disabilities have magnified needs. This raises questions about the allocation of responsibilities between individuals or between the individual and the collective as well as the need to confront the limits of responsibility.[125] Caring for children is currently predominantly a personal responsibility of parents. However, as the studies discussed in chapter 6 reveal, the abilities of parents to meet the needs of their child are limited by environmental obstacles, discriminatory attitudes and simply the inability of people to cope with illness or disability. The task is to examine how caring responsibilities can best be discharged in the face of conflicting needs, medical uncertainties, social expectations and limited practical, emotional and financial support.

---

[123] *Supra*, n. 109, at p. 124.
[124] Andrew Bainham, 'Resolving the Unresolvable: The Case of the Conjoined Twins' (2001) 60 CLJ 49, at p. 53.   [125] Sevenhuijsen, *supra*, n. 102, at p. 86.

Responsibility can be understood as a social practice but the concept is more than merely descriptive.[126] Whilst examination of caring practices does seek to identify who is re*sponsible for what in relation to others and what that involves, practices of caring responsibility are both determined by, and give definition to, societal norms of caring practices.[127] Whilst it can be argued that 'ought' should not be derived from 'is', parents do gain an understanding of what they ought to do in caring for their children from their understanding of common practice within their particular social, cultural and political environment.[128] Furthermore, it makes more sense to derive 'normative guidelines'[129] from caring practices than to establish norms of behaviour in abstraction. Examination of caring responsibilities to identify what parents do (therefore a descriptive process) provides a basis for establishing what parents ought to do (and is thus a normative process). As Janet Finch has argued, this is not to determine what should be done in a particular situation but rather to establish parameters by which to guide how to approach a particular problem: '*how you work out* the proper thing to do in given circumstances, rather than *specifying what* you should do'.[130] The majority of parents do, as they ought to do, more than the mere minimum for their children:

> To exercise parental responsibility is to put the interests and welfare of children or future children above one's own needs, desires or well-being. Welfare is, it must be accepted, an indeterminate and value-laden concept and the problems inherent in this cannot be ignored. But there is an irreducible minimum content to a child's well-being, and these must be satisfied by anyone carrying out the role of . . . parent . . . Responsible parents want their children to have good and fulfilling lives. They are prepared to forgo pleasures and make sacrifices to ensure their children are able to flourish.[131]

Taking responsibility involves more than doing just what is expected of us, it demands consideration of the particular needs of the person to whom

---

[126] As Debra Westlake and Maggie Pearson found in their research with mothers of young children: 'notions of "responsibility" were found to construct the way in which women respondents conceptualized their role as mothers: they were keen to present themselves to the outside world and to health and social services professionals as "responsible" parents'. Debra Westlake and Maggie Pearson, 'Child Protection and Health Promotion: Whose Responsibility?' (1997) 19 JSWFL 139–58, at p. 140.   [127] *Supra*, n. 48, at pp. 78–89.

[128] Janet Finch, 'The Proper Thing To Do' in John Eekelaar and Mavis Maclean (eds.), *A Reader on Family Law*, Oxford University Press: Oxford, 1994, at p. 68.

[129] The term used by Janet Finch in *ibid.*   [130] *Ibid.*, at p. 77.

[131] Freeman, *supra*, n. 59, at p. 180.

there is responsibility and concern with the 'outcome', whilst acting according to our values and self-imposed limits.[132]

In the context of the healthcare of children, a conceptual framework of relational responsibility would require that questions are asked about the particular child, about the parental experiences of, and knowledge gained through, caring for them, about the contribution of others to the care of the child and about the prevailing social, cultural and political context. This approach necessarily involves recognition that each child is different. And, rather than adopting abstract notions of the child as vulnerable and potential, it requires careful attention to the child as an individual. This is to look not to the psychological development of the child, their decision-making capacities, cognitive skills or thought processes, but to the child as a living and interdependent individual, the particular personality, character, spirit and experiences of whom, when very young, will be best articulated by those most intimately involved and closely concerned with them: in the majority of cases, by their parents. It also requires examination of the history of caring, by the child's parents and professional carers, to place specific healthcare decisions or provision within the existing practices of caring for the dependent child. Relational responsibilities are also determined by needs. What parents do, and what parents ought to do, in caring for a child changes according to the child's needs. It is notable that many, although not all, of the children who appear in the case law have siblings. The focus is, of course, upon the best interests or needs of the individual child and thus it is no surprise that the care of their brothers and sisters is not considered. Inevitably, in reality, parents will focus upon the needs of their seriously ill or injured child and family life changes to accommodate the needs of a disabled child. Siblings may be left in the care of grandparents or other relatives, they may spend much time at the hospital or they may help their parents to care. Consideration of responsibilities, what it is that families do in caring for a child with complex needs, should inform what ought to be done in the interests of the child.

To summarise the argument so far: A feminist concept of responsibility derived from the feminist ethic of care understands responsibilities to arise out of relationships. In any relationship, responsibilities are partly determined by social expectations, in part individually interpreted, and depend upon current needs. It is argued that the law regulating the provision of

---

[132] *Supra*, n. 78, at pp. 299–301.

healthcare to children should be based upon a conceptual framework of
relational responsibilities. In contrast to traditional philosophy, which
insists that what the individual ought to do should be determined according to abstract principles, it is argued that a moral concept of responsibility
should be informed by practices of caring responsibility. That is, that what
parents ought to do with regard to the care of their children's health should
be informed by guidelines developed through consideration of what
parents do in caring for their children's health.

   The majority of parents considered in this book have taken responsibility for the health of their children.[133] In some of the cases considered, there
is a difference of opinion with others concerned with the health of the child
about how that responsibility is best discharged. In other cases, the law can
be analysed to reveal what is expected of parents in meeting the caring
needs of their children. My concern is to present an argument for the way in
which the law can foster the relationships between all involved in caring for
children and support them in the discharge of their responsibilities to the
child. One important issue to confront is how a conceptual framework of
relational responsibility works with those small number of parents who fail
to take responsibility for their child and who neglect – fail in their caregiv-
ing – or even abuse or harm their child. Is it the case that the assumptions
upon which a conceptual framework of relational responsibility is based,
and in my argument the legal framework, may support the majority of
parents at the expense of ensuring the protection of children from irresponsible parents? A legal framework premised upon a conceptual framework of relational responsibility has not only to recognise the contribution
of parents who do take responsibility, but also to set clear expectations and
hold to account those who do not. By establishing norms out of caring
practices, reflecting the reality that the majority of parents do more than
the minimum in caring for their child, the responsibilities imposed upon
parents for care of their children holds them to account for taking responsibility and leads to blame for failure to do so.[134] The primary relationship
of the child will often be with their parents and thus the primary responsibility for care of a child will rest with his or her parents. Parents who neglect
or abuse their child have failed to fulfil their responsibilities to their child as
much as they have failed to respect their child's rights. To recognise that a

[133] Michael Freeman poses the interesting question whether children have a right to responsible
    parents, 'Do Children Have the Right Not to be Born?' in Freeman, *supra*, n. 59, at p. 183.
[134] *Supra*, n. 48, at p. 90.

particular parent or parents have failed to fulfil their moral responsibilities to their child is different from an approach which asserts that children have rights to a minimum standard of care. This is because the starting point is an assumption of a caring relationship rather than conflicting individualism and because consideration is given to the respective roles and responsibilities of parent and of professionals. Such an investigation may reveal culpability on the part of the parent or complexities in the circumstances which preclude the simple allocation of blame.

A further question arises in relation to parents who disagree. Both parents have responsibility to the child, to do their best for their child. Where parents disagree, it is necessary to scrutinise the extent to which each is considering the needs of the child as an individual and the history of caring practices within the particular family in the context of social expectations.

Parents: mothers and fathers

Alison Diduck contrasts the traditional conception of motherhood as based upon a bond, intimacy and the provision of care with that of fatherhood which has 'traditionally been grounded in sociality and legality; its roots lie in a notion of paternal proprietary rights over children and it thus sits more comfortably in the realm of rationality and choice'.[135] Despite the shift towards a model of the family in which there is, as Jane Lewis and Elaine Welsh have described, 'gender convergence', referring to the increased participation of women in the public realm of paid employment and the greater involvement of men in the work of care,[136] there is an abundance of social science research which makes it clear that it is still mothers who are primarily involved in meeting the everyday healthcare needs of their children.[137]

---

[135] *Supra*, n. 10, at pp. 84–5.

[136] Jane Lewis and Elaine Welsh, 'Fathering Practices in Twenty-Six Intact Families and the Implications for Child Contact' (2005) 1 *International Journal of Law in Context* 81–99, at p. 82.

[137] Clare Williams, *Mothers, Young People and Chronic Illness*, Ashgate: Hampshire, 2002, a study of forty adolescents with asthma and diabetes and the parent who was most involved in their everyday care. Four of the fathers took equal responsibility, one was the main carer, in all the other cases the primary caring role belonged to the mother. J. Read, *Disability, the Family and Society: Listening to Mothers*, Open University Press: Buckingham, 2000, a study of mothers of children with sensory or physical impairments; J. Brannen, K. Dodd, A. Oakley and P. Storey, *Young People, Health and Family Life*, Open University Press: Buckingham, 1994, at p. 99. As Debra Westlake and Maggie Pearson identified, this included 'diagnosing and treating childhood illnesses, taking children to the doctor, arranging vaccinations and child health screenings, planning the household diet etc.': *supra*, n. 126, at p. 146.

Despite an increase in the involvement of men in the domestic realm, the responsibility for the day-to-day running of the home and the family remains with women.[138] Fathers in the study by Jane Lewis and Elaine Welsh were principally involved in 'macro-responsibility': that is, responsibility for 'earning, guiding, leading and steering the child; imposing a moral code and imparting values', which is, as they identify, 'more "caring about" than "caring for" '.[139] In their study of parenting and step-parenting, Jane Ribbens McCarthy et al. identified 'an overall moral imperative, namely that *adults must take responsibility for children in their care and therefore must seek to put the needs of children first*'.[140] They found that the parents and step-parents they interviewed tried to abide by this, although inevitably it was lived out in a variety of ways. Fathers, they identified, considered putting the needs of the children first in terms of providing for them and by being an authority figure, role model or guide. Mothers, in contrast, focused upon the needs of the child – often putting their own happiness in second place to the needs of the child – and upon providing a home, involving 'emotional work, mediation of relationships and organisational skills'.[141] That is not to say, as Deborah Lupton and Lesley Barclay conclude from their study, that fathers do not have equal capacity with mothers for everyday caring. As the mothers inevitably spent more time caring for their newborn child and as the demands of providing financially took the father out of the home, the mother became more 'expert' and the father more distanced.[142] Ideal roles for the mother as nurturer and father as provider, protector and authority figure not only result in a failure to see the wide variety of roles undertaken and the extent to which fathers do contribute to the daily routine of care but also operate at a symbolic level to retain and reinforce distinct gender roles.[143]

There is, unsurprisingly, a parallel gender dimension to the responsibilities of mothers and fathers in relation to their children's health. It is

---

[138] *Supra*, n. 136, at p. 86.   [139] *Ibid.*, at pp. 85 and 89.

[140] Jane Ribbens McCarthy, Rosalind Edwards and Val Gillies, 'Moral Tales of the Child and the Adult: Narratives of Contemporary Family Lives under Changing Circumstances' (2000) 34 *Sociology* 785, at p. 789.   [141] *Ibid.*, at p. 793.

[142] Deborah Lupton and Lesley Barclay, *Constructing Fatherhood: Discourses and Experiences*, Sage: London, 1997, at p. 148. This study comprised at least six semi-structured interviews with sixteen couples across a period of time spanning from prior to the birth of their child to when the child was about eighteen months old.

[143] Sara Ruddick, 'The Idea of Fatherhood' in Hilde Lindemann Nelson (ed.), *Feminism and Families*, Routledge: New York, 1996, 205–20.

principally mothers who adopt the primary role in the everyday management of childhood health, whereas fathers become involved where the
illness is, or becomes, serious, or at those points where their child's condition necessitates negotiations with a new set of health professionals.[144]
Notably, the evidence of parents to the Bristol Inquiry revealed that the
allocation of responsibilities between fathers and mothers for the practicalities of caring for their child varied, depending upon such factors as the
length of time over which the child received treatment, how soon after
birth the child underwent surgery (when the expectation would be that
mothers would have a sustained period of time with their newborn child),
the father's job, and whether there were other children in the family who
needed to be cared for.[145] What was clear, however, was that both parents
tried to be involved in discussions and making decisions and both were
anxious to ensure that their child was provided with the best possible care.
Furthermore, both parents were equally emotionally involved in the
journey through treatment for their seriously ill child.

As Brian Lamb and Sarah Layzell observed from their study of 1,324
parents and carers of disabled people,[146] parenting brings with it responsibilities and changed priorities, whilst caring for a disabled child 'alters
the way in which people are viewed by others and by themselves'.[147] Daily
life changes when a child is born. Everyday life within the family is dis-
rupted by minor childhood illnesses. Parents caring for a seriously ill or
injured child or a child living with their disabilities try to make daily life as
normal as possible. Caring for a seriously ill child, or a child with complex
needs, can be a long-term responsibility which requires their parents, in
particular their mother, to re-assess their life plan because of the burden
of caring in the context of the allocation of primary responsibility to the
family:

> [W]hile struggling to reconcile the additional financial costs with the
> needs of their child, parents also had to confront new and unexpected
> experiences. In essence, they had to construct a new paradigm of family
> life so as to accommodate and include all aspects of their 'new' lives.
> Within this new paradigm, relationships, obligations, aspirations,

---

[144] Brannen et al., *supra*, n. 137, at p. 98.

[145] Jo Bridgeman, 'After Bristol: The Healthcare of Young Children and the Law' (2003) 23 *Legal Studies* 229–50.

[146] Brian Lamb and Sarah Layzell, *Disabled in Britain: Behind Closed Doors: The Carer's Experience*, Scope: London, 1995.   [147] *Ibid.*, at p. 1.

responsibilities, as well as one's sense of self, had to be redefined and renegotiated.[148]

The findings of these studies are consistent with the parenting responsibilities of the mothers and fathers in the cases considered in the chapters which follow. Whilst the cases concerned with the long-term care of children with disabilities clearly reveal the impact of meeting the child's needs upon both mother and father, they also reveal the greater burden upon the child's mother. In comparison, in the cases concerning seriously ill children it is not possible to distinguish between the caring responsibilities fulfilled by mothers or fathers, who usually appear in a united front on the legal issue for determination. Where a child is seriously ill, or severely injured, the child's needs become the focus of parental attention and concern.

Taking responsibility: parents, young children and healthcare law

As Katharine Bartlett has identified, when disputes arise the law forces the parties to present their positions and the court to decide through individualised, abstract, conflicting claims and not through responsibilities arising from relationships.[149] The role of the law is not just to establish the minimum standards of behaviour for individuals within society in order to protect the separate individual, nor merely to deter, punish or resolve conflict through an adversarial battle. Statutory obligations and common law principles also structure relationships and provide guidance for similar situations, making it unnecessary to resort to formal legal processes. The damaging effect of the current legal principles and framework is most clearly apparent in the treatment of David and Carol Glass considered in chapter 5, although I would suggest it was similarly experienced for many of the families involved in the cases considered in the other chapters. The chapters which follow seek to expose the limitations of the existing legal framework which is based upon ideas about the child and of the role of the law in protecting the child, which means that the model fails to cohere with the reality of children as individuals and of parental expertise gained through caring.[150] Furthermore, it is

---

[148] Barbara Dobson, Sue Middleton and Alan Beardsworth, *The Impact of Childhood Disability on Family Life*, Joseph Rowntree Foundation: York, 2001, at p. 25.

[149] *Supra*, n. 78, at p. 295.

[150] Bridget Young, Mary Dixon-Woods, Kate C. Windridge and David Heney, 'Managing Communication with Young People who have a Potentially Life Threatening Chronic Illness: Qualitative Study of Patients and Parents' (2003) 326 BMJ 305.

argued that it sets up parents and professionals in confrontation, damaging rather than supporting the relationship between them which is necessary for the shared endeavour of caring for sick children.

In the context of her examination of child custody, Katharine Bartlett suggests that the law can 'contribute to the creation of high expectations for parents, while leaving sufficient leeway so that parents are free to become responsible in the true sense'.[151] With a focus upon responsibilities arising out of relationships, the role of the state is to support those with responsibility and to foster the relationship between them as they work together to best meet the needs of the child. A caring perspective requires consideration of the question of how the state can create institutions which recognise the connections between individuals and provide support for those meeting the needs of the child. Furthermore, it demands very open and direct acknowledgement of expectations and limits of the individual and the state in taking care of the vulnerable and dependent. And the question which this raises for the law is whether the legal framework can recognise the caring work of parents in meeting their responsibilities to their child. From a position which accepts the critique provided by a caring perspective, the aim of this book is to critique the current law and present a framework which recognises the particular expertise of parents and professionals and to foster the relationship between them as they meet their responsibilities to children.

The chapters which follow provide a critical analysis of the law governing the provision of healthcare to babies, infants and young children. Childhood can be treated as a singular concept covering children from birth to the age of majority, or differentiations can be drawn between neonate, infant, toddler, schoolboy/girl and teenage child. All are unsatisfactory categorisations, suggesting there are clear divisions which do not exist in the real lives of children. Whilst wishing to stress that teenagers remain, to a different extent and in different ways, dependent upon their parents and parents remain responsible to their teenage children, this book does not consider the particular health issues and moral, social and legal questions surrounding the healthcare of teenage children.[152] For the majority of teenagers these issues may arise in relation to chosen behaviours or

---

[151] *Supra*, n. 78, at p. 301.
[152] The age of majority is eighteen: Family Law Reform Act 1969, s. 1. Section 8(1) of the Family Law Reform Act 1969 creates a rebuttable presumption that from the age of sixteen, children are competent to consent to surgical, medical or dental treatment.

lifestyle choices which have an impact upon their health and about which
they may wish their parents to remain ignorant – smoking, alcohol consumption, taking illegal drugs, diet, contraception and pregnancy[153] –
raising further questions about privacy and confidentiality and their ability
to access healthcare services for themselves. The judiciary has been asked to
resolve differences of opinion between teenage children and professionals
with regard to treatment for acute[154] or chronic illness,[155] accidental
injury[156] and mental health problems.[157] The legal issue, in comparison
with younger children whose ability to decide for themselves is not considered by the courts, has been whether they possess the capacity to decide for
themselves about their medical treatment. By virtue of the different issues
affecting their health and the extent to which teenage children approximate
adults in their ability to engage in rational and reasoned explanations for
their decisions, questions about the dependency of teenage children are
beyond the scope of this book. Furthermore, also beyond the scope of this
book is any examination of the legal framework for caring for children with
mental illness or of the responsibilities of children for their own health and
well-being, or to others. Rather, the focus is upon the responsibilities of
parents for maintaining, negotiating and securing the provision of healthcare for their dependent children and of professionals working together
with parents to care for children with physical illness. Consideration is also
given to the long-term caring needs of children with disabilities which, it is
alleged, resulted from negligence of healthcare professionals prior to,
during or after birth, to examine the caring responsibilities of parents.[158]

---

[153] The provision of advice and treatment and respect for the confidentiality of the child under the
age of sixteen consulting about contraception, sexually transmitted diseases and abortion was
recently at issue in *R (on the application of Axon) v Secretary of State for Health* [2006] EWHC
37, considering Department of Health, *Best Practice Guidance for Doctors and other Health
Professionals on the Provision of Advice and Treatment to Young People under Sixteen on
Contraception, Sexual and Reproductive Health,* July 2004 which re-affirmed the principles in
Gillick v West Norfolk and Wisbech AHA and another [1985] 3 WLR 830.

[154] *Re E (a Minor) (Wardship: Medical Treatment)* [1993] 1 FLR 386; *Re M (Medical Treatment:
Consent)* [1999] 2 FLR 1097.

[155] *Re S (a Minor) (Consent to Medical Treatment)* [1994] 2 FLR 1065; *Re P (Medical Treatment:
Best Interests)* [2003] EWHC 2327; [2004] 2 FLR 1117.

[156] *Re L (Medical Treatment: Gillick Competency)* [1998] 2 FLR 810.

[157] *Re R (a Minor) (Wardship: Consent to Treatment)* [1991] 3 WLR 592; *Re W (a Minor) (Medical
Treatment: Court's Jurisdiction)* [1992] 3 WLR 758.

[158] Without exploring the wider context of the services with which they have to engage in order to
secure the best possible care for their child, causing additional pressures and raising further
issues, although as Janet Read's study reveals, many similarities: Read, *supra*, n. 137.

Chapter 2 provides the context for the case law by outlining current developments in children's healthcare services. This is an area where there is currently much change arising from recognition, due to the 'Bristol Scandal' and the inquiry into the death of Victoria Climbié, that children's services, including healthcare services, have long been neglected. This chapter provides a brief account of the failings of care at the Bristol Royal Infirmary and outlines the recommendations of the Kennedy Report to develop child-centred healthcare services for children. It also briefly explains the Laming Report, as far as it relates to children's healthcare services. Within the overall agenda for improving children's services, *Every Child Matters*, delivery of improvement to children's healthcare services will primarily be through the *National Service Framework for Children, Young People and Maternity Services*. Within this chapter on the changing law and policy, the central theme will be the way in which the delivery of healthcare has to change to be child-centred, recognising the caring relationships within which the child is centred and children as unique individuals.

The implications for the law of a conceptual framework of relational responsibilities are outlined in chapter 7, with chapters 3–6 concentrating upon exploring the way in which recognition of responsibilities provides us with a different understanding of the disputes and problems which have arisen in relation to the healthcare of young children. In each of chapters 3, 4 and 5, there is an analysis of the cases through the critique of the perspective of child currently adopted in law and consideration of the questions which a focus upon responsibilities, rather than welfare or rights, requires us to address. Chapter 3 sets out the legal obligations imposed upon parents with regard to the health of their children, focusing upon everyday healthcare. These include examination of the boundaries set by the criminal law, the obligations imposed by civil law and the responsibilities imposed by the Children Act 1989. Chapter 4 provides an analysis of case law on healthcare decision-making for babies, infants and young children focused upon cases concerned with parental refusal of consent to treatment recommended by medical professionals. Chapter 5 examines cases concerning withholding or withdrawal of life-prolonging treatment from severely disabled children. It is argued that decisions about the future treatment of severely disabled children depend upon assessment of their quality of life and that an important part of that assessment is the views of the parents and those caring for the child of the child's current as well as their future quality of life – recognising the child as a living individual and not merely a potential being. This chapter also examines the responsibilities of healthcare professionals and of the judiciary.

Responsibility would underpin consideration of the child's welfare in the way that it is currently underpinned by consideration of rights. As a starting point, based upon feminist theories of care and accounts of parents taking care of their children, it is necessary to dismantle existing assumptions about the nature of child and the relationship between parent and child. This requires, first, attentiveness to the child as an individual with particular needs, wants and concerns.[159] Secondly, it demands consideration of the history of caring practices, who has provided what care for the child and examination of the quality of caring relationships. From their experiences of caring for the child, parents will develop 'deep and intimate knowledge of this child',[160] making them experts in the needs, wants and concerns of their child.[161] Furthermore, it requires examination of the contributions of others, such as healthcare professionals, to the well-being of the child. The attention to context adopted by a responsibilities approach directs consideration to the external factors affecting the abilities of those with responsibilities to care for the child and the individual and collective limits to care. The third factor to consider is thus the social context for the care of an individual, for example, societal norms and beliefs about the provision of medical treatment and the resources available to support the carers in the discharge of their responsibilities. It may be that full investigation of the circumstances will reveal additional or alternative factors for consideration or the need to modify the above factors.

Chapter 6 examines wrongful conception/birth actions, negligent treatment and failures in the provision of information. By way of a case study, consideration is given to the obligations of professionals, and the caring responsibilities of parents, to children suffering from severe brain damage alleged to have been caused by professional negligence at, or around, the time of the child's birth. Someone has to care for children born healthy or with severe impairments and the purpose of this chapter is to examine caring responsibilities and the consequential dependency of parents upon professionals.

Having provided a critical analysis of the law, in the final chapter the

---

[159] J. D. Baum, Sister F. Dominica and R. N. Woodward (eds.), *Listen. My Child Has a Lot of Living to Do: Caring for Children with Life-Threatening Conditions*, Oxford University Press: Oxford, 1990.   [160] *Supra*, n. 9, at p. 169.   [161] *Supra*, n. 159.

implications for the law of a conceptual framework of relational responsibility are considered. This framework – based upon relationships of care,
parental expertise and the uniqueness of each child – argues that the law
has an important role in creating the institutions and practices which
support and foster positive relationships between professional, parent and
child required for the delivery of child-centred healthcare.

2

Child-centred healthcare services for children

Introduction: children's healthcare services

Feminist analysis has exposed the misconception that there is a public realm of government and a private realm of the family which is beyond the scope of regulation. The extent to which parents are given the freedom to care for their children as they consider appropriate or there is intervention in the family to ensure that parents conform to norms of 'good' parenting is a matter for political determination.[1] The *Every Child Matters* agenda, to be implemented for healthcare services primarily through the *National Service Framework for Children, Young People and Maternity Services*, sets out a vision for children's services which may result in an unprecedented degree of intervention into the private realm of the family.[2] The specific context for this policy agenda is exposure of long-term neglect of children's healthcare services by the Bristol Royal Infirmary Inquiry,[3] the failure of health, social, education and policing services to work together to protect

---

[1] Katharine Bartlett, 'Re-Expressing Parenthood' (1988) 98 *Yale Law Journal* 293, at p. 297. The Home Office Consultation Paper, *Supporting Families*, 1998, was the first consultation paper on the family generally to be published by a British Government.

[2] Where previously issues concerning children and young people have been addressed by various government departments, the Minister for Children, Young People and Families within the Department for Education and Skills has been given overall responsibility for the co-ordination of policies affecting these groups. The Children Act 2004 further provided for the post of Children's Commissioner for England (in Wales in relation to matters beyond the remit of the Children's Commissioner for Wales, in Scotland in relation to reserved matters and Northern Ireland in relation to excepted matters) to which Professor Al Aynsley-Green was appointed in March 2005. The role of the Commissioner is to give a voice to children and young people, particularly vulnerable and disadvantaged children, nationally. The role will involve raising issues relevant to children and young people, enhancing awareness and understanding of the views of children in matters affecting them and representing the views and interests of children: Office of the Children's Commissioner, www.childrenscommissioner.org, visited 24 August 2005.

[3] Professor Sir Ian Kennedy, *The Report of the Public Inquiry into Children's Heart Surgery at the Bristol Royal Infirmary 1984–1995: Learning from Bristol*, CM5207(I), July 2001 (the Kennedy Report).

Victoria Climbié[4] and a commitment on the part of the Labour Government to delivering an NHS for the twenty-first century which is centred around the needs of the patient. This chapter will consider the recent history of the provision of healthcare to children through the findings of these reports and outline the standards for children's healthcare services currently in the process of implementation. Given the context of the background to these developments, it is possible to understand the four-fold aims of: developing child-centred services; providing targeted services embedded within universal services for all children; ensuring that services are 'joined-up' to ease the child's journey through health and social care; and recognition of the respective roles of parents/carers and professionals in securing the health and well-being of children. Consideration is also given in this chapter to challenges brought by parents to resource allocation decisions which deny their children access to medical treatment. First, a brief consideration of the state of health of children in England and Wales.

The health of children in England and Wales

Children living in England and Wales today generally enjoy healthier lives than any previous generation. Childhood death is now a rare occurrence. Children born at the beginning of the twenty-first century have a longer life expectancy than ever before. Improvements to children's health are a result of improved nutrition, better housing, a clean water supply and sanitation, a national programme of immunisation which has reduced the incidence of morbidity and mortality from infectious disease, preventative screening programmes and advancements in medical treatment and medical technology. Yet, children are frequent users of healthcare services. Healthcare services provided to children range from routine health promotion, through treatment for minor illness or unexpected injury and, for some children, medical management of much more serious or enduring health problems:

> Healthy children are seen for routine health checks and immunisations, and need care when they are briefly unwell – although over 80 per cent of all episodes of illness in childhood are managed by parents without reference to the professional health care system. In a typical

---

[4] Lord Laming (Chair), *The Victoria Climbié Inquiry: Summary and Recommendations*, HMSO, 2003.

year, a pre-school child will see their general practitioner about six times, while a child of school age will go two or three times;[5] up to half of infants aged under 12 months and one quarter of older children will attend an Accident and Emergency (A & E) Department. In any year, one in eleven children will be referred to a hospital outpatients clinic, and one in ten to fifteen will be admitted to hospital. The majority of children's admissions to hospital are unexpected, as is much surgery on children. Most of these children will have one short admission, but a few will spend long periods in hospital or be admitted often. Serious illness requiring intensive care will affect one in a thousand children. One in ten babies born each year will require admission to a neonatal unit, of whom about 2 per cent will need intensive care.[6]

Young children depend upon their parents to maintain their health through 'preventative action, health promotion, healthy living, and healthy life-styles'.[7] This begins before conception, with women planning a pregnancy recommended to take folic acid supplements and ensure they are immunised against rubella. It continues during gestation, with pregnant women advised to eat a healthy diet, take moderate exercise, minimise alcohol consumption, give up smoking and offered screening for foetal abnormalities.[8] Maintaining the health of young children centres around basic care – ensuring the child eats a healthy diet, exercises, gets sufficient sleep, keeping them safe from accidental injury and tending the child through minor childhood illness dealt with in the home without professional assistance.

The basic care of children, focused upon children's diets and activity levels, is currently a matter of priority for securing the health of all children and a primary objective of the government's public health strategy for

---

[5] The rate per 1,000 of the child population consulting their GP was 6,000–12,000 for children aged from birth to four years and 3,000–7,000 for children aged between five and fifteen: Office for National Statistics, *The Health of Children and Young People*, March 2004, ch. 2, 'Provision and use of services', table 2.14.

[6] Department of Health, *Getting the Right Start: National Service Framework for Children: Standard for Hospital Services*, Crown Copyright, April 2003, at p. 3.

[7] David Armstrong, 'From Clinical Gaze to Regime of Total Health' in Alan Beattie, Marjorie Gott, Linda Jones and Moyra Sidell (eds.), *Health and Wellbeing: A Reader*, Oxford University Press and Macmillan: Basingstoke & London, 1993, 55–67, at p. .65; David M. B. Hall and David Elliman (eds.), *Health for All Children* (4th edn.), Oxford University Press: Oxford, 2003, at p. 1, www.health-for-all-children.co.uk. All are key to the obligation imposed upon the state to recognise the 'right of the child to the highest attainable standard of health' in Article 24 of the United Nations Convention on the Rights of the Child.

[8] Department of Health, *National Service Framework for Children, Young People and Maternity Services: Standard 11: Maternity Services*, October 2004, paras. 6–7.

children,[9] given evidence of an increase in the number of children who are overweight and rising levels of childhood obesity. A survey published in 2000 of the diets of four- to eighteen-year-olds concluded that the majority of British children consumed more saturated fat, sugar and salt than the recommended levels.[10] In 2003, 13.7 per cent of two- to ten-year-olds were obese, and 27.7 per cent were overweight.[11] Weight problems in childhood can result in low self-esteem, place growing bodies under strain and can lead to heart problems. They also put children at risk of developing diabetes. Diabetes is a chronic metabolic disorder in which there is a raised blood glucose level resulting from insulin deficiency. Most children with diabetes have 'Type 1' diabetes requiring two to four insulin injections daily, although the incidence of 'Type 2' diabetes is rising due to obesity and insufficient exercise.[12]

The most common chronic diseases of childhood are asthma, eczema and hay fever. In England in 1996, 21 per cent of two- to fifteen-year-olds had been diagnosed as suffering from asthma, 24 per cent with eczema and 9 per cent with hayfever.[13] Asthma is a chronic inflammatory respiratory disease, the cause of which is uncertain. The effects of asthma range from mild to severe, with some children experiencing occasional mild episodes of coughing and wheezing whilst others suffer much more serious respiratory problems which have a detrimental effect upon their participation in physical activity and school attendance and hence upon performance. For many children, their condition will be managed under the supervision of their general practitioner, others require hospitalisation[14] and asthma can cause death.[15]

In contrast to the reduction in physical illness amongst children is an increase in the incidence of mental health problems.[16] The occurrence of

---

[9] Department of Health, *Choosing Health: Making Healthy Choices Easier*, November 2004, ch. 3, 'Children & young people – starting on the right path'.

[10] Laura McDermott, 'Food Promotion to Children: A Time for Action' (2004) *Childright* 14–16, referring to Food Standards Agency, *National Diet and Nutrition Survey: Young People aged 4–18 years*, 2000.

[11] Dhriti Jotangia et al., *Obesity Among Children under 11,* Department of Heath in collaboration with the Health and Social Care Information Centre, April 2005, using information from the Health Survey for England.

[12] Clare Williams, *Mothers, Young People and Chronic Illness,* Ashgate Hampshire, 2002, at pp. 22–6.   [13] *Supra,* n. 5, ch. 7, 'Asthma and allergic diseases'.

[14] In 2000, there were forty-eight annual hospital admissions per 10,000 children under five: *ibid.*

[15] *Supra,* n. 12, at pp. 18–22.

[16] *Supra,* n. 6, at para. 1.4. Mental health is a particular issue amongst older children for whom the consequences for their health of 'chosen behaviours' in relation to sexual activity, smoking and consumption of alcohol are further matters of concern.

mental disorder is higher in boys than amongst girls, with an incidence of 10 per cent in boys aged five to ten years compared with a rate of 6 per cent in girls of the same age, rising to 13 per cent and 10 per cent respectively in children aged eleven to fifteen. Rates of emotional disorder such as anxiety and depression are similar for girls and boys, whilst the occurrence of conduct and hyperkinetic disorders is greater amongst boys. The incidence of mental disorder is higher amongst children of families in Social Class IV (14 per cent) than in Social Class I (5 per cent) and is 21 per cent in families where neither parent has ever worked.[17]

Poverty remains an issue for the health and well-being of children, causing health inequalities amongst children not confined to their mental health.[18] The incidence of low-birthweight births, a major factor in neonatal death and with life-long consequences, is higher in areas of deprivation. Health inequalities persist throughout childhood, with higher rates of overweight and obese children, accidental injury and death in childhood amongst children from disadvantaged backgrounds.[19]

Serious illness amongst children is rare. There is, for example, a low incidence of cancer in childhood, occurring in 110–150 per million children per year. A third of these cancers are leukaemia, of which about 80 per cent are acute lymphoblastic leukaemia.[20] Treatment of childhood cancer has improved so that, by the mid-1990s, 75 per cent of children with cancer survived for at least five years after diagnosis and, in 2000, there were 15,000 adult survivors of childhood cancer. Cancer causes a similar number of childhood deaths each year to those caused by accidents. In 2000, there were three poisoning deaths and eight deaths from falls amongst children under the age of four in the UK.[21] More children died in that year in road accidents (thirty-eight children) and from drowning/choking/suffocating (sixty-six children). Whilst rarely fatal, the numbers of children injured in household accidents are much greater. In 2002, there were 26,179 children aged from birth to four years involved in poisoning accidents and 305,307 injured in falls.[22]

The incidence of children living with severe disability and complex needs has increased as a consequence of the ability to sustain the lives of children

[17] *Supra*, n. 5, ch.12, 'Mental health'.   [18] *Supra*, n. 6, at para. 1.4.
[19] Department of Heath, *National Service Framework for Children, Young People and Maternity Services, Core Standards*, October 2004, Standard 1, p. 24.   [20] *Supra*, n. 5, ch. 13, p. 3.
[21] Royal Society for the Prevention of Accidents, *Child Accident Statistics*, www.rospa.com/factsheets/child_accidents.pdf.   [22] Royal Society for the Prevention of Accidents, www.rospa.com.

born prematurely,[23] with disabilities following a serious accident or illness or with a life-limiting condition. Most children with severe disability and complex needs live at home, cared for by their parents, perhaps with help from other family members, raising important questions of social policy about the support provided to them to secure a quality of life for all.[24]

The Bristol Royal Infirmary Inquiry

Paediatric cardiac services at the Bristol Royal Infirmary

The Bristol Royal Infirmary Inquiry was established in June 1998, meeting the demands of parents who had expressed concerns about the quality of care provided to their children who had undergone cardiac surgery at Bristol.[25] The Bristol Inquiry was a public inquiry with terms of reference to examine the care of children undergoing cardiac surgery at the Bristol Royal Infirmary between 1984 and 1995 and, in the light of conclusions reached about the adequacy of care and action taken in response to concerns raised, to make recommendations to improve the quality of care provided by the NHS in the future.[26] The panel adopted a non-adversarial approach, emphasising that they were engaged in a different task from that of a court determining negligence liability in respect of harm to any one child.[27] The

---

[23] The EPICure study involving follow-up of all babies born in the UK and Ireland at less than twenty-six weeks' gestation and admitted to the neonatal intensive care unit between March and December 1995 aimed to learn about survival and disability in order to improve the care provided to pre-term babies. Of 4,004 babies, 314 survived to be discharged from hospital. In the follow-up study when the children were six years old, it was found that 20 per cent had cerebral palsy although only half severely, and 41 per cent had learning difficulties across the range from serious to requiring some learning support, www.nottingham.ac.uk/obgyn/EPICure/index. htm.   [24] *Supra*, n. 6, at para. 1.4.

[25] Announced by Frank Dobson, then Secretary of State for Health, Ministerial Statement to House of Commons, June 1998 (Hansard cols. 529–30). The panel members were Professor Sir Ian Kennedy (Chair), Rebecca Howard, Professor Sir Brian Jarman and Mavis Maclean.

[26] The evidence considered by the panel is available at www.bristol-inquiry.org.uk, including transcripts of oral evidence, witness statements, submissions, the clinical case notes report, background papers, expert papers and reports of the seven seminars. The Final Report and the Interim Report are also available from the website. All evidence, with the exception of the witness statements, was published on two CD-ROMs along with the report.

[27] *Supra*, n. 3, ch. 1, para. 31. By July 2001, 61 families had accepted compensation in the region of £20,000 where their child had died following surgery and about 100 claims were outstanding in relation to children who had died or suffered brain damage: Sean O'Neill, 'Payouts in heart babies scandal could top £50m', *Daily Telegraph*, 16 July 2001. Claims involving children whose treatment caused brain damage or disabilities such as those sustained by James and Bronwen Stewart's son Ian, in relation to whom the trust admitted they had failed to provide accurate

panel's method was that of systems analysis which, in contrast to the focus of a negligence action upon the acts of the individual in isolation from the circumstances, seeks to explain failings within the context of the system in which they occur.

The inquiry panel were clearly deeply touched by the evidence of the parents. Evidence was given to the Inquiry by parents of children who were successfully treated, of children who survived surgery but suffered mental or physical disability as a consequence and of children who died during or shortly after surgery. Although the inquiry panel provided a list of issues, parents identified those aspects of their experience of enduring importance to their views of the quality of care provided to their child and themselves. This parental evidence comprised both memories and current feelings about past events, with the benefit of hindsight and knowledge of subsequent revelations, centred upon the intense and emotional period of caring for an extremely ill child.[28] The conclusions of the Bristol Royal Infirmary Inquiry Report (hereafter, the Kennedy Report) are respectful of what the panel had learned from the parents, whilst the perspectives of the professionals involved are likewise acknowledged and both are tempered with views of experts and academic opinion.

The Kennedy Report states clearly the conclusion that the failures at Bristol were not the malicious acts of evil, callous or even uncaring individuals.[29] The

---

Footnote 27 (*cont.*)

information about the risks involved in the surgery, involve larger amounts of money: Keith Bradford, 'Not a penny', *Bristol Evening Post*, 4 July 2001. A settlement of £5.4m was approved by the High Court in December 2002, at which time Ian Stewart was the only child who had sustained brain damage during surgery for whom the United Bristol Healthcare Trust had admitted liability: Sarah Key, 'Huge payout "will open floodgates": 5.4m for heart-op boy who suffered brain damage', *Bristol Evening Post*, 7 December 2002.

[28] Parental evidence also provides important insights into the impact of organ retention without parental knowledge or consent considered in the Bristol Royal Infirmary Interim Report, *Removal and Retention of Human Material*, May 2000, and the way in which they and their child were treated after their child had died.

[29] The General Medical Council (GMC) found cardiac surgeons Mr James Wisheart and Mr Janardan Dhasmana and Chief Executive of the United Bristol Healthcare NHS Trust Dr John Roylance guilty of 'serious professional misconduct'. Mr Wisheart and Dr Roylance were removed from the medical register. Mr Dhasmana's registration was subject to the condition that he did not operate on children for three years. In June 2001, this restriction was extended for a further year and, as he had not performed cardio-thoracic surgery on adults since 1997, a restriction was imposed which permitted him to perform such surgery only under supervision: (2001) 322 BMJ 1441. The following year, the GMC removed this restriction permitting Mr Dhasmana to perform heart surgery upon adults unsupervised but continuing the ban preventing him from operating upon children: Martin Hickman, 'Dhasmana: Not allowed to operate on children', *Independent*, 20 June 2002.

conclusion that 'too many children died' was reached despite appreciation of the hard work, dedication, commitment and care of the professionals involved.[30]

The Inquiry found that the designation of Bristol as a supra-regional service for open-heart paediatric cardiac surgery in 1984 (until neonatal and infant cardiac services were de-designated in 1992) meant that parents of children, of all ages, who were referred to Bristol for cardiac surgery between 1984 and 1995 believed that their child was being provided with the very best available care. Bristol had failed to meet any of the criteria for designation but it was hoped that, with funding guaranteed, the case load would increase and expertise develop. The point is poignantly made: 'Set against these arguments is the simple proposition that if it had been put to parents that by travelling 80 miles further up a motorway, the chances of survival of their child could well be doubled (or more), the parents would probably have opted for elsewhere.'[31] The Kennedy Report concluded, from statistical and other evidence, that the standard of care between 1984 and 1995 for children undergoing open-heart surgery was 'less than adequate'.[32] The particular failings within paediatric cardiac services in Bristol were identified, within the context of a neglect of children's healthcare services generally.

The inadequacies of the Bristol paediatric cardiac services arose from failures in the organisation, lack of leadership and poor management, and from the culture in which it was delivered.[33] Division along lines of professional hierarchy, excessive workloads and a failure to work effectively as a team in the care of children with complex needs had a detrimental effect upon the quality of care provided. A culture of fear, blame and cover-up discouraged reflective practice, inhibited the sharing of information and precluded effective teamwork amongst the professionals involved in the care of children undergoing cardiac surgery. There was a failure to reflect upon the quality of care provided and a willingness to explain away poor

[30] *Supra*, n. 3, ch. 13, paras. 3–7; Summary.   [31] *Ibid.*, ch. 18, para. 2.

[32] *Ibid.*, Section 1, Conclusions, para. 6.

[33] An independent inquiry into paediatric cardiac services at the Royal Brompton and Harefield Hospitals, established as a result of concerns expressed by parents about their child's treatment, identified similar problems and demonstrated a comparable appreciation of the changed context for the delivery of healthcare services. The inquiry also considered allegations of discriminatory treatment of children with Down's Syndrome: Ruth Evans (Chair), *The Report of the Independent Inquiries into Paediatric Cardiac Services at the Royal Brompton Hospital and Harefield Hospital* (April 2001).

outcomes, attributing these to the presence of a 'learning curve', the fact that, given small numbers of children treated, the situation looked worse than it was when expressed in percentage terms, or that the children they treated had more complex problems than elsewhere.[34] In the absence of external or internal mechanisms for monitoring standards and assuring quality, these beliefs went unchallenged.[35] The Inquiry panel agreed with the parents who had identified the split site as a problem,[36] considering that it had resulted in a split service. Closed-heart surgery was performed at the Bristol Royal Hospital for Sick Children where the cardiologists were based. Seriously ill children were transferred to the Bristol Royal Infirmary for open-heart surgery where they were taken to the adult intensive care unit to recover before being returned to the children's hospital if further treatment was required prior to discharge. A further consequence of the split site was that the practice of cardiologists and surgeons meeting prior to operations to review notes and test results, described by one expert as 'imperative', 'fell by the wayside' and the cardiologists, based in the children's hospital, were not available to give advice during surgery.[37] A number of parents also pointed to the lack of facilities for children at the Bristol Royal Infirmary, where children recovered on an intensive care ward shared with adults, without dedicated paediatric intensive care beds or nurses and with equipment that was not always suitable.[38]

Improving the quality of healthcare services

The legacy of the children who died or suffered disability, injury or complications following open-heart surgery at the Bristol Royal Infirmary between 1984 and 1995 and of their parents and families goes beyond improvements in the standard of care in the paediatric cardiac services in Bristol. The Kennedy Report pointed to the general underfunding of the National Health Service as a whole and to the specific neglect of healthcare services for children. The panel made both general recommendations and those directed specifically at improving the standard of children's healthcare services. The 198 recommendations of the Kennedy Report,[39]

---

[34] *Supra*, n. 3, Section 1, Conclusions, para. 3. [35] *Ibid.*, ch. 14, para. 21.
[36] *Ibid.*, ch. 16, paras. 8–20. [37] *Ibid.*, ch. 16, paras. 21–30. [38] *Ibid.*, ch. 13, para. 8.
[39] Summarised in Jo Bridgeman, '"Learning from Bristol": Healthcare in the 21st Century' (2002) 65 MLR 241. The government response, Department of Health, *Learning from Bristol: The Department of Health's Response to the Report of the Public Inquiry into Children's Heart Surgery*

made in July 2001, were consistent with the direction of the Labour Government reform programme for the NHS aimed at putting 'the patient at the centre of the health service and the way in which care is delivered'[40] and the reform of self-regulation undertaken by the professional bodies, most notably the General Medical Council (GMC). The recommendations within the Kennedy Report ranged across medical education, reform of clinical negligence litigation,[41] systems for learning from mistakes, professional self-regulation, institutional monitoring and quality assurance, and public and patient participation. Taken as a whole, the recommendations of the Kennedy Report contribute to the development of a framework for the delivery of healthcare based upon the foundational values of the NHS,[42] shaped according to contemporary values and centred around the patient.

Improving the quality of children's healthcare services

The Kennedy Report concluded that children's services presented a particular cause for concern. The evidence indicated that the failures in children's acute healthcare services exposed in Bristol were widespread and that healthcare services for children remained a low priority at both national and local levels. The Kennedy Report noted reports going back to 1959 which shared as a recurring theme the importance of considering the specific needs of children within families in the planning and delivery of their healthcare. These set out good guiding principles, but ones which consistently had not been translated into changes in service delivery.[43] Given the existence of appropriate guidance, the Report focused upon how to achieve the shift in attitudes necessary to address the neglect of

at the Bristol Royal Infirmary 1984–1995, Cm 5363, January 2002, is considered in Jo Bridgeman, 'The "Patient at the Centre": The Government Response to the Bristol Inquiry Report' (2002) 24 JSWFL 347–61.

[40] Department of Health, *ibid.*, ch. 1, para. 26, but repeating the aim expressed in *The NHS Plan: A Plan for Investment, A Plan for Reform*, Cm 4818-I, 2000.

[41] *Supra*, n. 3, ch. 23, para. 54; ch. 26, paras. 23–35. Subsequent developments in this area are considered in chapter 6.

[42] '[T]hat the NHS be a publicly-funded service, free at the point of delivery, that it provide a comprehensive service and that there be equity in people's access to its services,': *ibid.*, ch. 21, para. 9.

[43] The Platt Report, *The Welfare of Children in Hospital*, Ministry of Health, Central Health Services Council, HMSO: London, 1959; *Fit for the Future: The Report of the Committee on Child Health Services*, volume 1, HMSO: London, 1976; *Children First: A Study of Hospital Services*, Audit Commission, HMSO: London, 1993; *Hospital Services for Children and Young People*, House of Commons Select Committee (Session 1996–7), Fifth Report, HMSO: London, 1997 noted in *ibid.*, ch. 29, para. 7.

healthcare services for children. Children are not, after all, merely small adults or indeed, as argued in chapter 1, non-adults. Neither is there a single model of 'the child' around whom services can be designed, as the needs of newborn, infant, toddler, pre-school, school-aged and teenage child are very different. Furthermore, beyond these categories, each child is an individual, whose needs depend upon their personality, state of health, previous experiences and their ability to cope with their condition. Welcoming the development of a National Service Framework for children, the Kennedy Report stressed the need for child-centred services which are responsive to the varied needs of children of different ages and which recognise the important contribution made by the child's parents or carers to the child's care. Hospital services for children had to be integrated with other services which might be required by the child or their family either before, or after, treatment. Hospital treatment should not be seen as an isolated episode but rather as a stage in a journey through children's services. To achieve integrated healthcare services structured not according to the needs of the organisation but according to the needs of sick or injured children and their parents,[44] leadership in relation to children's healthcare services was required at both national and local level.[45]

In their evidence to the Inquiry, parents had stressed the need for child-centred healthcare services. They had emphasised the importance, to the overall quality of care provided, of their child being treated as an individual, of recognition of the role of parents in contributing to the care of their child, and the need for support to be provided to the family throughout the child's journey through the healthcare system. Even where surgery was performed competently, failures within the overall system of care left parents with feelings of concern, distress or lasting doubts about whether they had done the best for their child. Whilst appreciating that professionals treated many patients, the ability of the professional to respond to the child as an individual affected judgment about the quality of care provided. As Paul Bradley, whose daughter Bethan died after undergoing a second operation at the age of five, said: '[w]e appreciate that hospital staff deal with count-

---

[44] Kennedy Report, *supra*, n. 3, ch. 29, para. 22.
[45] Publication of the Report was swiftly followed by the appointment of Professor Al Aynsley-Green as National Director for Children's Healthcare Services to lead the development of children's healthcare services and implementation of improvements, including the *National Service Framework for Children*. With his appointment to the post of Children's Commissioner, Dr Sheila Shribman took up the post from 1 December 2005.

less patients and that the individuality of the person may be lost amongst all the flesh and tissue . . . we feel it is important that Bethan is recognised as an individual with a personality, not just another statistic'.[46]

Parents appreciated that the doctors and nurses had many patients to care for, whilst their attention was focused upon their child. The overall quality of care was affected by the extent to which parents felt that their knowledge of their child, gained through the experience of caring for them, was recognised. Thus, many parents attached importance to being able to provide basic care for their child whilst in hospital and to conveying, to the professionals, information about their child's specific needs. Furthermore, given their knowledge of their child, any failure to take seriously parental concerns about their child's health prior to, or after, treatment contributed to a perception amongst parents that their child had not received the best possible care.

As the children whose care was under scrutiny all had heart conditions, any hospital treatment was merely one episode in the management of their child's condition. Parents spoke of feeling alone and unsupported in the care of their child both before and after surgery. Even where surgery appeared to have been successful, the overall quality of care depended upon the information, advice and support provided to parents to guide them in their care of their child after discharge. Furthermore, whilst surgeons were focused upon the particular medical problem presented by the child, parents were concerned for the well-being of the whole child. Consequently, descriptions by surgeons of operations as successful but which left their child with physical or mental problems, even where parents were aware of the possibility of the risk which materialised, had an impact upon overall perceptions of the quality of care. As Penelope Plackett, whose daughter Sophie suffered brain damage during an operation to repair her heart defect, explained, 'My Sophie is still classed as a success even though she cannot walk, talk, move or do anything for herself. Under their criteria because she lived for thirty days after the operation she is still counted as one of their successes and I think that is a travesty.'[47]

In addition to their knowledge and experience of their child and the need for support before, during and after hospital treatment, parents also commented upon their decision-making responsibilities. Evidence from

---

[46] Written statement of Paul Bradley with regard to the treatment of his daughter, Bethan, to the Bristol Royal Infirmary Inquiry, paras. 99 and 104.

[47] BBC News, 'Travesty of brain-damaged success', 22 March 1999 (http://news.bbc.co.uk).

parents reflected the distinction identified by Priscilla Alderson between the legal obligation imposed upon professionals to impart information and parental understanding of the information provided. This does not refer to the level of comprehension of the technical aspects of treatment but that, even where sufficient information had been provided to fulfil the professional obligation, parents lacked 'experience [of] knowledge as awareness'.[48] In other words, there is a difference between fulfilling a duty by providing information and parents receiving such information and appreciating the meaning of that information for their care of their child. It was important that parents understood the seriousness of their child's condition and the risks of the surgery not only so that they could make a decision about treatment (often, there was really little choice) but also so that they could make decisions about the time they spent with their child. As one mother, Rowena Cutter, said:

> [T]he doctors gave me almost no information on Scott's condition during his period of unconsciousness. I think . . . it is incumbent upon the doctors themselves to make sure that a patient has all the information and that they understand that information. I think the doctors forget that whilst the child is their patient, that child is the son or daughter of the parent . . . Furthermore, had I known that Scott's condition was worsening and that they had genuine cause for concern, I would have been able to prepare myself for the inevitable outcome.[49]

Parents were critical of false hope and words of reassurance which meant that understanding, and thus acceptance, was not a possibility.[50] The function of the provision of information was more than merely fulfilling legal obligations to avoid a negligence action, it was necessary for parents to make decisions about how they spent time with their child, and to enable them and other family members to come to terms with the possibilities of success, or failure, of treatment.

Sadly, professional arrogance on the part of the surgeons was a central fault in the failings of the paediatric cardiac service in Bristol. In order to secure improved children's healthcare services for the future, the

---

[48] P. Alderson, *Choosing for Children: Parents' Consent to Surgery*, Oxford University Press: Oxford, 1990, at p. 116.

[49] Written statement of Rowena Cutter with regard to the treatment of her son, Scott, to the Bristol Royal Infirmary Inquiry, para. 35.

[50] Expressed by Andrew Hall, Penelope Plackett, Sandra Rundle, Mary Thorn and Brenda Rex in their written statements to the Bristol Royal Infirmary Inquiry.

Kennedy Report stressed the need to change the nature of the relationship between parents and professionals in the shared endeavour of caring for the child.

Parents and professionals: partnership and tensions

In the case of *Re J* (1990), Lord Donaldson MR portrayed the relationship between parent and healthcare professional in making decisions about the care of a child as a partnership:

> No one can dictate the treatment to be given to the child, neither court, parents nor doctors. There are checks and balances. The doctors can recommend treatment A in preference to treatment B. They can also refuse to adopt treatment C on the grounds that it is medically contra-indicated or for some other reason is a treatment which they could not conscientiously administer. The court or parents for their part can refuse to consent to treatment A or B or both, but cannot insist on treatment C. The inevitable and desirable result is that choice of treatment is in some measure a joint decision of the doctors and the court or parents.[51]

Lord Donaldson MR's characterisation of the relationship between parent and professional as a partnership recognises that professionals and parents have different roles in relation to the healthcare of children. Parents and professionals have different responsibilities (arising from their relationship with the child), knowledge and expertise (medical/technical and of the needs of the individual child) and functions in caring for a sick child. The doctor has a professional relationship with the child and is an expert in relation to the medical condition of the child – the diagnosis, prognosis and treatment options. The focus of the doctor will be upon the particular medical problem within his or her expertise and upon all of the children within his or her care. The relationship between parent and child is an intimate one of care, in which the parent has knowledge of their child as an individual, their experiences of health and illness, and their ability to cope with both their condition and treatment. Parents will be focused upon their child's treatment within the context of the past and their hopes for the future. Inevitably, the partnership between professional and parent is not an equal one. The doctor is equipped with knowledge about their field of expertise and will impartially administer to the child's medical needs.

---

[51] *Re J (a Minor) (Wardship: Medical Treatment)* [1991] 2 WLR 140, at p. 145.

Where the professional is exercising their skills in relation to a very sick child with a complex condition, they are inevitably faced with uncertainty about their ability to treat the child. The parent may be upset and extremely anxious, particularly where they have recently been presented with bad news about their child's health. The emotional intensity for parents caring for an extremely ill child was noted in the Kennedy Report:

> To each parent, these were times of the highest intensity. This was their child and their child's life. Each moment was an eternity and yet everything passed in a dizzying whirl. Each word and gesture were noted and repeatedly weighed and assessed for significance. But, paradoxically, sometimes words might be forgotten and gestures disregarded if hope lay elsewhere.[52]

In these circumstances, parents are dependent upon the professional upon whom they rely to provide their child with the best possible care.

In the past, the doctor/patient relationship may have been one of professional paternalism, in which the patient was an unquestioning beneficiary of treatment determined by the doctor who 'knew best'. Increasing recognition of the importance of patient autonomy, a market-driven health service and talk of patient rights (such as in the Patients' Charter) in the late twentieth century resulted in a shift from a model of professional paternalism without arriving at the logical conclusion of professional servitude to patient demand. The Kennedy Report characterised the model for the future as a partnership between professional and patient based upon the values of openness, honesty and mutual respect. These values should apply throughout to the process of securing consent, exchanging information and responding to concerns and complaints before, during and after treatment. To abide by these values, professionals need to be honest with themselves, and their patients, about the limits of the treatment and not give false hope or reassurance. In turn, parents have to accept the limitations of medical science in treating a child with complex needs. Where the patient is a child, openness, honesty and mutual respect in the relationship are vital for the proper discharge of the caring responsibilities of both professional and parent.

Rather than structure services and provide care according to, and upon, the demands of the adults concerned or their perceptions of what children require, the Kennedy Report argued that child-centred healthcare

---

[52] *Supra*, n. 3, ch. 2, para. 25.

CHILD-CENTRED HEALTHCARE SERVICES FOR CHILDREN   61

services have to be planned, structured and delivered according to children's assessments of their needs and that children have to be treated as partners in their care. That requires being responsive to the individual child, involving them to the extent that they wish to be involved and, where they do, informing them in an appropriate way to an appropriate extent. Priscilla Alderson, in her research, found that most children wanted their parents to be involved in the decision whether they should undergo surgery.[53] And as primary carers of, and advocates for, their children, parents will normally want to be involved not only in decision-making but also as participants in the care of their child and by contributing their expertise which they have gained through their particular interest in, and attention to, their child:

> Overwhelmingly, they [the parents] emphasised the need for parents with a child in hospital to be involved in their child's care and for parents' expertise, as the people who know the child best and who care for the child, to be fully acknowledged and appropriately engaged. This approach is now regarded as good practice when children are in hospital. We believe that it should be standard, routine practice. We have no doubt that this approach, whereby parents and patients are alongside and in partnership with the professional, rather than following and doing what they are told, is the way forward for modern care in hospital.[54]

It is, however, important to ensure that the interests of the individual child are recognised, as these may be different from the interests of the parents or the family:

> Children's needs are ordinarily expressed through their parents, who are usually the primary providers of their care. But there are also important differences between children and their families. Their interests do not always coincide.[55]

Unfortunately, before the Kennedy Inquiry reported, another public inquiry had been established which raised fundamental questions about children's services. This inquiry arose, not as a result of concerns expressed by parents who had done their best for their child, but from the neglect and abuse of a child by those who had assumed responsibility to care for her.

---

[53] Priscilla Alderson, *Children's Consent to Surgery*, Open University Press: Buckingham, 1993.
[54] *Supra*, n. 3, ch. 23, para. 15.   [55] *Ibid.*, ch. 29, para. 17.

Victoria Climbié, the Laming Inquiry and *Every Child Matters*

The death of Victoria Climbié from the cruelty, abuse and neglect of the woman into whose care she had been entrusted, her father's aunt Marie-Therese Kouao, and her boyfriend, Carl Manning, was the subject of a public inquiry chaired by Lord Laming.[56] Victoria died, at the age of eight, in the paediatric intensive care unit at St Mary's Hospital, Paddington on 25 February 2000 from heart, lung and kidney failure due to hypothermia caused by malnourishment and living in damp conditions with her movement constrained.[57] The neglect and cruelty inflicted upon Victoria went back over a period of some nine months commencing soon after she arrived in the UK in April 1999. The Inquiry concluded that the last four months of her life had been spent in a black bin bag in the bath in an unheated bathroom, lying in her own urine and excrement. Victoria had also been beaten. The post-mortem found 128 injuries to her body.

Victoria died as a consequence of the deliberate cruelty, the abhorrent actions, of Marie-Therese Kouao, the woman to whom her parents had entrusted their daughter and the woman who had promised that, by providing her with an education, she could offer Victoria the chance of a brighter future. Thus Victoria's death and the conviction of Kouao and Manning for her murder serve as an horrific reminder that children will not always receive love, nurturance and protection from those adults entrusted to care for them. After the event, these adults were punished through the processes of the criminal justice system for the harm they had caused. The Laming Inquiry concentrated upon the role of the public services responsible for protecting children from harm: primarily the police, social services and health authorities to whom she was referred as a result of concerns about deliberately inflicted injuries. Among the issues raised by the tragic events leading to the death of Victoria Climbié are the three questions central to this book: What are the responsibilities of parents or those undertaking the daily care of children? What are the responsibilities of professionals involved in the delivery of children's services? What is the function of public authorities with respect to the care of children?

Lord Laming considered the social services responsible for child protection to have been 'under-funded, inadequately staffed and poorly led'.[58] Condemnation of the failures of ill-trained, or overworked, front-line staff

---

[56] *Supra*, n. 4.   [57] *Ibid.*, at pp. 2 and 31.   [58] *Ibid.*, at p. 4.

was placed in the context of criticism of inadequacies in management and leadership. Lord Laming concluded that child protection had, in the future, to be secured through support for the family and that multi-agency working had an essential role in effective child protection.[59] The Laming Report had a direct impact upon family policy in the Green Paper, *Every Child Matters*, published at the same time as the government's reponse to the Laming Report.[60] The Green Paper proposed a programme of change to ensure that all children have the opportunity, through promotion and preventative strategies, to fulfil their potential, whilst providing specific safeguards for children vulnerable to neglect or abuse or vulnerable because of illness or disability.[61] Children's well-being is framed by five goals set out in *Every Child Matters* developed through a consultation process in which children and parents were participants:[62]

1. Being healthy: achieving physical, mental, emotional and sexual health and enjoying a healthy lifestyle (including choosing not to take illegal drugs) – the key mechanism for delivery of which is the *National Service Framework for Children, Young People and Maternity Services*;

2. Staying safe: protecting children from neglect, violence and sexual exploitation, accidental injury or death, bullying or discrimination, crime and anti-social behaviour, whilst providing children with security, stability and care;

3. Enjoying and achieving: preparing for school, enjoying school and leisure, achieving educational standards and personal and social development;

4. Making a positive contribution: to community and society and not engaging in anti-social or offending behaviour, developing enterprising behaviour, positive relationships and self-confidence to deal with changes and challenges in life;

5. Economic well-being: participating in further education, training or employment upon leaving school, living in decent homes free from

---

[59] *Ibid.*, at p. 7.

[60] *Keeping Children Safe: The Government's Response to the Victoria Climbié Inquiry Report and Joint Chief Inspectors' Report Safeguarding Children*, Cm 5861, Crown Copyright, September 2003 considered that the Children Act 1989 provided a sound basis for safeguarding children but that there needed to be a greater focus upon prevention and early intervention and for child protection to be linked to support for parents through a 'spectrum of services': para. 4.

[61] Chief Secretary to the Treasury, *Every Child Matters*, Cm 5860, HMSO: London, September 2003.

[62] Developed into twenty-five outcomes set out in Department for Education and Skills, *Every Child Matters: Change for Children*, 2004, p. 9.

poverty with access to transport and material goods in sustainable communities.

Covering a wide range of issues, including poverty, truanting, sport in schools, bullying and child offending, *Every Child Matters* sets out a vision of integrated children's services and support for parents to fulfil their responsibilities in the context of a seamless web between universal services to promote children's well-being and targeted services for children in need.

Integrated children's services

The result of Bristol, Laming and *Every Child Matters* is an ambition to achieve a 'reconfiguration of children's services creat[ing] a complex structure that extends and modifies existing arrangements'.[63] Sue Penna suggests this involves a reconceptualisation from traditional understandings of child protection to 'the protection of children from failing to achieve their "potential"' in relation to health, education, poverty and anti-social behaviour.[64] The focus of services will be upon support for all parents, prevention and early intervention.

Central to these developments is a response to the failure identified by both Kennedy and Laming to provide joined-up services – in which professionals communicate with each other and work together – for children across health, social care and education. The key means by which to 'address the fragmentation of responsibilities for children's services'[65] is multi-agency working. Given legislative effect in the Children Act 2004, local authorities are required to have established joined-up children's services by 2008. How this is achieved is not prescribed but it is to be developed according to local needs. As a minimum there must be integrated educational and social services with others, including statutory services, voluntary and community providers, and sport, culture or play organisations, as appropriate. These services may be delivered through Children's Trusts, which are partnerships of organisations planning, commissioning, and providing, universal and targeted services and sharing processes to ensure integrated services. All local authorities must have arrangements in place by 2008 which integrate services, strategies and processes, for

---

[63] Sue Penna, 'The Children Act 2004: Child Protection and Social Surveillance' (2005) 27 JSWFL 143, at p. 146.   [64] *Ibid.*, at p .146.
[65] See www.everychildmatters.gov.uk/aims/childrenstrusts/faq (visited 24 August 2005).

commissioning services, pooling of budgets, co-ordination of staff and governance according to local need. To achieve this and address the fragmentation of services, co-location of services is recommended through, for example, Sure Start Children's Centres and Extended Schools.[66] The Children Act 2004, s. 10, imposes a duty upon the local authority to promote co-operation with partners such as the Primary Care Trust, NHS Trust, Strategic Health Authority, police, youth offending team and local probation board to improve outcomes for children. A reciprocal duty is imposed upon these partner agencies to co-operate with the authority. Sharing of human and physical or other resources and the pooling of budgets is permitted, as appropriate. A duty is imposed upon all agencies providing children's services to discharge their functions having regard to the need to safeguard and promote the welfare of children.[67] The Children Act 2004 therefore establishes the legislative framework to encourage and facilitate integrated commissioning, and delivery, of children's services.

Each local authority is required, by 2006, to have developed a Children and Young People's Plan setting out the local strategy for children's services following analysis of local need and determination of local priorities. Each area is required to appoint a Director of Children's Services accountable for children's services across the local authority and as a minimum for educational and social service functions. At the political level, each local authority is required to appoint a Lead Member for Children's Services.[68] Within each area, there must be a Local Safeguarding Children Board to co-ordinate and monitor the work undertaken by the partner service organisations to safeguard and promote the welfare of children, focused upon the goal of 'staying safe'.[69] Section 12 of the Act gives the Secretary of State the power to issue regulations requiring local authorities to establish and operate a database of information about children and young people or to establish a corporate body to do so. Shared information is aimed at facilitating the delivery of integrated services by making relevant information about a child available to all professionals involved in his or her care. *Every Child Matters* also proposes a common assessment framework and that there should be a lead professional where the child is receiving services from more than one agency.

The Children Act 2004 further provides for an integrated inspection framework of children's services, focused upon the extent to which they

[66] *Supra*, n. 9, at paras. 15–30.   [67] Children Act 2004, s. 11(2)(a).
[68] *Ibid.*, ss. 18 and 19.   [69] *Ibid.*, s. 13(1).

improve the well-being of children and young people.[70] The Act makes provision for joint reviews undertaken by inspectorates, according to this framework, focused upon how well the services work together to improve the well-being of children.[71]

Rather than offer fragmented services and an episodic approach to hospital treatment, the Kennedy Report emphasised the need to provide joined-up services for children, bringing together health, social and voluntary services. In the future, hospital treatment should be delivered as a stage on a journey through health and social care systems, with support (counselling, information and practical) provided before, and after, treatment. The vision of the Kennedy Report, shared by *Every Child Matters*, is for development of child-centred healthcare services which are no longer organised around the needs of the institution or the professionals working within the service but structured according to the needs of the child or young person and their family. The primary mechanism for achieving this for children's healthcare services is the ten-year plan set out in the *National Service Framework for Children, Young People and Maternity Services* published in October 2004.[72]

The *National Service Framework for Children, Young People and Maternity Services*

The *National Service Framework for Children, Young People and Maternity Services* (NSF) sets out a long-term strategy for improving the health and well-being of children and young people (and thus the 'being healthy' goal of *Every Child Matters*) by setting the *standards* of care which should be offered by 2014. The purpose of the framework is to establish standards which promote high-quality child-centred care which meets the needs of children, parents and families, working towards the 'delivery of appropriate, integrated, effective and needs-led services'[73] and the eradication of differences in the quality of care. The standards are not legally binding and are deliberately designed to allow local variation in implementation, which does leave uncertainty as to the extent to which the NSF will result in

---

[70] *Ibid.* s. 21.   [71] *Ibid.* s. 20.

[72] Department of Health, *National Service Framework for Children, Young People and Maternity Services*, October 2004.

[73] Professor Aynsley-Green, Presentation, 'Practical Implications of the Emerging NSF for Children', Conference, 22 January 2003, at p. 9, www.dh.gov.uk.

positive change to children's healthcare services. The evidence that children today are healthier than ever, that social, environmental and economic factors have a greater impact upon the health of children than biological disorders[74] but that health inequalities exist, explains the focus of the NSF upon health promotion with early intervention. The first five standards apply universally to children, Standards 6–10 to children with particular needs and Standard 11 to maternity services.

Universal standards

Health promotion

Promotion of children's health and teaching children to adopt a healthy lifestyle are to be brought within the integrated approach to children's health services, delivered through the Child Health Promotion Programme. This will include raising awareness about, and providing information and support services in relation to, health promotion, including immunisation. Given the evidence of the impact which the social, economic and environmental circumstances in which children live has upon their health, and the health inequalities which occur due to poverty, this standard seeks to bring about a shift from the traditional model of surveillance of children's health to an approach which integrates health visiting, general practice care and use of school nurses. The aim is to assess every child's physical, emotional and social development, by the time of their first birthday, and to provide services to meet the assessed needs of child and family.[75] Central to the promotion of the health of children will be a schedule of checks and a programme of immunisation, supported by health promotion.[76] The stated aim is for services to be universal yet personalised. Additional support will be provided to children and families in need, delivered in partnership with parents. Schools are also expected to play an important role in the development of children's skills to live a healthy life through the National Healthy Schools Programme. The programme seeks to foster health across school provision, including policies on healthy and nutritious food, provision of time and facilities for physical activity within the curriculum and out of school hours and through personal, social and health education (PSHE) supported by the *Healthy Living Blueprint*.[77]

---

[74] Hall and Elliman, *supra*, n. 7, at p. 1, www.health-for-all-children.co.uk.
[75] *Supra.*, n. 72, Standard 1, at p. .22.   [76] *Ibid.*, at p. .25.
[77] See www.teachernet.gov.uk/healthyliving.

Since 2004, all four- to six-year-olds attending LEA maintained schools have been offered a piece of fruit or vegetable every day, new nutritional standards for school meals have been issued and funding has been provided for the development of school travel plans. A further element of this standard is a reduction in the number of children injured and killed in accidents in the home resulting from falls, scalding, burns, drowning, choking and poisoning.[78]

Supporting parents/carers

The standards relating to supporting parents recognise that parents face different challenges depending upon the age of their child so that the information which is helpful to a parent with a newborn child is different from that which may be of assistance to parents of a teenage child. The aim is to improve universal services (primarily through the provision of information, guides and materials) whilst targeting services to support parents with particular needs, whether these are due to their socio-economic situation, parental problems, or arise from the special needs of their children. The focus of this standard is upon support for parents to improve the parent/child relationship and enhance their confidence in, and skills of, parenting. This will be done through the provision of information, by alerting parents to sources of support within the voluntary sector and community, and referring parents to appropriate specialist services.[79] The controversial challenge presented by this standard is to change understanding about the need for parenting support and advice. The message is that all parents at some time need support, information or advice about parenting. To seek support should not be understood as an indication of having failed as a parent but as the behaviour of good, responsible parents.

Provision of services which are focused upon the child, young person and family

This standard, which clearly responds to the findings of the Bristol Royal Infirmary Inquiry and the recommendations of the Kennedy Report, sets out the general principles for the development of child-centred healthcare services for children. These are that services must be structured around the (changing) needs of the child or young person, differentiating according to their 'individuality, developmental age and social circumstances' and

---

[78] *Supra*, n. 72, at p. 50.   [79] *Ibid.*, Standard 2.

caring for the whole child (and not merely dealing with the illness or medical problem). In addition, healthcare services must recognise the role of parents, the importance of families and, furthermore, that the child has a life beyond their specific health problem.[80] Children and young people must be able to contribute to discussions about their care and treatment and to the planning and evaluation of healthcare services.[81] The relationship between child, parent and professional must be understood as a partnership. Information must be shared within this partnership throughout the child's 'journey' according to legal and ethical principles on consent and confidentiality.[82]

Children with particular needs

Everyday illnesses and primary care

This standard covers acute illness or injury and long-term conditions which are not disabling – including Accident and Emergency treatment, minor childhood illness and management of chronic conditions such as asthma.[83] Adopting the general principles outlined in Standard 4, this standard focuses upon the provision of information to enable children and their parents to make judgments about management of the child's condition and when professional assistance is required. It also emphasises the importance of ensuring that staff are skilled in the care of children and do not merely treat them as mini-adults.

Acute illnesses and hospital care

The standards for hospital care were the first to be developed as a direct response to the Kennedy Report.[84] These standards aim to reconfigure services around the child rather than the needs of the organisation, recognising that these differ depending upon the stage which the child is at in their journey through illness or injury, from prevention, through diagnosis, treatment, support or rehabilitation.[85] Hospital services should be child-centred, meaning that the child is treated, not the illness, that children are treated as children and young people as young people, and that the child

---

[80] *Ibid.*, Standard 3, at p. 89.   [81] *Ibid.*, at p. 91.
[82] *Ibid.*, Standard 4, at pp. 118–43 addresses the different issues of consent and confidentiality which arise as the child becomes a young person who should be supported to take responsibility for their health and may wish to seek advice or use services without the presence of their parent.
[83] *Ibid.*, Standard 6.   [84] *Supra*, n. 6.   [85] *Ibid.*, at paras. 1.7–1.8.

and parents are understood as partners in care. Services should also be delivered by staff trained in the treatment and nursing of children.[86] The standard stresses the entitlement of the child to privacy and respect, to explanations and to be asked for their permission for medical examination. The role of parents, who are 'usually the experts on their child',[87] must be respected. Children and their parents must be provided with 'accurate information that is valid, relevant, up-to-date, timely and understandable and developmentally, ethically and culturally appropriate', using a range of communication methods to equip them to make decisions about treatment.[88] The aim is to limit disruptive hospital stays as far as possible through co-ordinated care, including planning for discharge.[89] With obvious reference back to the events at Bristol, this standard stresses the importance of learning from adverse events not only through reports to the National Patient Safety Agency but also by discussion at trust board level of particular incidents which offer 'a learning opportunity'.[90]

Children with disabilities and complex needs

This standard aims to secure high-quality, integrated and co-ordinated care for disabled children and children with complex needs.[91] It emphasises that all children are entitled to enjoy 'ordinary lives', participating as members of a family and a community and with opportunities to reach their potential. This is an aim consistent with that detailed by parents in the study on *The Impact of Childhood Disability on Family Life* by Barbara Dobson, Sue Middleton and Alan Beardsworth, who found that:

> In compensating for their children's conditions, parents were doing their utmost to reconstruct a normal family life. Life had shown parents that there was considerable discrimination, as well as numerous physical barriers, which prevented their children from achieving their potential. They simply wanted their children, disabled or non-

---

[86] *Ibid.*, at paras. 2.5–2.7.

[87] *Ibid.*, at para. 3.13, but who may have other children to care for and for whom hospitalisation of their child may cause material hardship.   [88] *Ibid.*, at para. 3.15.

[89] *Ibid.*, at para. 3.30.   [90] *Ibid.*, at para. 4.6.

[91] *Supra*, n. 72, Standard 8. The aim is that '[c]hildren and young people who are disabled or who have complex health needs receive co-ordinated, high-quality child and family-centred services which are based on assessed needs, which promote social inclusion and, where possible, which enable them and their families to live ordinary lives'. This aim is consistent with Article 23(1) of the United Nations Convention on the Rights of the Child: 'States Parties recognize that a mentally or physically disabled child should enjoy a full and decent life, in conditions which ensure dignity, promote self-reliance and facilitate the child's active participation in the community.'

disabled, to have the same opportunities and experiences as others and they were prepared to do whatever was required to achieve this.[92]

If achieved, integrated children's services which bring together social services with education and possibly health services offer the potential to improve substantially the conditions under which disabled children, and children with complex needs, and their families live. Common assessment, co-location of services and multi-agency packages of care which are 'flexible and responsive to children's and families' needs' offer the possibility of improving the overall standard of care provided to children, and support for parents upon whom the primary caring role falls. Material improvements (housing, the provision of equipment and assistive technology) could make a difference to their lives. Better access to local mainstream children's services and to childcare could help parents to work and thereby improve their financial well-being. Services structured around the needs of the child, minimising the disruption to family life and schooling caused by the need to attend hospital or primary care services, would likewise enhance the quality of life within the family. The standard provides a focus for these services directed at giving 'children maximum opportunities to participate in family life and to achieve their optimal development',[93] including participation in leisure, sport and play activities.

Other standards

Standard 5 is directed at the safety of children through standards for safeguarding children and promoting their welfare throughout childhood. It is hoped that the likelihood of children being harmed or neglected will be reduced by the provision of specialist services embedded within universal services to support all families.[94] Mental illness affects 10 per cent of five- to fifteen-year-olds, which means that there are 1.1 million children who could benefit from mental health services. Standard 9 addresses the improvement of the mental health of all children by promoting mental health, early intervention and ensuring that complex mental health needs are met through 'timely, integrated, high quality, multi-disciplinary mental health services'. In the child's early years, the standard stresses the

---

[92] Barbara Dobson, Sue Middleton and Alan Beardsworth, *The Impact of Childhood Disability on Family Life*, Joseph Rowntree Foundation: York, 2001, at p. 35.   [93] *Supra*, n. 72, at p. 16.
[94] *Ibid.*, Standard 5, at p. 147.

importance of attachment and bonding between parent and child, and appropriate child-rearing practices, for the child's psychological well-being.[95] Standard 10 is directed towards securing safe, effective medicines administered in ways which are appropriate given the age of the child. Medicines should also be supported by information to permit parents and children to be partners in decision-making and to ensure safe and effective use of medicines. Appreciating that the well-being of children commences before birth and hence moral obligations are owed to the unborn, Standard 11 focuses upon high-quality maternity services responsive to the needs of mother and baby and assisting in preparation for parenthood.

The standards set out in the *National Service Framework for Children, Young People and Maternity Services* are not legally binding, although the expectation is that they will be implemented by 2014. The lessons learnt from Bristol and the failures identified in the Laming Report are apparent in the aims of the NSF. The standards are clearly aimed at establishing universal and targeted, child-centred, integrated healthcare services respectful of children as individuals and of the role of parents as partners with professionals in the care of children. The Kennedy Report observed that guidance on the provision of children's healthcare had been persistently unimplemented; whether the NSF successfully secures child-centred healthcare services for children depends upon local leadership under the national direction of the National Director for Children's Healthcare Services and the Children's Commissioner.

The Kennedy Report emphasised that its conclusions about the quality of the care provided at the Bristol Royal Infirmary had to be put into the context of a history of under-funding of the NHS generally.[96] The Report welcomed the commitment of the Labour Government to invest in the NHS, enabling the recruitment of more staff, refurbishment of hospitals and purchase of new equipment, whilst emphasising that investment had to be accompanied by attitudinal change if child-centred healthcare services for children were to be developed. The political question of the resources – human, material and technical – available is clearly a further factor upon which the future development of children's healthcare services depends. The next section considers cases in which parents have challenged

---

[95] *Ibid.*, Standard 9, at para. 2.2.

[96] That is, the level of funding was insufficient to meet the promises made about the services provided by the NHS, *supra*, n. 3, Section 1, Conclusions, ch. 4, para. 4.31; ch. 22, paras. 5–6.

the failure to provide their children with the medical treatment which they need because of the lack of available resources.

Challenging resource allocation decisions

Formally, this issue arrives in the public domain in the context of proceedings brought by parents to challenge decisions of hospital management in relation to the allocation of scarce NHS resources. These cases therefore raise the question of the limits of state-provided healthcare challenged by parents who are seeking to secure treatment for their child. In 1987, the courts refused an application for leave to apply for judicial review of the decision of Central Birmingham Health Authority to postpone the operation to repair the hole in the heart of six-week-old David Walker.[97] The hospital accepted that the baby required the operation and that it had been postponed a number of times due to a shortage of paediatric intensive care nurses to staff all the beds and as a result of more urgent cases being a higher priority for surgery when a bed did become free. Understandably, his mother wanted the operation he needed to be performed immediately; the hospital had to consider his needs alongside those of other patients in light of the resources available. Their evidence was to the effect that David would not be harmed by waiting but, if his case became an emergency, the operation would be performed even without the necessary aftercare being available. In contrast to the cases in chapter 5, where doctors formed the view that further treatment was not in the child's best interests, the doctors in this case were of the opinion that the surgery was in David's best interests but that it was only in his best interests to perform the operation without the necessary aftercare if his condition deteriorated to the point that emergency surgery was required. The issue was understood by MacPherson J to be a question of funding of the National Health Service and not a decision about a particular patient. As stated by Sir John Donaldson MR in the Court of Appeal, the question for the court in reviewing the decision of the hospital was whether it was *Wednesbury* unreasonable.[98] Their Lordships' were of the opinion that it was not.

This was followed by an application for leave for judicial review by the father of four-year-old Matthew Collier. Having previously had two heart operations, Matthew was assessed as being in desperate need of open-heart

---

[97] *R v Central Birmingham Health Authority, ex parte Walker; R v Secretary of State for Social Services and another, ex parte Walker*, QBD, 3 BMLR 32, 24 November 1987 (web.lexis-nexis.com/professional/).   [98] *Ibid.*

surgery and placed at the top of the waiting list. His operation had been arranged, and cancelled, three times in a four-month period because of a shortage of intensive-care beds and nurses. The application sought to distinguish this case from the previous one on the grounds that Matthew urgently needed surgery. In strident terms, Stephen Brown LJ stressed that the court was not the appropriate forum in which to consider the national allocation of resources and, in the absence of any evidence of *Wednesbury* unreasonableness on the part of the health authority, the court could, and should, not intervene in decisions about the allocation of resources.[99] Stephen Brown LJ expressed sympathy for the child and his parents and understanding of their anxiety. However, he was forthright in his criticism of the 'misconceived' judicial review proceedings brought against the same hospital, with respect to the same specialism, experiencing the same resourcing problem, as in *Walker*. Legal proceedings, he speculated, may merely have been an instrument with which to put pressure upon the hospital. He noted that to make the order sought would have the effect of shifting scarce resources from the provision of treatment to the defence of resource allocation decisions.

Surgery was performed upon both children soon after the refusal of the court to order a reconsideration of the decision: David underwent his operation on the evening of the Court of Appeal judgment and Matthew in the week following the judgment of the court.[100] Newspapers reported that Matthew's parents had received three offers of funding for a private operation but it was performed within the NHS a few days after the court's decision. Heart surgery is a risky and complex procedure performed upon children who are seriously ill and both David and Matthew died without being discharged from hospital. Matthew's family maintained that the delay in performing the surgery may have been a material factor in his death.[101] In both of these cases, there was agreement between parents and doctors that the surgery, which was delayed for lack of specialised nurses, was in the child's best interests. In such circumstances, court proceedings served as a practical step which parents, desperate to secure the best possible care for their child, could take to challenge the decision.

---

[99] *R v Central Birmingham Health Authority, ex parte Collier*, CA, 6 January 1988 (web.lexis-nexis.com/professional/).

[100] 'Heart baby's surgery success', *The Times*, 26 November 1987; '10-hour operation to save heart boy', *The Times*, 14 January 1988.

[101] Craig Seton, 'Mother talks of "cruel fate": Heart baby's death', *The Times*, 7 December 1987; Craig Seton, 'Hole in heart boy is dead', *The Times*, 15 February 1988.

A policy of judicial non-intervention in the allocation of NHS resources was re-affirmed by Lord Donaldson MR in the context of the care of a child requiring intensive medical and nursing care due to severe disabilities. The case of *Re J* (1992) concerned an appeal against an interim injunction granted by Waite J to the effect that, in the period prior to the hearing, if J, who had been severely brain damaged in a fall when he was one month old, should suffer a life-threatening event he should be given life-prolonging treatment, including artificial ventilation.[102] Lord Donaldson MR expressed the opinion that for the court to make an order requiring doctors to treat contrary to their professional judgment would fail to 'adequately take account of the sad fact of life that health authorities may on occasion find that they have too few resources, either human or material or both, to treat all the patients whom they would like to treat in the way in which they would like to treat them. It is then their duty to make choices.'[103] His Lordship explained that the court did not have information about the competing claims on the health authority and was not able to express an opinion as to how resources should be used. Although Lord Donaldson MR referred to the allocation of scarce resources in his armoury of reasons why the order should be discharged, this case was not directly concerned with resource allocation. The central issue was whether it was in J's best interests to be ventilated in the event of a life-threatening episode.[104] The cost of caring for a severely disabled child in intensive care is extremely high, resources devoted to his care are not available to others and J was occupying a bed in intensive care to the exclusion of other children who might need it. These are important factors for decisions about the allocation of scarce resources, none of which were relevant to the question whether life-prolonging treatment was in his best interests.[105]

Whilst the Court of Appeal maintained this approach in considering the refusal of the health authority to fund further treatment against leukaemia for ten-year-old Jaymee Bowen, Laws J at first instance was prepared to

---

[102] *Re J (a Minor) (Child in Care: Medical Treatment)* [1992] 3 WLR 507.

[103] *Ibid.*, at p. 517.

[104] Decisions to withhold or withdraw treatment from children with severe disabilities are considered in chapter 5.

[105] Although Antje Pedain argues that in such cases the best interests of the child are determined with a 'subtext of resource allocation' which should be openly acknowledged: 'Doctors, Parents, and the Courts: Legitimising Restrictions on the Continued Provision of Lifespan Maximising Treatments for Severely Handicapped, Non-Dying Babies' (2005) 17 CFLQ 535–44.

hold the health authority to account by requiring rather more by way of explanation for their decision. Jaymee had first been treated for acute lymphoblastic leukaemia at the age of five and had undergone two courses of chemotherapy, total body irradiation and a bone marrow transplant.[106] When she was ten, Jaymee suffered a relapse, developing acute myeloid leukaemia. The doctor who had been treating her considered that further treatment was not in her best interests, a view shared by those who had been involved in her earlier treatment. However, her father's research identified a possible course of treatment involving intensive chemotherapy and a bone marrow transplant. The view of the health authority was that the treatment was not in Jaymee's best interests and that palliative care was to be preferred to uncomfortable and distressing treatment which, further, would not be an effective use of limited resources given competing claims upon them. The treatment was experimental, expensive (£15,000 for the first stage – an intensive course of chemotherapy – and £60,000 for the bone marrow transplant) and carried only a small chance of success (estimates ranged from 1 to 20 per cent).

Laws J considered that the case was to be determined by reference not to the *Wednesbury* principle but to her fundamental right to life.[107] In his opinion, a rights-based approach required consideration of whether the health authority's decision interfered with her right to life and, if it did, whether there was a 'substantial objective justification on public interest grounds'. As the health authority's decision 'materially affected for the worse the applicant's chances of life', her right to life was interfered with. Laws J was critical that the conclusion as to Jaymee's best interests appeared to be a clinical decision:

> Of course it may readily be assumed that a 10-year-old child, in circumstances like those of this case, cannot make for herself an informed decision upon the question which course of action is in her best interests. That being so, someone else must take the decision for her. But it should not be the doctors; it should be her family, here – her father. He has duties and responsibilities to her shared by no one else. The doctors' obligation is to ascertain and explain all the medical facts, and in the light of them articulate the choice that must be faced. Their expert views on the medical issues, however, do not constitute the

---

[106] Her younger sister, Charlotte, was the donor, raising questions about the duties of parents in balancing the best interests of their children.
[107] *R v Cambridge District Health Authority, ex parte B* [1995] 1 FLR 1055.

premises of a syllogism from which an inevitable conclusion as to what is in the best interests of the patient may be deduced. It is not at all a matter of deduction from the medical facts. It is a personal question which the patient, if he is of full age and capacity, will decide in the light of medical advice. In the case of a little child, others must decide it – not the experts, but those having, legally and morally, overall care of the patient.[108]

His Lordship considered that the decision as to her best interests had been incorrectly approached as solely a clinical assessment and not one to which her father's views were pertinent. He was of the opinion that, even if his human-rights approach was not the correct one to adopt, Jaymee's father's views must be 'a relevant consideration' to a reasonable decision. Accepting that healthcare resources are limited, Laws J went on to say that the health authority had not explained what treatment might be unavailable if Jaymee was treated, nor had it stated the priorities of the health authority, nor given an account of the health authority budget or its budget for extra-contractual funding. His conclusion was that 'where the question is whether the life of a 10-year-old child might be saved, by however slim a chance, the responsible authority must in my judgment do more than toll the bell of tight resources. They must explain the priorities that have led them to decline to fund the treatment.'[109] Furthermore, in his judgment, the health authority had mistakenly approached the funding issue as a commitment to the entire £75,000 rather than to the initial £15,000. Laws J quashed the health authority's decision not to fund Jaymee's treatment, requiring them to reconsider it and expressing the opinion that the possibility of saving the life of a ten-year-old child must be a high priority in the competition with others for limited resources.

Immediately, that afternoon, the Court of Appeal allowed the health authority's appeal against the order. Sir Thomas Bingham MR countered each of Laws J's objections: the health authority could not help but consider the wishes of the family who were putting them under pressure to fund the treatment; the authority could not be expected to explain to the court their budget allocation; and the authority had rightly considered whether to fund the whole of the treatment course and not merely the first stage. The £75,000 required for the proposed course of treatment was provided by an anonymous benefactor, with the health authority funding further care and

---

[108] *Ibid.*, at pp. 1062–3.   [109] *Ibid.*, at p. 1065.

routine treatment as she went into remission. Jaymee died fifteen months later in May 1996.[110]

As her case was brought to court by way of judicial review proceedings, the merits of the experimental treatment were not subjected to independent scrutiny. It is important not to confuse the two issues of whether experimental treatment was in her best interests and whether the court should ask the health authority to reconsider its decision not to fund it, given the competing demands upon its resources. Jaymee's subsequent period in remission followed by her death makes it difficult not to feel sympathy for the positions of all involved. Jaymee, who was initially adamant that she wanted further treatment, underwent painful, invasive treatment to enjoy some months with her family and friends before dying from her condition. Her father fought hard, using the law and the media,[111] to secure medical treatment for his daughter to give her a small chance of life. But it is also possible to understand the refusal of the health authority, under a duty to use a restricted budget to meet the needs of all in the area, to fund expensive, experimental and unproven treatment. Sympathy is, of course, no basis for a decision, although consideration of the circumstances from the differing perspectives may permit a better understanding of the complexities of the situation. Importantly, it highlights the different roles and responsibilities of her father, doctors and the health authority. Whilst some were critical of Jaymee's father's determined pursuit of further treatment, there is no evidence to suggest that he was doing anything other than what he thought was best for his daughter. He was, however, dependent upon the doctors who had formed a view that the treatment he wanted her to receive was not in her best interests and upon the resources being made available to deliver that treatment. If treatment was to be denied because expensive, experimental treatment was not in her best interests, her father was at least entitled to an explanation of the reasons for that decision. However, the approach of Laws J, rather than that adopted by the Court of Appeal and in

---

[110] Carol Midgley, 'She wanted to come back as a butterfly', *The Times*, 23 May 1996.
[111] The original order ensuring anonymity for Jaymee Bowen was discharged at the application of her father in order to sell their story to the press to raise further money for her ongoing treatment: *R v Cambridge District Health Authority, ex parte B (No. 2)* [1996] 1 FLR 375. Discharging the order, Sir Thomas Bingham commented, 'I greatly regret the necessity to exploit the medical problems of this child for purposes of financial gain. I do not, however, think that the maintenance of a reporting restriction could be justified if the consequence were the denial of treatment which might and, in the father's judgment, would be of therapeutic and possibly life-saving benefit to the child.'

the previous cases, is better suited to securing an understanding of the decision of the health authority not to fund experimental, expensive treatment offering a small chance of success.

As Christopher Newdick explains in his book, *Who Should We Treat?*,[112] the courts in subsequent cases[113] have demonstrated greater willingness to require health authorities to provide reasons for their decisions. This would suggest that the kind of explanation about funding decisions which Laws J wanted in the case of Jaymee Bowen may be required in the future. The lack of any explanation for the failure to treat Matthew Collier, who spent four months at the top of the waiting list for surgery he desperately needed, is notable.[114] It is of no doubt that the parents in all of these cases were seeking to secure the best possible treatment for their seriously ill child. Their ability to do so was dependent upon working together with healthcare professionals and was limited by, amongst other things, the resources available. Legal principles which require a full explanation to be given to parents as to why treatment will not be provided to their child rightly foster an effective partnership between parent and professional and support them in their care for the child. The respective functions and roles of both professionals and parents in doing their best to meet the child's healthcare should be recognised and the external factors affecting their abilities to do so openly acknowledged.

Conclusion

Oliver Quick suggests that the events at the Bristol Royal Infirmary between 1984 and 1995 amounted to a disaster of larger proportions than the 'classic sudden disaster'. It was of greater magnitude because there were repeated failings by 'experts' whom parents had entrusted to care for their child, opportunities to prevent the disaster which went unheeded and resulted in the deaths of children, deaths 'outside the natural order'.[115] The very cruel and unnecessary death of Victoria Climbié at the hands of her carer was

---

[112] Christopher Newdick, *Who Should We Treat? Rights, Rationing and Resources in the NHS*, Oxford University Press: Oxford, 2005, ch. 5.

[113] For example, *R v North Derbyshire Health Authority, ex parte Fisher* (1997) 38 BMLR 76 (web.lexis-nexis.com/professional/); *R v NW Lancashire Health Authority, ex parte A, D, and G* (2000) 8 Med Law Rev 129.

[114] *Supra*, n.112, at p. 127.

[115] Oliver Quick, 'Disaster at Bristol: Explanations and Implications of a Tragedy' (1999) 21 JSWFL 307, at p. 317.

likewise a subversion of the natural order which occurred within the context of missed opportunities to prevent it. Both are likely to have a profound effect upon the shape of children's services in the years to come.

Clem Henricson has identified a shift, in the family policy of the Labour Government, from family-centred to child-centred policy, which she suggests is an approach which encompasses both *care* through support to families and *control* of family behaviour.[116] It is important to understand current healthcare policy for children's services within the context of the circumstances to which it responds. Both the Bristol Inquiry and the Laming Inquiry centred upon failures in services provided to children. The Bristol Inquiry concerned children whose parents were seeking to secure the best possible care for their child's complex health needs and were failed by the professionals whom they trusted to care for their child. Victoria Climbié's death, at the hands of the adult entrusted with her care, should have been prevented by services whose function it is to protect children. Consequently, the goal is to develop services which are child-centred rather than parent- or family-centred, to deliver universal and targeted services which enable children to fulfil their potential and which protect them from harm. Both parents and professionals have responsibilities to children arising out of their relationship with the child. The welfare of children depends upon parents and professionals working together, in partnership, each respectful of the role, function and expertise of the other. There is no fundamental challenge within these policy developments to the primary responsibility of parents for the care of their children. Parental autonomy and state intervention are balanced through the availability of information, advice and support services. These proposals do, however, recognise the role of the state in the creation of institutions which support adults with caring responsibilities arising from their relationship with the child and which foster the relationship between parent and healthcare professional in the shared endeavour of meeting the needs of the child.

---

[116] Clem Henricson, *Government and Parenting: Is there a Case for a Policy Review and a Parents' Code?*, Joseph Rowntree Foundation: York, 2003, at p. 8.

3

Child health and parental obligations

What is a parent and what does being a parent involve?

This chapter provides an analysis of the legal obligations imposed upon parents for the management of the health of their children. There is an examination of the boundaries established by the criminal law, the obligations imposed by civil law and the responsibilities enacted in the Children Act 1989. The aim of this chapter is to examine the obligations upon parents for the everyday care of their children's health, usually left to parents to fulfil within the privacy of the home according to their preferences, values and priorities. Parents will usually resolve any disagreements about their children's healthcare, between themselves, in private. The chapter ends with two examples which were brought into the public sphere of the courtroom as a consequence of disagreement between the mother and father, both of whom had parental responsibility.

The first issue to consider in an account of the current law is an examination of the legal status of parent and the concept of parental responsibility. In common use, reference to 'parent' may encompass parentage (the genetic link), parenthood (ongoing responsibility for a child)[1] or parenting (the activity of being a parent). Although each has a different focus – upon biology, accountability or practice respectively – all are relational, that is, they depend upon the existence of a child.

In law, to have the status of parent brings with it financial responsibility for the child and rights – including to oppose a change of the child's surname, to object to removal of the child from the jurisdiction, to apply for a specific issue order – and is material for the purposes of succession.[2]

---

[1] Andrew Bainham, 'Parentage, Parenthood and Parental Responsibility: Subtle, Elusive Yet Important Distinctions' in Andrew Bainham, Shelley Day Sclater and Martin Richards (eds.), *What is a Parent? A Socio-Legal Analysis*, Hart: Oxford, 1999, 25–46, at pp. 28–30.
[2] *Ibid.*, at pp. 33–4.

All of these, Andrew Bainham observes, 'relate to fundamentals which go beyond the everyday decisions involved in upbringing'.[3] Generally, the legal status of parent follows the genetic link. This is the case for the woman who gives birth to a child, for her husband by virtue of the rebuttable presumption that the father is the husband of the child's mother, and for her partner. The Human Fertilisation and Embryology Act 1990, ss. 27 and 28, confers the legal status of mother and father respectively upon adults to whom a child is born following assisted reproduction services which may result in the birth of a child who is not genetically linked to the adults involved in his or her creation.

Parental responsibility is a 'sort of trusteeship over the child'.[4] It is a status conferred by law which can be held by those not biologically connected to the child[5] and by adults not actively involved in the everyday parenting of the child. Parental responsibility is automatically vested in the mother of the child and shared by married fathers.[6] Notably, for children born before 1 December 2003 to unmarried couples, the genetic father, who may also be a social father, will not automatically be conferred with parental responsibility. Unmarried fathers of children born before December 2003 can gain parental responsibility by entering a parental responsibility agreement with the mother, through a court order (parental responsibility order),[7] residence order, by marrying the mother of the child, or guardianship in the event of the mother's death. For children born after 30 November 2003, the Adoption and Children Act 2002 amends s. 4 of the Children Act 1989 so that, in addition to the methods of acquiring parental responsibility, it is automatically vested in unmarried fathers who are registered as the father on the child's birth certificate.[8] Where parental responsibility is shared it can either be exercised jointly or alone,

---

[3] *Ibid.*, at p. 34.   [4] *Ibid.*, at p. 35.

[5] For example, if a residency order is granted: Children Act 1989, s. 12(2).

[6] Children Act 1989, s. 2(1).

[7] According to Ward LJ in *Re S (Parental Responsibility)* [1995] 2 FLR 648, conferring upon him the 'status of parenthood' which involves sharing the burden of care without giving him the right to override the day-to-day decisions made by the mother.

[8] The Adoption and Children Act 2002, s. 111, amending s. 4 of the Children Act 1989, came into force on 1 December 2003: the Adoption and Children Act 2002 (Commencement Order No. 4) Order 2003 (SI 2003/3079). Although the existing position was compliant with the ECHR, *B v UK* [2000] 1 FLR 1, this change to the law is compatible with Article 18 of the United Nations Convention on the Rights of the Child which provides:

   1. States Parties shall use their best efforts to ensure recognition of the principle that *both* parents have common responsibilities for the upbringing and development of the child.

permitting each person holding parental responsibility to care for the child.[9] Whilst parents cannot divest themselves of their status as parents,[10] they can agree for another to exercise parental responsibility on their behalf.[11]

What is meant, in English law, by parental responsibility is set out in s. 3(1) of the Children Act 1989: 'In this Act "parental responsibility" means all the rights, duties, powers, responsibilities and authority which by law a parent of a child has in relation to the child and his property.' The responsibilities of parents are sketched out in broad, vague terms:[12]

> The definition does not tell us what these are, which is why some question its usefulness, but it is, in a broad sense, fairly clear what it is talking about. At the risk of over-simplification, the person possessing parental responsibility will have a right to look after the child (unless this has been removed by a Court order) and the right and duty to take all major decisions relating to the child's upbringing including such matters as where the child is to live, which school the child should attend or what medical treatment the child should, or should not receive.[13]

Case law considering parental responsibility invariably arises in the context of claims by unmarried fathers to parental responsibility of children following the breakdown of their relationship with the children's mother or in the context of disputes between parents sharing responsibility for their children. The day-to-day exercise of parental responsibility within families does not come before the courts, as disagreements about which school the child should attend, whether the child should have a brace fitted on their teeth, or have their ears, lips or belly button pierced, whether the child should attend Sunday School or play in the football team are resolved in the privacy of the home rather than in the public realm of the courtroom.

---

[9] Children Act 1989, s. 2(7). Exceptions occur in those instances where it has been provided by statute or, as Dame Elizabeth Butler-Sloss P identified, 'the small group of important decisions made on behalf of a child', including sterilisation, change of surname and circumcision, which must be determined by the court in the event of disagreement amongst holders of parental responsibility: *Re J (Child's Religious Upbringing and Circumcision)* [2000] 1 FLR 571.

[10] Except by adoption or a parenting order under s. 30 of the Human Fertilisation and Embryology Act 1990.   [11] Children Act 1989, s. 2(9).

[12] Clem Henricson, *Government and Parenting: Is there a Case for a Policy Review and a Parents' Code?*, Joseph Rowntree Foundation: York, 2003, considers the arguments for and against a statement of parental rights and responsibilities and provides a draft statement.

[13] *Supra*, n. 1, at p. 35.

Minimum standards of parenting

In his renowned article written soon after the enactment of the Children Act 1989, John Eekelaar argues that there were two facets to the shift effected in that legislation from parental rights to parental responsibilities: first, that parents have responsibility to act in the interests of their children rather than rights over their children; secondly, that the responsibility for children rests with their parents as opposed to elsewhere, such as with the state.[14] Parents and not their children make the decisions and the state has allocated to parents the duty of raising their children.[15] Children are entrusted to the care of their parents as those presumed most likely to be concerned for the welfare and well-being of the child. It would be impractical for the state to undertake the rearing of all children[16] and any other allocation of children – for example, to adults considered better able to raise the child – would be socially unacceptable. Having placed the responsibility with parents, formally the state leaves parents to exercise their responsibilities according to their own values, priorities and beliefs given their abilities and resources.[17] However, the state does have an interest in the discharge of parental responsibility and in the raising of children.[18] First, the state has a general interest in the development of the generation who are the citizens of the future. Secondly, the state places limits upon parental autonomy, for example through laws making the education of children compulsory, establishes minimum standards of parental care through the criminalisation of neglect of child health and abuse, and provides for state intervention to protect the individual child at risk of, or caused, significant harm. To provide an account of the legal obligations imposed upon parents for the care of their children's health, it is necessary to explore the current principles of the criminal, civil and family law systems within the context of their distinct functions in the regulation of family life.[19]

---

[14] John Eekelaar, 'Parental Responsibility: State of Nature or Nature of the State?' (1991) 13 JSWFL 37–50. This is consistent with Article 18(1) of the United Nations Convention on the Rights of the Child: 'Parents or, as the case may be, legal guardians, have the primary responsibility for the upbringing and development of the child.'

[15] Michael Freeman, *The Moral Status of Children: Essays on the Rights of the Child*, Martinus Nijhoff: Netherlands, 1997, at pp. 318–19.

[16] David William Archard, *Children, Family and the State*, Ashgate: Hampshire, 2003, at p. 66.

[17] *Supra*, n. 14.   [18] *Supra*, n. 16, at pp. 121–2.

[19] As discussed in the previous chapter, the minimum obligations established by the law are backed by norms of good parenting disseminated through professional advisers and other sources of information and advice, such as the National Family and Parenting Institute.

Criminal law

All too regularly, we are reminded that parents and other adults entrusted with the care of children do not always love, nurture and provide for them and of the failures on the part of professionals whose role is to intervene to protect children from abuse, harm or neglect. It is, however, the case that most parents do not treat their children in this way, rather they love, care for and protect them.[20] Section 1 of the Children and Young Persons Act 1933 and, where death occurs, the common law offences of murder and manslaughter set the boundaries of minimally acceptable conduct for those responsible for the care of children.[21] The former makes it an offence:

> S1(1)   If any person who has attained the age of sixteen years and has responsibility for any child or young person under that age, wilfully assaults, ill-treats, neglects, abandons, or exposes him, or causes or procures him to be assaulted, ill-treated, neglected, abandoned, or exposed, in a manner likely to cause him unnecessary suffering or injury to health (including injury to or loss of sight, or hearing, or limb, or organ of the body, and any mental derangement) . . .

Subsection 2 makes it clear that failure to seek medical advice can amount to neglect:

> (2)   For the purposes of this section –
> (a)   a parent or other person legally liable to maintain a child or young person, or the legal guardian of a child or young person, shall be

[20] In 2000, 41 infants (under the age of 1) and 19 children aged 1–4 died as a result of unlawful killing or in circumstances where an open verdict was returned. There were 40 accidental deaths of infants (7 in road accidents, 2 in falls, 2 in fire, 25 from drowning, choking or suffocation) and 102 accidental deaths amongst children aged 1–4 (31 in road accidents, 6 in falls, 15 in fire, 41 from drowning, choking or suffocation and 3 from poisoning). *Child Accident Statistics*, Royal Society for Prevention of Accidents, www.rospa.com/factsheets/child_accidents.pdf, visited 14 February 2006.

[21] The Domestic Violence, Crime and Victims Act 2004, s. 5, creates the offence of causing or allowing the death of a child or vulnerable adult. This section makes it an offence for members of the household who have had frequent contact with a child or vulnerable adult to cause their death by an unlawful act or to fail to take reasonable steps to protect the victim whom they were aware or ought to have been aware was at significant risk of serious physical harm: s. 5(1). To address the situation where a child has died and the prosecution is unable to establish which of two adults caused the death of the child, subsection (2) provides that the prosecution does not need to prove which of two defendants caused the death and which failed to take reasonable steps to prevent the death. Subsection (3) provides that no offence is committed by someone under the age of sixteen unless that person is the child's mother or father (making it clear that no offence would be committed by siblings in the circumstances set out in s. 5(1)).

deemed to have neglected him in a manner likely to cause injury
to his health if he has failed to provide adequate food, clothing,
medical aid or lodging for him, or if, having been unable otherwise to provide such food, clothing, medical aid or lodging, he
has failed to take steps to procure it to be provided under the
enactments applicable in that behalf;

The leading case is that of *R v Sheppard*, in which the parents of sixteen-
month-old Martin Sheppard, who died of hypothermia associated with
malnutrition, were convicted of an offence contrary to this section. The
basis of the charge of wilfully neglecting Martin in a manner likely to cause
him unnecessary suffering or injury to health was that in the previous seven
months and, in particular, in the week prior to his death they had failed to
secure medical aid for him. His parents, who were described by Lord
Diplock as of low intelligence, living on a 'meagre income' in poor accom-
modation, explained that they thought that he had a childhood illness for
which medical treatment was neither available nor necessary. As is clear
from the statutory provisions, 'neglect' includes an omission: 'to omit to act,
to fail to provide adequately for [his] needs; and, in the context of s 1 of the
1933 Act, [his] physical needs rather than [his] spiritual, educational, moral
or emotional needs'.[22] The 'neglect' alleged fell within that defined in s. 1(2),
which left for the court the question whether, as a matter of fact, his parents
had failed 'to provide for Martin in the period before his death medical aid
that was in fact adequate in view of his actual state of health at the relevant
time'.[23] The majority (Lords Diplock, Edmund-Davies and Keith) over-
turned the principle established in the earlier case of *R v Senior*[24] that 'wilful
neglect' created an absolute offence. In the words of Lord Diplock:

> Such a failure as it seems to me could not be properly described as
> 'wilful' unless the parent *either* (1) had directed his mind to the ques-
> tion whether there was some risk (though it might fall far short of a
> probability) that the child's health might suffer unless he were exam-
> ined by a doctor and provided with such curative treatment as the
> examination might reveal as necessary, and had made a conscious deci-
> sion, for whatever reason, to refrain from arranging for such medical
> examination, *or* (2) had so refrained because he did not care whether
> the child might be in need of medical treatment or not.[25]

[22] *R v Sheppard and another* [1981] AC 394, at p. 404 (Lord Diplock).
[23] *Ibid.*, at p. 403 (Lord Diplock) – the *actus reus* of the offence.   [24] *R v Senior* [1899] 1 QB 283.
[25] *Supra*, n. 22, at pp. 404–5.

The appeal of Martin Sheppard's parents was successful as they were genuinely unaware of his need for medical attention. As Lord Keith expressed it, as far as the mental element of the offence was concerned:

> [A] parent who knows that his child needs medical care and deliberately, that is by conscious decision, refrains from calling a doctor, is guilty . . . A parent who fails to provide medical care which his child needs because he does not care whether it is needed or not is reckless of his child's welfare. He too is guilty of an offence. But a parent who has genuinely failed to appreciate that his child needs medical care, through personal inadequacy or stupidity or both, is not guilty.[26]

The cases in which parents have been charged with manslaughter rather than the statutory offence of child neglect are dominated by parental beliefs rather than inadequacy. The older cases are of constructive manslaughter committed where an unlawful and dangerous act, which amounts to a criminal offence, causes death. The father of the deceased child in *The Queen v Robert Downes*[27] was a member of the 'Peculiar People', a sect which, 'in literal compliance with the directions in the 14th and 15th verses of the 5th chapter of the Epistle of St James', did not seek medical advice in the event of illness. Rather, the elders of the church prayed over the sick child and anointed him with oil. Despite the father's sincerely held beliefs that this course of action was in the best interests of the child, it amounted to wilful neglect to provide medical aid (an offence contrary to the Poor Law Amendment Act 1868, s. 37) which, when it resulted in the child's death, was manslaughter. *R v Senior*[28] again involved a member of the 'Peculiar People' who neglected to seek medical advice for his son who consequently died from the effects of diarrhoea and pneumonia at the age of eight or nine months. In *Senior* 'wilful neglect' contrary to the Prevention of Cruelty to Children Act 1894, s. 1, a 'deliberate and intentional' 'omission of such steps as a reasonable parent would take, such as are usually taken in the ordinary experience of mankind' was held to be an absolute offence. Although, as Lord Diplock pointed out in *R v Sheppard* (above), Senior did know that there was a risk in failing to secure medical aid, he took that risk in order to comply with his religious beliefs. Phillimore LJ in the Court of Appeal in *R v Lowe* held that an offence contrary to the Children and Young Persons Act 1933 committed by omission did not suffice for constructive manslaughter.[29]

---

[26] *Ibid.*, at p. 418.   [27] *The Queen v Robert Downes* 1 QBD 25.   [28] *Supra*, n. 24.
[29] *R v Lowe* [1973] QB 702.

A more recent and complicated case, based upon parental neglect of their child's medical needs, is the conviction for gross negligence manslaughter of Dwight and Beverley Harris in respect of the death of their nine-year-old daughter Nahkira.[30] In December 1991, Nahkira's GP referred her to hospital, suspecting juvenile diabetes. According to the law report, Nahkira's father refused to allow her to be treated with injections of insulin because 'he was a Rastafarian and would prefer to accept treatment from someone of his own belief'. Told, in Nahkira's presence, that without treatment she would eventually die, her parents left the hospital to return with her later to speak with the registrar. When they returned, the registrar was busy elsewhere in the hospital and by the time the registrar was available her parents had taken Nahkira home. Over the six weeks which followed, Nahkira's parents made unsuccessful attempts to secure a consultation in which to discuss the treatment of their daughter's condition. At the same time, unsuccessful attempts were made to contact the family by a community diabetic nurse and a social worker. Whilst waiting for an appointment, and at the suggestion of a friend, her parents gave Nahkira a homeopathic remedy. A month later, they contacted a different homeopath and made an appointment for two days later. Nahkira became increasingly unwell and, the next day, her father telephoned the homeopath three times for advice. When they arrived for their consultation with him, Nahkira was unconscious in a diabetic coma. Still, the homeopath spent an hour and a half with her parents before referring her to hospital – time, he explained, spent building a relationship with Nahkira's parents and gaining their confidence. Nahkira died later that day.

Nahkira's father informed the court that they believed that her diabetes could be managed through diet and homeopathic treatment and that she had been well until the day before her death. The medical evidence was that she would have gradually deteriorated, that upon admission to hospital she was severely dehydrated and 'her body had consumed all of her reserves of energy'. The judge directed the jury that for the purposes of conviction for gross negligence manslaughter it had to be established:

1. That her parents had a duty to care for her health and well-being (which was not in doubt);

---

[30] *R v Harris and another* 23 BMLR 122, CA, 1994 (web.lexis-nexis.com/professional/). Her father, Dwight Harris, was sentenced to thirty months' imprisonment; her mother, Beverley Harris, to an eighteen-month suspended sentence.

2. They had breached that duty by failing to do as they ought to have done for her health and well-being. That breach was 'gross' in the sense of being 'obviously or exceptionally culpable' and justified a criminal conviction; and

3. This failure was a substantial and operative cause of her death.

The judge emphasised that these were the important questions to be answered for the purposes of determining the criminal liability of her parents which, applying the established principles of criminal law, had to be decided irrespective of the actions of others which may have contributed to the circumstances of her death. For example, there was evidence before the court from a paediatrician to the effect that, given the symptoms reported to the homeopath on the day before her death, he would have advised urgent hospital treatment at the first telephone call and immediately rung 999 himself at the last. This evidence clearly raises questions about the culpability of others involved in her care but which were irrelevant for the purposes of determining the criminal culpability of her parents who were convicted of the offence. The Court of Appeal could not fault the direction of the judge, and quoted with approval from the direction of Tucker J:

> The defence say, you may think with justification, that Dr Hammond was negligent, and grossly so, in his treatment of Nahkira and in his dealings with the defendants. They say that his negligence, either by itself or taken together with the earlier failures by the hospital authorities and the social services to counsel and contact the defendants and to bring proceedings to have Nahkira taken into care and the general lack of communication, were the causes of her death.[31]

In upholding the convictions, the Court of Appeal considered that the prosecution had rightly singled out the failures of the parents despite errors having been made by a number of people, not confined to the homeopath who was consulted in the days leading to her death. The principles of criminal law which resulted in the conviction of her parents for the manslaughter of their daughter located the blame for Nahkira's death solely with her parents: a conclusion that, as rational adults aware of their daughter's condition, they neglected their obligation to secure appropriate treatment.

It is, however, illuminating to consider the circumstances leading to Nahkira's death from the perspective of her parents. The account given of

---

[31] *Ibid.*

the circumstances of her death by Beverley Harris to the *Independent* newspaper suggests a more complicated situation than the one of culpable neglect constructed in the appeal court judgment.[32] First, she explained, they did not reject the administration of insulin to Nahkira out of Rastafarian beliefs but wanted someone to discuss the proposed treatment with them. They had questions about the insulin treatment, for example whether insulin was derived from animal products and whether it could be tested with Nahkira's blood prior to administration as she suffered from a number of allergies, which they wished to discuss prior to commencing life-long administration. According to their story as told in the *Independent*, Nahkira's father was a moderate Christian who also adhered to Rastafarian teachings, was a vegetarian who avoided additives but had no objection to modern medicine and had not previously used homeopathic remedies. Nahkira's mother told the *Independent*: 'No one at any point told us that Nahkira needed insulin now. We knew diabetes was something she was developing, but she was nine and had been fine. We thought insulin was something she would need eventually.' Having sought an appointment with the consultant, returned to their GP and responded to the note left by the community diabetic nurse, they believed that an appointment would be sent to them. They did not realise the urgency of the need for treatment. Nahkira appeared well. She had lost some weight but they attributed this to a carefully monitored diet. What they did not know then was that the homeopathic remedy they were giving her had the effect of masking her symptoms and making her appear well as her condition deteriorated.

Within the terms of the criminal law, Beverley and Dwight did fail in their duty to care for their daughter's health and well-being and this failure was a contributory cause of her death. Whether their breach was 'gross', that is 'obviously and exceptionally culpable', was a matter upon which the jury was asked to make a judgment upon consideration of all of the evidence and in light of the direction from the trial court judge which the Court of Appeal could not fault, according to their view of norms of parental care. The function of the criminal law is to ascribe responsibility for past conduct, making a judgment about the culpability of her parents as the adults primarily responsible for the health and well-being of their child, taking the fact of Nahkira's death out of the context in which it occurred.

---

[32] Steve Boggan, 'The girl that nobody saved', *Independent*, 6 December 1993. The points which follow in this paragraph come from this newspaper account.

Nahkira died a preventable death. The jury passed their judgment. Her parents served the sentence imposed by law. However, in the circumstances of this case, blaming the parents for the death of their child enabled questions to be avoided about the responsibilities of others involved in her care. It precluded examination of whether those with responsibilities to her, arising out of their relationship with her, did their best to meet her caring needs. The law does impose obligations upon parents to secure medical treatment for their child, which means that parents have to be aware that their child might be ill, decide when the child's condition requires professional help, seek help, explain symptoms, take advice and, with professionals, upon whom they depend for medical expertise, agree how to treat. In addition to the failure on the part of her parents, there were failures on the part of the professionals to work together with her parents to ensure that she had appropriate care for her diabetes. Their MP told the *Independent*:

> I don't believe the Harrises were bad parents. They may have made some poor judgements, but the mechanisms were there to avoid putting them in the position where they could make those judgements. The hospital, which knew more than the Harrises about how ill Nahkira really was, and the social services had the power to seek an emergency protection order, but they did not do so. The Harrises were convicted for supposedly being negligent. But if they failed that child, they were not alone.[33]

A child died in circumstances which, as with the death of Victoria Climbié, raises questions about the roles of parents (or primary carers) and of health and social care professionals working to meet the needs of the child which require thorough examination. The function of the criminal law is to punish past conduct. The process of allocating blame through the criminal justice system does not involve a full examination of the failure of all with responsibilities to the child. This is not to argue that parents should be above the law, rather it is to emphasise the importance of understanding their responsibilities within the context of their relationship with the child and the knowledge and expertise of others with responsibilities to her.

Section 1(2) of the Children and Young Persons Act 1933 deems a failure to seek medical attention to be neglect.[34] This suggests that if a child is in

---

[33] *Ibid.*

[34] *R v Hayles* [1969] 1 QB 364; *R v Wills* [1990] Crim LR 714. Fear of being blamed for the injuries is no defence: *R v Young* 97 Cr App Rep 280. The argument that doctors could not give treatment will not excuse failure to seek assistance where the failure results from recklessness as to whether the child might need medical treatment: *R v S and M* [1995] Crim LR 486.

hospital receiving medical care parental responsibility to seek adequate medical aid is fulfilled.[35] It was held in the case of *Oakey v Jackson* that refusal of consent to medical treatment can amount to wilful neglect if, in the circumstances, it is unreasonable to withhold consent.[36] A further question is whether parents can be guilty of manslaughter in the event of death following a refusal to consent to medical treatment. Notably, it was Dr Arthur, not the child's parents, who stood accused of the murder of John Pearson, a baby born with Down's Syndrome who was rejected by his parents at birth and died following the provision of 'nursing care only' and administration of a sedative.[37] This issue – whether parents who are under a duty to care for their child are liable for manslaughter if their refusal to consent to medical treatment leads to the death of the child – was directly confronted, but left unresolved, by Ward LJ in the case of the conjoined twins, *Re A*. It is worth setting out his deliberations at length:

> I seem to be the lone voice raising the unpalatable possibility that the doctors and even – though given the horror of their predicament it is anathema to contemplate it – the parents might kill Jodie if they fail to save her life by carrying out the operation to separate her from Mary. Although I recoil at the very notion that these good people could ever be guilty of murder, I am bound to ask why the law will not hold that the doctors and the parents have come under a duty to Jodie. If the operation is in her interests the parents must consent for their duty is to act consistent with her best interests . . . I know there is a huge chasm in turpitude between these stricken parents and the wretched parents in *R v Gibbins and Proctor* (1918) 13 Cr App Rep 134 who starved their child to death. Nevertheless I am bound to wonder whether there is strictly any difference in the application of the principle. They know they can save her. They appreciate she will die if not separated from her twin. Is there any defence to a charge of cruelty under section 1 of the Children and Young Persons Act 1933 in the light of the clarification of the law given by *Reg v Sheppard* [1981] AC 395 which in turn throws doubt on the correctness of *Oakey v Jackson* [1914] 1 KB 216? Would it

---

[35] Jonathan Montgomery, *Health Care Law*, Oxford University Press: Oxford, 2003, at p. 431.

[36] *Oakey v Jackson* [1914] 1 KB 216, 220. It should be noted that Ward LJ in *Re A (Children) (Conjoined Twins: Surgical Separation)* [2001] 2 WLR 480 doubted this remained good law in the light of *R v Sheppard and another* [1981] AC 394.

[37] *R v Arthur* 12 BMLR 1 (web.lexis-nexis.com/professional/), summing up to the jury of Farquharson J. The charge was changed to attempted murder following evidence of another potential cause for the baby's death from bronchial pneumonia at the age of three days. Dr Arthur was acquitted.

not be manslaughter if Jodie died through that neglect? I ask these insensitive questions not to heap blame on the parents. No prosecutor would dream of prosecuting. The sole purpose of the inquiry is to establish whether either or both parents and doctors have come under a legal duty to Jodie, as I conclude they each have, to procure and to carry out the operation which will save her life. If so then performance of their duty to Jodie is irreconcilable with the performance of their duty to Mary. Certainly it seems to me that if this court were to give permission for the operation to take place, then a legal duty would be imposed on the doctors to treat their patient in her best interests, i.e. to operate upon her. Failure to do so is a breach of their duty. To omit to act when under a duty to do so may be a culpable omission. Death to Jodie is virtually certain to follow, barring some unforeseen intervention. Why is this not killing Jodie?[38]

The point Ward LJ raises is not confined to, although it is complicated by, the particular circumstances of the rare dilemma presented by the conjoined twins.[39] More usually, the question of liability for manslaughter following refusal of consent will be answered by acknowledgement that rarely will there be just one view of what is in the best interests of the child and that as long as the refusal of treatment is reasonable the parents have discharged their duty. This is reflected in the opinion expressed by Ward LJ that surgeons at St Mary's in Manchester would have been acting lawfully had they let 'nature take its course in accordance with the parents' wishes'. Ward LJ was right to point out that once the court has determined that the treatment, surgery or procedure is in the best interests of the child, there is no longer any scope for differences of opinion as to what is best. However, it must be the case that if parents have not discharged their duty by securing medical advice, their duty is discharged once the responsibility for the treatment decision becomes that of the court.[40]

S. I. Strong argues that the court in *Re C (a Child) (HIV Test)*[41] should have considered analogous criminal law cases.[42] C's parents refused their consent to a blood test to determine whether she was HIV positive because

---

[38] *Re A (Children) (Conjoined Twins: Surgical Separation)* [2001] 2 WLR 480, at pp. 532–3.

[39] Ischiopagus twins, amounting to 6 per cent of conjoined twins, which are estimated to occur, as a result of failure of monozygotic twins to separate during gestation, in 1 in 100,000 births: Andrew Bainham, 'Resolving the Unresolvable: The Case of the Conjoined Twins' (2001) 60 CLJ 49–53, at p. 49.   [40] *Ibid.*, at p. 53.

[41] *In re C (a Child) (HIV Testing)* [2000] 2 WLR 270, discussed in chapter 4.

[42] S. I. Strong, 'Between the Baby and the Breast' (2000) 59 CLJ 259–63.

they rejected dominant medical explanations and treatments of HIV. C's mother was HIV positive and she had adopted an 'holistic' approach to her care, seeking to maintain a healthy lifestyle and using complementary therapy. Approving of the decision of the court to order C to undergo a blood test and questioning the court's refusal to order C's mother to stop breast-feeding in the event that the child tested HIV negative, S. I. Strong asked 'if religious beliefs (which are greatly respected in law and society) cannot negate a charge of manslaughter, why should controversial beliefs about medical treatment be allowed to prevail here? Must one wait until the child dies to demonstrate that the parents' beliefs were not sufficient as a matter of law to justify their actions? Surely not.'[43]

The argument being made is that criminal law cases such as *Sheppard* and *Senior* provide illustrations of parental beliefs which should not be permitted to dictate the healthcare provided to children. Had the parents deliberately avoided any contact with the healthcare services and had their daughter died from an AIDS-related illness without having been diagnosed or treated, it is possible that a jury might consider that her parents had neglected to secure medical treatment for her in contravention of s. 1 of the Children and Young Persons Act 1933 or had committed gross negligence manslaughter. Factually, the case is different from both *Sheppard* and *Senior*. C's parents had consulted a general practitioner so that their daughter could have her developmental checks and it was her mother's status and not the health of the child which prompted the request for a blood test to be carried out. The parental refusal of consent was grounded in carefully formed opinions, based upon research, albeit not those shared by mainstream medical opinion. The comparison of *Re C* with *Sheppard* and *Senior* highlights the importance of full consideration of all the circumstances and the dangers of deductions based on broad categorisations.

To insist upon a full examination of all the circumstances in which parents make decisions about whether to seek the advice of professionals, and whether to accept or reject the advice provided, is not to seek to excuse neglectful parents. It is to argue for a challenge to existing assumptions of individualism and selfish pursuit of individual interest. It is to suggest that the starting point is to recognise the connections between parent and child in which the young child is dependent upon their parent's care. It is to require an examination of parental fulfilment of responsibilities within the

---

[43] *Ibid.*, at p. 262.

context of the responsibilities of others to the child arising from their relationship with them and an appreciation of the dependency of parents
upon, in this context, the support and advice of healthcare professionals.
This requires a full examination of all the circumstances from the perspective of the child as a person, the history of practices of caring and the wider
societal context.

Civil law

Negligence

It is commonly asserted that the special relationship between parent and
child places parents under a duty to act in addition to a duty to take care
when they act. There exists the possibility of a child bringing an action
against a parent for damages alleging that they sustained injuries as a result
of failure of the parent in control of the child to take reasonable care. The
judiciary have expressed difficulty in setting the standard of care in
reported cases when children have been in the care of either foster carers[44]
or schools, with the local authority as the defendant. There are no reported
cases brought against parents. Consequently, to date, despite the 'special
relationship', the common law of negligence presents a theoretical possibility, rather than a reality, in shaping the legal obligations of parent to child.

In *Surtees v Kingston-upon-Thames Borough Council; Surtees v Hughes
and another*, the standard of care imposed upon parents was considered in
an action brought in respect of severe burns sustained to the claimant's foot
as a two-year-old child in foster care. Much of the judgment is concerned
with the disputed facts surrounding the injuries which occurred twenty-
three years prior to judgment. The factual issue was whether the foster
mother left the child alone with a bowl of very hot water, left the child alone
in the bathroom with a sink containing very hot water (the claimant's contention), or left the child alone in the bathroom standing on a laundry
basket by the sink and the child placed her foot in the sink to reach for
something, knocking the hot tap on as she did so (the foster mother's
version). Sir Nicholas Browne-Wilkinson VC elegantly expressed the

---

[44] Although in *S v Walsall MBC and others* [1986] 1 FLR 397 damages were awarded against a foster
mother in respect of severe burns to the soles of the feet of the claimant when she was two and a
half. The judge refuted any suggestion that the injuries were deliberately inflicted and invoked
the doctrine of *res ipsa loquitur* in the absence of any explanation to hold the foster mother liable
in negligence for the injuries.

difficulties of identifying the standard of care owed within the normal chaos of everyday life within the family home. Not only did the court have to consider the public policy issues of the impact upon the family of legal proceedings brought against each other but:

> Moreover, the responsibilities of a parent (which in contemporary society normally means the mother) looking after one or more children, in addition to the myriad other duties which fall on the parent at home, far exceed those of other members of society. The studied calm of the Royal Courts of Justice, concentrating on one point at a time, is light years away from the circumstances prevailing in the average home. The mother is looking after a fast-moving toddler at the same time as cooking the meal, doing the housework, answering the telephone, looking after the other children and doing all the other things that the average mother has to cope with simultaneously, or in quick succession, in the normal household. We should be slow to characterise as negligent the care which ordinary loving and careful mothers are able to give to individual children, given the rough-and-tumble of home life.[45]

The other case was brought against the local authority for failing to prevent the child injuring the deceased and, thus, was more specifically concerned with the standard of care owed by parents, or those caring for children, to control the child and thereby prevent the child from causing harm to others. In an action brought by the dependants of the deceased, the court considered whether a nursery teacher had been negligent when she left two children, aged between three and four, ready to go for a walk to get ready herself. Her return was delayed as she stopped to tend to a child who had cut himself. Whilst she was away from the room, one of the children went outside through unlocked gates and on to the road. The driver of a lorry who swerved to miss him was killed. Lord Goddard held that:

> Her duty was that of a careful parent. I cannot think that it could be considered negligent in a mother to leave a child dressed ready to go out with her for a few moments and then, if she found another of her children hurt and in need of immediate attention, she could be blamed for giving it, without thinking that the child who was waiting to go out with her might wander off into the street. It is very easy to be wise after

---

[45] *Surtees v Kingston-upon-Thames Borough Council; Surtees v Hughes and another* [1991] 2 FLR 559, at p. 583. The case is discussed by Jane Wright, 'Negligent Parenting – Can My Child Sue?' (1994) 6 *Journal of Child Law* 104.

the event and argue that she might have done this or that; but it seems that she acted just as one would expect her to do, that is to attend to the injured child first, never thinking that the one waiting for her would go off on his own.[46]

Factually the case of *Stubbings v Webb and another*[47] was based upon the positive duty of parent to child. The claimant brought an action in trespass to the person against her adoptive father and adoptive brother, arising from sexual abuse carried out when she was a child, and an action in negligence against her mother. The basis of the claim against the mother was that she had failed in her duty of care to her daughter by failing to remove her from the home, inform the authorities or prevent the abuse. The substantive issue was not considered. The issue which was considered was the limitation period and the case was out of time.[48] Obiter, in the subsequent case of *Barrett*, Lord Woolf expressed the opinion that *decisions* made by parents, or by local authorities in the place of parents, about the care of a child should not give rise to a duty of care: '[P]arents are daily making decisions with regard to their children's future and it seems to me that it would be wholly inappropriate that those decisions, even if they could be shown to be wrong, should be ones which give rise to a liability for damages.'[49] In the House of Lords, Lord Hutton shared the view that children should not be able to sue their parents in negligence in relation to decisions about their upbringing (whilst being of the opinion that the responsibilities of parents are different from those of local authorities so that it did not follow that children could not bring an action against local authorities in relation to decisions such as placing the child in care or for adoption).[50]

To date, the courts have adopted a policy-driven approach in which concerns about the impact of litigation upon family life and of opening the floodgates to trivial claims have prevailed over the use of negligence to establish parental standards of care. Susan Maidment argues that 'A common law duty of care on parents would be an additional positive

---

[46] *Carmarthenshire County Council v Lewis* [1955] AC 549, at p. 561.

[47] *Stubbings v Webb and another* [1993] AC 498.

[48] In the subsequent case of *S v W and another (Child Abuse: Damages)* [1995] 1 FLR 862, both the judge at first instance and the Court of Appeal judges thought it illogical that a claim could be brought against the mother alleging failure to protect her daughter from abuse whilst a claim against the father for damages resulting from his abuse was statute-barred. The father had admitted abuse of his daughter for which he had been sentenced to a term of four years' imprisonment.   [49] *Barrett v Enfield LBC* [1997] 3 WLR 628, at p. 635.

[50] *Barrett v Enfield LBC* [1999] 3 WLR 79, at pp. 111–13.

weapon in the hands of the state (through its judicial system) to enforce the statutory "parental responsibility" which the law imposes upon parents.'[51] In contrast, Claire McIvor argues that parental liability should be confined to positive acts which cause harm to the child and not extend to liability for failings in parental care. She considers that the protective duty of parents is a moral, but not a legal, duty.[52]

Trespass to the person

Parents who cause their children actual bodily harm through the use of physical force to punish their child may find themselves the defendant in civil proceedings. However, where legal proceedings are brought in response to the use of unreasonable force in the punishment of a child, they usually take the form of criminal proceedings brought on behalf of the state rather than an action for damages initiated by the child.[53] Consequently, the principal function for the tort of trespass to the person is in respect of the parental role in decision-making about medical treatment. In such circumstances, it would be the healthcare professional who would commit a battery in the absence of consent to treatment provided on behalf of young children by their parents.[54] Parental responsibility for securing healthcare for their child requires parents of young children (who cannot decide for themselves) to decide if treatment, and which of the treatments available, is in the best interests of their child, including:

> those day-to-day health care decisions made by all parents of small children – the giving of an aspirin, the spoonful of cough syrup, or even agreeing to a course of antibiotics. Parental judgment reigns here whether it stems from clinical advice, family, cultural or religious traditions, or simply personal preference. Society allows parents to act

---

[51] Susan Maidment, 'Children and Psychiatric Damages – Parents' Duty of Care to their Children' (2001) 31 *Family Law* 440–4, at p. 444.

[52] Claire McIvor, 'Expelling the Myth of the Parental Duty to Rescue' (2000) 12 CFLQ 229–37.

[53] The Children Act 2004, s. 58 provides that actual bodily harm cannot be justified in either criminal or civil proceedings on the grounds that it was inflicted as reasonable punishment, and s. 1(7) of the Children and Young Persons Act 1933 is repealed. Thus, a limit is placed upon the harm which may be inflicted in smacking children but smacking is not unlawful. On the issue of the physical punishment of children, the ECHR failed to bite as hard as it could have done. In *A v United Kingdom* [1998] 2 FLR 959, the European Court of Human Rights held that the United Kingdom had failed to fulfil its obligation to protect children against inhumane and degrading treatment. However, the Court did not hold that all physical punishment of children amounted to a violation of the rights under Article 3, rather it depended upon the degree of severity involved.   [54] Unless carried out in an emergency.

on their own perceptions of what is best for their child in day-to-day matters.[55]

As Lord Fraser said in *Gillick*, 'Nobody doubts, certainly I do not doubt, that in the overwhelming majority of cases the best judges of a child's welfare are his or her parents.'[56] In the event of a disagreement between parents and healthcare professionals,[57] the court must be asked to consent to the provision, withholding or withdrawal of treatment as required in the best interests of the child.[58] Inevitably, it is the difficult cases which end up in court by application to the High Court either for a declaration under the court's inherent jurisdiction or for a specific issue order under section 8 of the Children Act 1989. Generally, these cases are difficult cases either because the healthcare professionals believe that refusal by the parents is putting the child at risk of significant harm, or because the decision is whether to continue life-sustaining treatment. Without explicitly doing so, cases considering parental refusal of consent to medical treatment or those in which parents are seeking to secure a particular treatment of their child, expose the standard of care provided by parents to judicial scrutiny. In other words, there is a judicial assessment as to whether the parents are acting as responsible parents.

Michael Freeman rightly argues that there must be constraints upon parental autonomy through intervention by the state in the form of independent review by the courts, according to established principles developed through case law, and not confined to cases where parents fail to meet minimum standards.[59] He provides the example of the case of *Re D*[60] to demonstrate the value of judicial scrutiny of decisions made not in neglect but, possibly, due to over-protectiveness.[61] In *Re D*, Heilbron J held that the proposed sterilisation of D, an eleven-year-old girl who had Sotos Syndrome, was not, in the circumstances, in her best interests. Michael Freeman suggests that, by virtue of their close involvement with the child

---

[55] Caroline Bridge, 'Religion, Culture and Conviction – the Medical Treatment of Young Children' (1999) 11 CFLQ 1–15, at p. 1.

[56] *Gillick v West Norfolk and Wisbech AHA and another* [1985] 3 WLR 830, at p. 843.

[57] Doctors can proceed to treat with the consent of one person with parental responsibility (Children Act 1989, s. 2(7)). In the vast majority of cases, parents will discuss and make decisions together about the appropriate treatment for their child.

[58] *Glass v United Kingdom* [2004] 1 FLR 1019.

[59] Michael Freeman, 'Freedom and the Welfare State: Child-Rearing, Parental Autonomy and State Intervention' (1983) JSWL 70–91.

[60] *Re D (a Minor) (Wardship: Sterilisation)* [1976] 1 All ER 326.   [61] *Supra*, n. 59, at p. 84.

and personal interest, professionals and parents are in no position to make a rational decision. Consequently, such decisions are best left to independent assessment. It is the premise of this book that currently insufficient attention is given by the courts to the role and expertise of parents gained as they care for their child and to the differences between parental and professional knowledge of, and relationship with, the child: hence the argument for a conceptual framework of relational responsibilities to inform independent assessment by the courts.

Whether decisions are made by parents or by the courts, the legal principle governing decisions about children's healthcare is the same: the welfare or best interests principle.

The welfare or best interests principle

As Lord Scarman explained in *Gillick*, the welfare, or best interests, principle acts as a guide for the actions and decisions of parents and court alike:

> [W]hen a court has before it a question as to the care and upbringing of a child it must treat the welfare of the child as the paramount consideration in determining the order to be made. There is here a principle which limits and governs the exercise of parental rights of custody, care and control. It is a principle perfectly consistent with the law's recognition of the parent as the natural guardian of the child: but it is also a warning that parental right must be exercised in accordance with the welfare principle and can be challenged, even overridden, if it be not.[62]

Where decisions are made by the court under the Children Act 1989,[63] relating to the upbringing of the child,[64] section 1 provides that 'the child's welfare shall be the court's paramount consideration'.[65] Section 1(3) pro-

---

[62] *Gillick v West Norfolk and Wisbech AHA and another* [1985] 3 WLR 830, at p. 845.

[63] Such as a section 8 specific issue order.

[64] And to issues relating to the administration of the property of the child or use of income from it: Children Act 1989, s. 1(1)(b).

[65] Whereas the United Nations Convention on the Rights of the Child, Article 3 provides that:

  1. In all actions concerning children, whether undertaken by public or private social welfare institutions, courts of law, administrative authorities or legislative bodies, the best interests of the child shall be *a primary* consideration [emphasis added].

  Michael Freeman points out that s. 1(1) of the Children Act 1989 goes further in making the child's interests *the paramount*, rather than *a primary*, consideration but that it is of much more limited application than Article 3(1): *supra*, n. 15, at p. 107.

vides the court with a welfare checklist as a guide to factors relevant to assessment of the welfare of the child in section 8 order cases, or cases concerning care and supervision orders under Part IV:

s 1 (3) (a) the ascertainable wishes and feelings of the child concerned (considered in the light of his age and understanding);

(b) his physical, emotional and educational needs;

(c) the likely effect on him of any change in his circumstances;

(d) his age, sex, background and any characteristics of his which the court considers relevant;

(e) any harm which he has suffered or is at risk of suffering;

(f) how capable each of his parents, and any other person in relation to whom the court considers the question to be relevant, is of meeting his needs;

(g) the range of powers available to the court under this Act in the proceedings in question.

In section 8 cases concerning the medical treatment of children, the courts make reference to the welfare checklist but tend not to apply it systematically, preferring a more holistic approach. Furthermore, in these cases, the courts tend to treat the welfare principle and best interests test as synonymous. In the case of the conjoined twins, Jodie and Mary, Ward LJ quoted with approval from the judgment of Lord Hailsham in the earlier case of *Re B*: 'There is no doubt that, in the exercise of its wardship jurisdiction the first and paramount consideration is the well being, welfare, or interests (each expression occasionally used, but each, for this purpose, synonymous) of the human being concerned.'[66] Ward LJ continued to say that this was the test by which the court was to determine the issue given legislative basis, since *Re B*, in s. 1(1) of the Children Act 1989. The Court of Appeal has recently expressly adopted the formulation of best interests from cases concerning incompetent adults, to whom the welfare principle does not apply, as 'manifestly' applicable to cases concerning children.[67] 'Best interests are not limited to best medical interests'[68] rather 'best interests encompasses medical, emotional and all other welfare issues',[69] including whether

---

[66] *Re A (Children) (Conjoined Twins: Surgical Separation)* [2001] 2 WLR 480, at p. 512, quoting the Lord Chancellor, Lord Hailsham of St Marylebone, in *Re B (a Minor) (Wardship: Sterilisation)* [1988] AC 199, at p. 202.

[67] *Wyatt and another v Portsmouth Hospital NHS and another* [2005] EWCA Civ 1181, para. 79.

[68] *Re MB (Medical Treatment)* [1997] 2 FLR 426, per Butler-Sloss LJ, at p. 439.

[69] *Re A (Male Sterilisation)* [2000] 1 FLR 549, per Dame Butler-Sloss P, at p. 555.

the proposed treatment is 'to the emotional, psychological and social benefit'[70] of the child.[71]

Furthermore the Court of Appeal, in the Charlotte Wyatt case, specifically approved the approach to determination of best interests suggested in *Re A* (which considered whether sterilisation was in the best interests of a male with Down's Syndrome) by Thorpe LJ who said that 'the evaluation of best interests is akin to a welfare appraisal' but that, in the absence of a checklist, the responsibility of the judge was to draw up a balance sheet. Actual benefits from the proposed course of conduct should be set against any dis-benefits, followed by possible benefits and disadvantages with an estimate of their probability to arrive at a sum of certain and possible benefits against certain and possible disadvantages.[72] In his judgment, Holman J explained that he had found just such a balance sheet to have been of enormous assistance in deciding whether ventilation should be withdrawn from eighteen-month-old MB. His Lordship suggested that, in the future, lists should be drawn up by all parties in their preparation of the case. Holman J included in his judgment the balance sheet prepared on behalf of the guardian as 'the most comprehensive list' and as it was 'put forward on behalf of the child himself'.[73]

Deciding which course of action is in the welfare or best interests of the child seeks to be a particularistic – not a universal – assessment and is thus dependent upon the facts. Although, as discussed in the final chapter, a concern to 'do their best' pervades parental accounts of their roles with regard to their child's health and well-being, we do not have evidence of day-to-day application of the best interests principle by parents in uncontested cases. It is, therefore, necessary to rely upon consideration of the parental positions adopted, and the content of the principle, in the contested cases determined in court. As Waite LJ rightly identified in *Re T*: 'The law's insistence that the welfare of a child shall be paramount is easily stated and universally applauded, but the present case illustrates, poignantly and

[70] *Re Y* [1997] 2 WLR 556, at p. 562.
[71] The General Medical Council guidance, *Seeking Patients' Consent: The Ethical Considerations*, November 1998, stresses the importance of trust, effective communication and continuing dialogue in the process of obtaining consent to medical treatment. Guidance from the Department of Health to professionals, *Guide to Consent for Examination or Treatment*, March 2001 and parents, *Consent – What You Have a Right to Expect: A Guide for Parents*, July 2001 states current English law.
[72] *Wyatt and another v Portsmouth Hospital NHS and another* [2005] EWCA Civ 1181, para. 56, referring to the judgment of Thorpe LJ in *Re A (Male Sterilisation)* [2000] 1 FLR 549.
[73] *An NHS Trust v MB* [2006] EWHC 507, paras. 58–60.

dramatically, the difficulties that are encountered when trying to put it into practice.'[74]

The welfare principle has been criticised as uncertain,[75] 'indeterminate',[76] 'adhocery',[77] 'individualistic'[78] and as providing a 'convenient cloak for bias, paternalism and capricious decision-making'.[79] In contrast, John Harrington suggests that the principle is a 'guiding standard' which enables identification of the relevant factors to be considered without demanding a particular decision.[80] Thus, he considers it to provide a helpful checklist giving sufficient flexibility to achieve the best possible outcome in each instance. As such, he argues, 'a kind of prudential reasoning has to be undertaken which is highly responsive to the particularity of the given case and dependent to a significant extent on the intuitive sense of reasonableness of the deciding judge'.[81] This permits judges to give effect to 'a distinctively judicial common sense'. However, leaving matters to judicial intuition and common sense inevitably results in decisions shaped by experience and assumptions.[82] Application of the welfare principle and determination of the best interests of the child can legitimately result in different conclusions, depending upon such factors as the weight accorded to the medical evidence and the values or beliefs of the decision-maker.

The welfare principle has been criticised for leaving open the possibility of merely giving effect to what others consider to be in the interests of the child from their perspective as adults, drawing upon their ideals of what it is to be a child and their memories of their own childhood re-interpreted from their position as adults.[83] Further, the principle has been criticised for

---

[74] *Re T (a Minor) (Wardship: Medical Treatment)* [1997] 1 WLR 242, at p. 253.

[75] Jonathan Herring, 'Farewell Welfare?' (2005) 27 JSWFL 159–71, at pp. 160–4.

[76] Stephen Parker, 'The Best Interests of the Child – Principles and Problems' in P. Alston (ed.), *The Best Interests of the Child: Reconciling Culture and Human Rights*, Oxford University Press: Oxford, 1994, at p. 26.

[77] Ian Kennedy, *Treat Me Right: Essays in Medical Law and Ethics*, Clarendon Press: Oxford, 1988, at p. 395.

[78] Jonathan Herring, 'The Welfare Principle and the Rights of Parents' in Andrew Bainham, Shelley Day Sclater and Martin Richards (eds.), *What is a Parent? A Socio-Legal Analysis*, Hart: Oxford, 1999, 89–105.   [79] *Supra*, n. 76, at p. 26.

[80] John A. Harrington, 'Deciding Best Interests: Medical Progress, Clinical Judgment and the "Good Family"' [2003] 3 Web JCLI.   [81] *Ibid.*

[82] Regina Graycar, 'The Gender of Judgments: An Introduction' in Margaret Thornton (ed.), *Public and Private: Feminist Legal Debates*, Oxford University Press: Melbourne, 1995, 262–82.

[83] Ann Oakley, 'Women and Children First and Last: Parallels and Differences between Children's and Women's Studies' in Berry Mayall (ed.), *Children's Childhoods: Observed and Experienced*, Falmer Press: London, 1994, 13–32, at pp. 16 and 28.

letting in to the decision the interests of others and for failing to admit the interests of others.[84] Having a child, and becoming a parent, makes a significant difference to the lives of adults, but it is neither possible nor desirable for daily family life to be lived with the interests of the child as *paramount.* Generally, parents will act in the best interests of their child as far as possible depending upon the child's needs, the needs of other family members, the resources available, the demands of employment, their abilities, individual interpretation of expectations of parent and child, and according to social expectations. When a child is seriously ill priorities change; that much is apparent from a reading of the written statements of parents to the Bristol Royal Infirmary Inquiry. As the studies considered in chapter 6 demonstrate and the account of the care provided to MB by his mother indicate, the daily life of parents of a disabled child is very different to that of parents caring for a child without impairments. The responsibilities of parents caring for a child who has become seriously ill or a child with disabilities – what the parents do and what they ought to do – are determined by the child's needs, social expectations and individual interpretation.

An issue of importance, upon which there is a lack of clarity within the case law, is the relevance of the interests of others, parents and siblings, to determination of the interests of the child.[85] Parents who argue for continued treatment of a sick child have been criticised for putting their own interests above those of their child, as have parents who refuse treatment or wish for treatment to be withdrawn.[86] In *Children, Families and Health Care Decision-Making,* Lainie Friedman Ross rejects the best interests

---

[84] John Eekelaar, 'Beyond the Welfare Principle' (2002) 14 CFLQ 237–49, at pp. 237–8.

[85] The interests of the family of a twenty-five-year-old woman with mental and physical handicaps were considered in *Re Y* [1997] 2 WLR 556 by Connell J who was keen to stress the unusual circumstances. The question was whether it was in Y's best interests to undergo a procedure to collect bone marrow for donation to her sister. Y benefited from her relationship with her sister, although it had suffered as a consequence of her sister's illness. However, Y's closest relationship was with her mother, who was in poor health herself exacerbated by the worry of her daughter's illness. Without a transplant, her sister was unlikely to live, which would have an adverse effect upon her mother's health and her ability to visit Y would be further compromised as Y's mother would then have to care for her granddaughter.

[86] Both the parents of six-year-old Samantha Irwin and the parents of Laura Davies were subjected to criticism. Samantha Irwin's parents refused consent to a third liver transplant for their daughter which offered a 3–5 per cent chance of success. Samantha had told her parents, 'I'm really fed up with this. I want to go home.' Laura Davies underwent a liver and bowel transplant and, when that was unsuccessful, a seven-organ transplant: Angela Neustatter, 'Children: should their lives be in their own hands?', *Independent*, 3 October 1993.

principle (as she understands it to be stated by Allen Buchanan and Dan Brock in *Deciding for Others: The Ethics of Surrogate Decision Making*), arguing that it requires parents to consider only the self-regarding interests of the child. Consequently, she suggests, there is no scope for consideration of the child within the family which may mean that the child has an interest in the interests of other family members being fulfilled and there may be family interests which are not commensurate with the interests of any individual within the family.[87] Allen Buchanan and Dan Brock argue that for newborns (and it would apply for older children who lack legal competence) best interests is the appropriate principle to guide decision-making.[88] They separate the young child's interests into experiential, functional and developmental. The child has current, and future, interests in pleasure, avoiding pain and discomfort, and maintaining bodily functions. Further, it is in the interests of the young child to develop their capacities for independent existence and for relationships with others. They therefore have an interest in having the opportunities to develop their capacity and form relationships with others.[89] As a guiding principle, and contrary to Lainie Friedman Ross's reading of their work, they argue that best interests do not require that the interests of the individual child are always optimised. What is best may not be possible because of the expense or, they suggest, the interests of other children in the family.[90]

Jonathan Herring explains that the welfare of those to whom the child is intimately connected is considered to be irrelevant because:

> the present law's understanding of the welfare principle is individualistic. By this is meant that the child and his or her welfare are viewed without regard for the welfare of the rest of his or her family, friends and community. The claims of the other members of the family and of the community are only relevant to the extent they directly affect the child's welfare.[91]

---

[87] Lainie Friedman Ross, *Children, Families and Health Care Decision-Making*, Oxford University Press: Oxford, 1998, at p. 42. She presents an alternative model for children's healthcare decision-making which is based upon parental autonomy exercised according to respect for their child's personhood.

[88] Allen Buchanan and Dan Brock, *Deciding for Others: The Ethics of Surrogate Decision Making*, Cambridge University Press: Cambridge, 1989, at p. 246.   [89] *Ibid.*, at pp. 247–58.

[90] *Ibid.*, at p. 259.

[91] Jonathan Herring, 'The Human Rights Act and the Welfare Principle in Family Law – Conflicting or Complementary?' (1999) 11 CFLQ 223–35, at p. 225.

In *Re A*, Ward LJ quoted from Lord MacDermott in *J v C*:

> when all the relevant facts, relationships, claims and wishes of parents,
> risks, choices and other circumstances are taken into account and
> weighed, the course to be followed will be that which is most in the
> interests of the child's welfare as that term has now to be understood.
> That is the first consideration because it is of first importance and the
> paramount consideration because it rules upon or determines the
> course to be followed.[92]

Whilst this clearly restates that it is the best interests of the child which
prevail, it fails to clarify how the 'claims and wishes' of the child's parents
are relevant to the assessment of the child's welfare. The clearest exposition
is provided by Butler-Sloss LJ in *Simms*, a case in which the court was asked
to determine whether treatment, which was new and not tested on humans,
was in the best interests of two teenagers 'changed from normal, energetic
teenagers into helpless invalids lying in bed and with a severely limited
enjoyment of life' by probable variant Creutzfeldt–Jakob disease. Butler-
Sloss LJ stated the task of the court as being to assess:

> in the widest possible way to include the medical and non-medical
> benefits and disadvantages, the broader welfare issues of the two
> patients, their abilities, their future with or without treatment, the
> views of their families, and the impact of refusal of the applications.[93]

Applied to the facts of that case, it meant that:

> [T]he views of both families should carry considerable weight in the
> circumstances of these two young people. I have no doubt that the
> family of A have their feet firmly on the ground and understand very
> well the limitations on the prospects of benefits and the risks attached.
> They would not wish to prolong her life if she were suffering as a result
> of the treatment but they feel very strongly that this treatment should
> be carried out . . . If the treatment were not to be given, both families
> would be deeply distressed. They would, of course, continue to care for
> their children with the same dedication . . . The impact of refusal by
> this court of granting the declarations on each set of parents and, in

---

[92] *J v C* [1970] AC 668, per Lord MacDermott at p. 711, considering the scope and meaning of the
Guardianship of Infants Act 1925, 'shall regard the welfare of the infant as the first and paramount consideration'.

[93] *Donald Simms and Jonathan Simms v An NHS Trust and Secretary of State for Health; PA and JA v
An NHS Trust and Secretary of State for Health* [2002] EWHC 2734, at para. 60.

one case, 5 siblings, and in the other case, one sibling, would in my view be enormous and palpable.[94]

This is to say that determination of the best interests of the child was reached in consideration of the interests of the child, the views of the child's parents and family and the likely impact upon both child and family. In taking this approach, Butler-Sloss LJ here appreciated the importance of caring relationships to the upbringing of the child and expressed this far more convincingly than she had in the earlier case of *Re T*.[95] Three important points emerge. First, in cases concerning medical treatment of young children it is impossible to determine their best interests in isolation from the views of those caring for them. But, secondly, what is important to take into account is the *views* of those caring for the child of the interests of the child and *not*, when deciding the best interests of the child, the *interests* of those caring for the child. The views of the child's parents may be influenced by their beliefs or the values by which they raise their child. As Wilson J noted in *Re C*, 'the views of these parents, looked at widely and generously, are an important factor in the decision, even, to some extent, irrespective of the validity of the underlying grounds for their views'.[96] Thirdly, for children cared for by their parents, within families, the impact upon those with whom they have relationships has also to be considered.

The chapters which follow explore whether judicial application of the best interests principle is affected by assumptions about the child and about parents; in other words, whether a perception of the child as vulnerable and dependent and in need of protection, including from their parents, influences the approach to, and conclusions about, the best interests of the child. A different understanding of the child as connected and interdependent, situated within caring relationships, introduces into assessment of the welfare of the child the expertise of parents and their concerns, beliefs and values. This is not to say that the decision is what is in the best interests of the parents, or any other, but that the interests of the child have to be

---

[94] *Ibid.*, at para. 64.

[95] *Re T (a Minor) (Wardship: Medical Treatment)* [1997] 1 WLR 242, at p. 250. Butler-Sloss LJ's judgment is analysed in chapter 4.

[96] *In re C (A Child) (HIV Testing)* [2000] 2 WLR 270. Andrew Downie suggests this is 'startling' on the grounds that s. (1)(3)(f) of the Children Act 1989 requires the court to consider the ability of the parents to meet the needs of the child, not the parents' wishes or opinions. This interpretation suggests that the views related to the preferences of the parents as opposed to their views about the interests of their daughter: Andrew Downie, '*Re C (HIV Test)*: The Limits of Parental Autonomy' (2000) 12 CFLQ 197.

assessed in the context of their relationships with those caring for them and taking care of them. Considering the best interests of the child situated within caring relationships means that the views of others – parents, siblings – will also be relevant to assessment of the best interests of the child. My view is that decisions about everyday healthcare of children and treatment for more serious conditions are rightly determined according to the best interests of the child. However, as the central question, it makes a difference whether best interests are determined according to assumptions of individualism, abstraction or according to responsibilities established in relationships. The latter requires a different set of questions to be asked to determine the best interests of the child. In particular, the concern of parents for the well-being of their child directs consideration to the needs of the individual child. The responsibilities of parents arising from their relationship with their child directs consideration to the expertise of parents, their knowledge of the child, gained as they care for them. It illuminates the fact that the medical evidence is partial evidence about the best interests of the child, focused upon the medical condition, prognosis and treatment options. Finally, it requires the court directly to confront, and examine, limits to caring: these may not be simply a matter of personal choices but occur within the context of external factors. They may arise, for example, due to the support available to parents and human, material or technical resources available.

One issue which confronts all parents is the question whether their child should be immunised against childhood diseases.

Childhood immunisation: in the best interests of the child?

Public health, private harm?

A comprehensive public health programme of immunisation of children has contributed to the eradication of smallpox, and reduced the incidence of Haemophilus Influenzae type b (Hib) infections, diphtheria, whooping cough and measles within England and Wales.[97] This has the undoubted good of reducing the incidence of children catching these diseases which are not only unpleasant to experience but present the risk of serious harm to the child. Yet, alongside general parental concerns about the unknown

---

[97] Helen Bedford and David Elliman, 'Concerns about Immunisation' (2000) 320 BMJ 2401. The routine vaccination schedule is set out at www.immunisation.nhs.uk.

consequences of overloading their child's immune system[98] are specific concerns arising from studies published in medical journals, inevitably followed by much press coverage. In the 1970s there were concerns about a link between the pertussis (whooping cough) vaccine and brain damage[99] and, more recently, there have been concerns about a link between the MMR vaccine and autism and bowel problems. In the context of different conclusions upon scientific evidence, parents have to decide whether their child should be immunised, balancing risk, uncertainty and the possibility of the child suffering serious harm from either immunisation or from the infectious disease. In 1978, the Pearson Commission recommended a system of state compensation for vaccine-induced injury.[100] The Vaccine Damage Payments Act 1979 provides a lump sum payment for children who are severely injured as a result of immunisation by a prescribed vaccine.[101] Given a government anxious to ensure sufficient uptake of immunisation on the understanding that immunisation rates of 95 per cent need to be achieved in order for the programme to be effective, uncertainties arise about trust in the sources of information available.[102] How to fulfil parental responsibility on this public health issue, privately determined, is a question confronted by every parent.

Children can suffer harm from immunisation or from contracting the disease against which they are not immunised. *Thompson v Bradford*[103] concerned an action for damages brought by the parents of Hamish Thompson who was severely disabled, as a consequence of contracting polio after immunisation, at the age of eight weeks. The court found that his GP was not in breach of his duty of care when he failed to advise

---

[98] In particular, whether there is a link with the increased incidence of asthma.

[99] A report in 1974 linking the vaccine to brain damage gained much publicity and resulted in parental concern and a drop in vaccination levels. The findings of this study have been disputed and further research has refuted the link. Slowly public confidence has returned so that by 1995 there was a 94 per cent rate of vaccination: Office for National Statistics, *The Health of Children and Young People*, March 2004, ch. 5, 'Infectious diseases', at p. 13.

[100] Pearson Report, *The Report of the Royal Commission on Civil Liability and Compensation for Personal Injury*, Cmnd 7054, 1978.

[101] A one-off payment of £100,000 is made to a person who is severely disabled (60 per cent disabled) and whose disability was caused by vaccination: Department for Work and Pensions, *Vaccine Damage Payments* (HB3), April 2004.

[102] For children reaching their second birthday in 2004–5, 81 per cent had received the primary course of the MMR vaccine and 93 per cent had received vaccinations against diphtheria, tetanus, polio, whooping cough, Hib and Meningitis C: Health and Social Care Information Centre, *NHS Immunisation Statistics England 2004–05*, 2005.

[103] *Thompson v Bradford* [2005] EWCA Civ 1439.

Hamish's parents against immunisation given that Hamish had a boil which required treatment. Whilst added discomfort to a sick child or ineffective vaccination was foreseeable, it was not foreseeable that he would contract polio. For parents who were clearly concerned and seeking guidance from professionals about whether immunisation should go ahead given their child's state of health, the legal principles must seem to miss the point about their dependence upon professional advice and their feelings of responsibility for agreeing to a course of action which ultimately caused their child to suffer severe disabilities. We are merely left to speculate that if his parents had known that the reason acutely, or systemically, unwell children are not immunised is because to do so would be 'adding insult to injury'[104] they would have agreed to subject their child, who had a boil, was uncomfortable and irritable and was in receipt of a prescription for antibiotics, to immunisation. In contrast, Emma Thomson's parents had decided that Emma should not be immunised against measles given an episode in her infancy when she may have had a fit.[105] Emma subsequently contracted measles and sustained brain damage as a consequence of the disease. The legal issue in the case was whether her parents had been provided with information about immunisation and it was held that her parents had been informed that the risks of immunisation could be reduced by the simultaneous administration of immunoglobulin. However, the case is striking for the failure to examine the understanding amongst the three GPs consulted that her parents were anxious to avoid immunisation given their daughter's history as against the claim of her parents that they were anxious that she should be immunised if it was not contra-indicated. Although just two examples, both children were left with severe impairments and, as such, these cases serve to demonstrate the burden upon parents to make a decision in the face of enormous uncertainty about the risks of immunisation as against the risks of contracting the disease.

These individual personal tragedies occur against the background of widespread concern about the harms of immunisation. The claims brought by parents against the manufacturers of the whooping cough vaccine, alleging that it caused their children to suffer brain damage, are a precursor to the current controversy over MMR. The claims raised difficult issues of causation, which were decided against the families in the case of *Loveday v*

---

[104] *Ibid.*, at para. 15, quoting from the Education Health Guide.
[105] *Thornson* [*sic*] *v James and others*, 29 July 1997 (web.lexis-nexis.com/professional/).

Renton.[106] The current controversy over the causative link between the MMR vaccine and autistic spectrum disorders and bowel disorders has resulted in protracted, complicated group litigation involving in excess of 1,000 families. Although legal proceedings commenced in September 1998, the substantive issue of liability of the manufacturers under the Consumer Protection Act 1987 has yet to go to trial to determine issues upon which there is scientific uncertainty. As of April 2006, there had been in excess of fifteen case management proceedings, decisions upon procedural issues and judicial review proceedings brought as a result of the decision, in September 2003, of the Legal Services Commission to withdraw funding from claimants alleging a link between the vaccine and autistic spectrum and bowel disorders.

Parental disagreement

In the majority of the cases considered in this book the child's parents are in agreement about which course of action is in the best interests of their child. The determination of the best interests of the child in the face of disagreement between parents about their child's healthcare is demonstrated by the case of *A and D v B and E*.[107] The Court of Appeal considered that the issue of immunisation came within the category of issues which required parental agreement or, in the face of their inability to agree, an order from the court as to the best interests of the child.[108] The case concerned two girls, aged four and ten, unrelated but both of whom lived alone with their mothers. Their fathers, who had parental responsibility by virtue of a parental responsibility order, wanted their daughters to be immunised. In the face of disagreement about the best interests of their daughters between parents both of whom had legal responsibility, the dispute was determined by a section 8 specific issue order in which:

> the court has to determine whether immunisation is in each of the girls' best interests as their welfare is the court's paramount consideration. If it is in their best interests, the court has next to consider whether there are good reasons why that declaration should not be made. Such reasons might arise if making the declaration would so affect the mother that her ability to care for the child would

[106] *Loveday v Renton and another*, 30 March 1988 (web.lexis-nexis.com/professional/).

[107] *A and D v B and E* [2003] EWHC 1376 (Fam); *B (Child)* [2003] EWCA Civ 1148 (CA).

[108] *B (Child)* [2003] EWCA Civ 1148, para. 17.

be impaired, or it would be otherwise adverse to the child's best interests.[109]

Sumner J considered at length the medical evidence and the differences in the expert medical opinion as to the risk of contracting the disease, the potential harms from the disease and the risks of vaccination to reach a conclusion in relation to each vaccination as to whether it was, medically, in the best interests of each child before considering the other factors. Upon the medical evidence advanced, he concluded that it was in the medical interests of both children to be immunised against diphtheria, tetanus, polio,[110] meningitis C, and to receive the triple vaccine MMR.[111] The medical evidence also pointed to the immunisation of four-year-old C against pertussis[112] and HIB.[113] If F tested tuberculin negative, the medical evidence was to the effect that she should be immunised against TB. Sumner J then considered the evidence of both mother and father in each case before concluding that the best interests of each child were coterminous with the medical best interests. In reaching this conclusion, his Lordship stressed that '[t]his decision should not be seen as a general approval of immunisation for children. It does not mean that at another hearing a different decision might not be reached on the facts of that case.'[114]

Whether Sumner J had adopted the correct approach to determination of the issue, by considering first whether immunisation was in the girls' medical best interests and, having reached the conclusion that it was, whether there were factors which weighed against that conclusion, was the subject of appeal.[115] Counsel's argument was that this approach effectively created a presumption in favour of immunisation which placed the onus upon the children's mothers to rebut. Thorpe LJ could not fault what he

---

[109] *A and D v B and E* [2003] EWHC 1376 (Fam), para. 5.

[110] Although there had been no cases in the UK for many years, there was a risk of exposure when travelling.

[111] Measles, mumps and rubella. Sumner J considered the views of the medical experts on the merits, and risks, of the single and triple vaccinations. He also appreciated that decisions about administration of the MMR vaccine have currently to be made against the backdrop of the ongoing litigation brought on behalf of children with autistic spectrum disorders and bowel disorders noted above.

[112] Whooping cough – but not for F as there was no licensed vaccine for children over seven.

[113] The expert opinion provided to the court was that children under the age of five are at the greatest risk.   [114] *A and D v B and E* [2003] EWHC 1376 (Fam), at para. 358.

[115] *B (Child)* [2003] EWCA Civ 1148.

considered to be the 'conscientious and comprehensive' judgment of Sumner J. Thorpe LJ said that, in determining the best interests of the child, the task of the judge is to consider all relevant factors, but it is for the judge to determine how to do so as long as 'he keeps each in its proper proportion and ultimately conducts a comprehensive survey attaching to each relevant factor the weight that he deems it deserves'.[116]

A preference for holistic health and natural parenting was at the heart of the dispute between the parents A and B over whether their daughter C should be submitted to a programme of immunisation. A, the father, accepted that there were risks and benefits to be weighed but, in light of the possibility of serious illness or death, felt that the balance was 'in favour of the scientific approach as against a spiritual or other alternative approach'.[117] The mother, B, had adopted an holistic way of life, had read about immunisation and preferred for C to develop a natural immunity, to assist with which she had continued to breast-feed to the age of four. As Sumner J acknowledged, the specific issue before the court went 'against everything she believes to be the right approach to child rearing'.[118] The refusal of the mother of ten-year-old F was as genuine, if not so principled. She was concerned about the risks of immunisation and, as F was a healthy child, did not consider immunisation to be necessary, preferring her to develop natural immunity.

Sumner J set out ss. 1(1) and 1(3) of the Children Act 1989, noting that the court could take into account other relevant considerations. He considered the views of F, who was in favour of immunisation against meningitis, as a friend had been seriously ill with the disease, and against the MMR, although willing to follow the order of the court. Sumner J considered four-year-old C to be too young to have her views taken into account. In addition to the medical evidence, consideration was given to the possible harms if unvaccinated and to the emotional needs of the children. His Lordship accepted that both of the mothers were refusing immunisation in their judgment of the best interests of their daughter. As the matter had been referred to court, it was now for the court to determine whether immunisation was in the best interests of each child and to give an order accordingly, as long as there were no overriding reasons against giving the order. This meant that if the court considered medical treatment was in the best

[116] *Ibid.*, at para. 24.   [117] *A and D v B and E* [2003] EWHC 1376 (Fam), at para. 204.
[118] *Ibid.*, at para. 247.

interests of the child but would damage the child's relationship with her mother no order would be made if the benefit was minor or the risk of harm high. The opposition of the mother who was the principal carer was a matter of considerable concern but, Sumner J concluded, it was not sufficient to deter him from making the order.

There are a number of important points of note in this judgment. Sumner J stressed that immunisation is not compulsory. Where parents are in agreement whether their child is vaccinated or not, it is a matter for parental choice. In this case, arising in circumstances in which the parents were in dispute about other matters including contact, Sumner J acknowledged that the mothers would be making the everyday decisions involved in raising their daughters but the fathers, who enjoyed parental responsibility, were to be consulted on major decisions. Moreover, Sumner J expressed the opinion that '[w]here parents do not live together, the court recognises the importance of the particular bond which exists in most cases between a child and the parent with the principal care of the child. It exists with both children here. It does not give that parent greater rights. It does mean that the court will take care to safeguard and preserve that bond in the best interests of the child.'[119] However, exactly what that means is not clear from either his judgment or his decision.

The difference of opinion in this case was not between parents and doctors. It is currently accepted that, as an issue upon which there is genuine debate, decisions about immunisation are to be made by parents. The disagreement in this case was between the girls' parents in relation to an issue upon which there is a clear government policy, a fairly well-entrenched but not universally held view within the medical profession, and much uncertainty amongst parents. The judgment arguably gave insufficient attention to the fact that immunisations are a public health issue. The benefits of immunisation are partially to the individual but partially to the community as a whole in reduction of the incidence of disease amongst all, including those who have not been immunised or for whom immunisation is contraindicated. Richard Huxtable has suggested that where the issue is one of public health, the best interests principle is not appropriate for determination of the welfare of the individual child.[120]

---

[119] *Ibid.*, at para. 304.
[120] Richard Huxtable, '*Re C (A Child) (Immunisation: Parental Rights)* [2003] EWCA Civ 1148' (2004) 26 JSWFL 69–77.

As a case brought under the Children Act 1989, the focus of the decision was upon the welfare of the child. Article 8 of the ECHR was mentioned only in passing.[121] Hannah Baker has argued that a rights-based approach would have recognised the parent's right to raise her child according to her values and beliefs in balancing the rights of the child and the rights of the parent (or in this case, the rights of the mother and the rights of the father).[122] The result is unlikely to be any different. The rights of the child may prevail. But a rights-based conclusion is dependent upon the weight ascribed to the different arguments to determine whether the child's right to preventative healthcare, or her right to be protected from invasive and risky treatment of disputed benefit, prevails. Parents are invited to bring their children for immunisation. The majority do, although they may not agree to the administration of all vaccines available and they have the opportunity to discuss their concerns about immunisation with their GP, health visitor or others before doing so. Despite the benefits to public health generally, children are not immunised against the wishes of their parents. This is not because of any rights of the parents but because parents are entrusted to raise their children according to their beliefs and values. The mother of one of the girls expressed the inconsistency of the order with the beliefs and values according to which she was raising her child:

> This ruling makes it possible for officials to take my child and inject her with MMR jabs against my beliefs and my will – against the will of her mother, who lives with her, cares for her and looks after her . . . And who is willing to take responsibility if something terrible happens? Not the judge, nor the vaccination company, not the doctor injecting my child, and not the father who has not paid child maintenance.[123]

She provided the daily care for her daughter and would continue to do so should immunisation harm her daughter. Yet, her judgment about the best interests of her child reached according to her beliefs and values was overridden.

Whilst treatment can be provided with the consent of one person with parental responsibility, usually parents are at one in difficult treatment

---

[121] Without, as Kath O'Donnell points out, any analysis: 'Case Commentary – *Re C (Welfare of Child: Immunisation)* – Room to Refuse? Immunisation, Welfare and the Role of Parental Decision Making' (2004) 16 CFLQ 213–29, at p. 228.

[122] Hannah Baker, 'MMR: Medicine, Mothers and Rights' [2004] CLJ 49–52.

[123] Lorraine Fisher, 'Judge tells mums: give your girls MMR jabs; outrage at ruling', *Mirror*, 14 June 2003.

decisions, perhaps needing the support of each other in dealing with the tragedy of a seriously ill child. In this instance the child was not very sick, rather the specific issue was one of a day-to-day, yet major issue, regarding the upbringing of a child. The judgment details some of the background to the application for a specific issue order based in the breakdown of the relationship between the parents in each case, ongoing hostilities between them, and the use of litigation to structure their parenting.[124]

A focus upon responsibilities takes us away from the dichotomy – immunise or not – and requires more detailed consideration of the circumstances of the dispute. I argue in chapter 1 that, as a starting point for a conceptual framework of responsibilities, consideration should be given to the needs of the child as an individual, to the quality of relationships of care and external factors affecting the ability of those with responsibilities to the child to care for the child. Unanswered questions remain in this case about the needs of the two girls, about the ongoing relationship between the mother, father and daughter[125] and about the history of caring for the children. Had the parents genuinely reached a conclusion about how best to meet their child's needs on this issue? This must include a willingness to discuss the matter with the child's other parent, with whom they shared parental responsibility, and to consider the arguments for, and against, immunisation. The refusal of F's mother was based in her own experience – she had not been immunised and felt that she had not suffered as a consequence. Her daughter was healthy and she had no reason to think that she would be infected with any of the diseases. Her daughter was ten and had not yet suffered any harm whilst the immunisations carried risks themselves. Although she would accept the order of the court, F's mother did not think it would be helpful to hear the medical evidence because she had already made up her mind.[126] B, mother of C, raised her daughter according to holistic health

---

[124] In an earlier case, the Court of Appeal considered the sole issue of whether a four-year-old boy should receive the pertussis vaccine following a County Court hearing on the range of immunisations. Thorpe LJ expressed enormous exasperation that this was a matter which the parents were unable to resolve without the assistance of the court and expressed the hope that 'common sense would prevail'. *Re W (A Child)* CA, 8 March 2000 (web.lexis-nexis.com/professional/).

[125] The circumstances of this case would appear to be a good illustration of a willingness to resort to court to resolve differences rather than resolve them 'within the dynamic of the entire relationship'. As Mavis Maclean and John Eekelaar observed, where the relationship has broken down, differences take on greater importance and resort to law appears more attractive as the damage which this can cause to the relationship has already been done: Mavis Maclean and John Eekelaar, *The Parental Obligation: A Study of Parenthood Across Households*, Hart: Oxford, 1997, at p. 2.   [126] *A and D v B and E* [2003] EWHC 1376 (Fam), at paras. 261–8.

and natural parenting. She pointed to the inconclusive nature of the medical evidence and the dissenting views, expressing the judgment that main-stream medical opinion had not provided sufficient information. She was interested in the medical evidence as her views were not entrenched.[127] Full examination of the circumstances would have revealed the differences between them. It is notable that the medical experts, whilst supportive of the immunisation programme, were anxious to address the concerns of the mothers. The order of the court failed to do this. Surely the court should ensure that parents have been provided with sufficient information to enable them to take the responsibility of consenting to preventative health measures which carry risks? Determination of best interests of the child through a conceptual framework of responsibility would require the court to confront the wider context. On the facts of this case, the context is widely shared uncertainty amongst parents about the risks of subjecting their child to a public health programme, the success of which depends upon wide-spread take-up and the benefits of which are partly to their child and partly to the community as a whole.

Circumcision: in the best interests of the child?

Whilst female circumcision has been criminalised within English law,[128] male circumcision is currently permitted for both medical and ritual/reli-gious reasons. The Law Commission in its consultation paper, *Consent in the Criminal Law*, expressed the view that male circumcision is lawful, a com-monly accepted exception to the principle that an effective consent cannot be given to the infliction of actual bodily harm.[129] Marie Fox and Michael Thomson argue that the polarisation of analysis between female and male circumcision has served to mask proper analysis in medical, ethical and legal debate of the risks and harm involved in ritual (non-medical) male

---

[127] *Ibid.*, at paras. 210–12.
[128] The Female Genital Mutilation Act 2003 replaced the Prohibition of Female Circumcision Act 1985, making it an offence to carry out female genital mutilation except in a surgical procedure performed by a registered medical practitioner in the interests of the physical or mental health of the girl or woman, or performed by a registered medical practitioner or registered midwife upon a girl or woman in labour or who has just given birth and connected to the labour or birth. The 2003 Act introduces a new offence of aiding, abetting, counselling or procuring another to perform female genital mutilation outside the UK, upon a UK national or per-manent resident, in circumstances which would amount to an offence contrary to section 1.
[129] Law Commission Consultation Paper No. 139, *Consent in the Criminal Law* (1995), at para. 9.2.

circumcision. They ask why circumcision, 'the excision of healthy tissue from a child unable to give his consent for no demonstrable medical benefit', should be a private matter of parental choice.[130] The British Medical Association's guidance to doctors stresses that consent of both parents is required for non-therapeutic male circumcision of young children, that consent must be obtained from competent children, and all children must be given the opportunity to express their views which must be taken into account.[131] They explain that the health benefits are unproven and, as the procedure carries medical and psychological risks, other factors must be present to justify non-therapeutic circumcision.[132] Parental preference is likewise insufficient: justification must be based upon the best interests of the child, with due consideration to social and cultural factors.

The issue of parental disagreement about circumcision came before the court in *Re J (Child's Religious Upbringing and Circumcision)* in which a father sought a specific issue order that his son, aged five years, should be circumcised.[133] The order was refused by Wall J in the Family Division and upheld by the Court of Appeal, Thorpe LJ referring to the judgment of Wall J as 'impregnable'.[134] J's father was a non-practising Muslim of Turkish origin permanently living in the UK. His mother was a non-practising Christian. It was accepted that the mother had agreed, whilst pregnant, that if their child was male he would be circumcised. However, J was being brought up in 'an essentially secular lifestyle'. Wall J acknowledged the existence of differing views about circumcision. Some considered ritual circumcision to be 'an assault on the bodily integrity of the child'. Yet, it is a common, and accepted, practice within the Muslim and Jewish communities. Wall J concluded that 'where two parents, jointly exercising parental responsibility for a male child cause him to be ritually circumcised in

---

[130] Marie Fox and Michael Thomson, 'Short Changed? The Law and Ethics of Male Circumcision' (2005) 13 *International Journal of Children's Rights* 161–81, at p. 170.

[131] BMA, *The Law and Ethics of Male Circumcision: Guidance for Doctors*, 2006.

[132] Damages were awarded to a child for the physical injury, and to his parents for the psychological injury, following negligence in the performance of a ritual circumcision in *Ibrahim (a Minor) v Muhammad; Ibrahim and another v Muhammad*, 21 May 1984 (web.lexis-nexis.com/ professional/).

[133] *Re J (Child's Religious Upbringing and Circumcision)* [1999] 2 FLR 678. The father also sought an order requiring J to be brought up in the Muslim religion. Wall J did not consider that it would be better for J for an order to be made on this issue (s. 1(5) Children Act 1989) given that the father did not actively practise his religion, or mix with Muslims. He merely sought to teach J about Islam which could be done during periods of contact.

[134] *Re J (Child's Religious Upbringing and Circumcision)* [2000] 1 FLR 571.

accordance with the tenets of their religion, that exercise of parental responsibility is lawful'.[135]

Wall J considered each of the factors in the welfare checklist set out in s. 1(3) of the Children Act 1989, noted GMC[136] and BMA guidelines to the effect that circumcision should only be performed with the consent of both parents, that in J's case it was not medically indicated and that the procedure was not risk, or pain, free. His father argued that circumcision would be a celebratory event which would enable J to identify with his father and as a consequence of which he would be 'confirmed in the eyes of Islam as a Muslim'. This was weighed against the evidence that the practice was not common amongst J's peers and, given his mother's objection to the procedure, would cause stress and tension between his parents and might cause J to suffer psychological damage. The judgment clearly appreciates that the child's best interests are dependent upon those caring for him. Wall J noted: that as he was five years old, J's views about the procedure would be determined by how it was presented to him by those he trusted; J's emotional needs required that his relationships with both of his parents be maintained; that his mother was meeting his caring needs but to order circumcision would be likely to damage further her relationship with J's father and add to the hostility between them which was a cause of harm to J. Wall J made an order prohibiting the father from arranging for, or permitting, J to be circumcised in England, Wales or elsewhere. In the subsequent case of *Re S (Specific Issue Order: Religion: Circumcision)*,[137] Baron J considered it was in the best interests of children, a girl aged ten and an eight-year-old boy, to continue to be exposed to both the Muslim and Jain religions as they had been during their parents' marriage. Whilst the Jain religion considers circumcision to be a form of mutilation and hence unacceptable violence, the Muslim religion requires circumcision during childhood. It was up to the child, K, to decide, once he was *Gillick* competent, if he wished to adhere to any one religion and to undergo circumcision.

These cases raise the issue of the relevance of the religious beliefs of parents to decisions about the best interests of the child. The right to freedom of thought, conscience and religion under Article 9 of the ECHR and the requirement that states 'take all effective and appropriate measures with a view to abolishing traditional practices prejudicial to the health of

---

[135] *Re J (Child's Religious Upbringing and Circumcision)* [1999] 2 FLR 678.
[136] GMC, *Guidance for Doctors who are Asked to Circumcise Male Children*, 1997.
[137] *Re S (Specific Issue Order: Religion: Circumcision)* [2004] EWHC 1282.

children' under Article 24(3) of the United Nations Convention on the Rights of the Child were both considered by Wall J in *Re J*. The father's right under Article 9 to manifest his religion was limited by the rights and freedoms of the boy's mother and the best interests of the child.[138] Despite living in a country respectful of cultural diversity, religious opinion and alternative beliefs, the relevance of these views to determination of the best interests of the child has not been worked through by the courts.[139]

The responsibilities which arise out of relationships are in part individually interpreted, partly determined by social expectations, but respond to the needs of the child as a living being rather than an abstract ideal. Parents care for, have responsibilities towards, and raise their children. What parents do clearly has an influence upon who their children are. Parental beliefs expose their children to ideas, practices and experiences which children may, or may not, accept or follow. Religious beliefs may provide the backdrop for parental views about the best interests of the child but a focus upon responsibilities requires examination of their conclusion. Have the parents given sufficient consideration to the needs of their child as an individual connected to, and dependent upon, his or her parents but also separate from them? Further, on the specific issue of circumcision, that it is a practice undertaken within some cultures, or according to some religious beliefs, is not in itself a sufficient reason. It is necessary to interrogate those beliefs, thereby exposing the reasons for them.[140] As a social, rather than medical, procedure non-therapeutic circumcision must be addressed with consideration of the individual child as a person rather than an ideal, thorough examination of the quality of the relationships between the child and his parents and the history of practices of caring, and investigation of the reasons for the parental decision, or difference of opinion.

Taking responsibility: parents and professionals

The healthcare needs of most young children will be met by their parents, working with the health visitor, practice nurse and GP, with the occasional visit to Accident and Emergency. Whilst working in partnership with

---

[138] Jane Fortin argues that non-therapeutic circumcision amounts to a breach of Article 8 of the ECHR as a violation of the child's right to bodily integrity which would not necessarily be justified under Article 8(2): *Children's Rights and the Developing Law*, Reed Elsevier: London, 2003, at p. 332.   [139] *Supra*, n. 55.   [140] *Supra*, n. 15, at p. 139.

healthcare professionals in primary care, parents have expressed awareness that their care of their child is being monitored and surveyed. Yet, their expertise gained through the provision of care for their child is not recognised. Parents have expressed frustration where their child's development – physical, mental and social – is tested and compared against the 'norm' whilst their own experiences of their child are ignored as subjective anecdote against objective evidence.

The study by Debra Westlake and Maggie Pearson identified the particular tensions arising in the relationship between health visitors and mothers. Health visitors provide a mainly preventative service, monitoring physical and emotional well-being, advising parents about child health and good parenting. The health visitor's role is thus a peculiar one involving advising, supporting and judging:

> [o]n the one hand, health visitors are expected to establish a caring and supportive relationship with families, while, on the other, they are charged with the responsibility of monitoring the occurrence of abuse, neglect and inadequate parenting . . . [T]his contradiction greatly reduces the health visitor's acceptability and effectiveness.[141]

Debra Westlake and Maggie Pearson found that, contrary to assumptions within health policy that parents did not know their responsibilities and needed to be educated about them, mothers did know and took them very seriously; even though, for some mothers, circumstances of material deprivation made fulfilment of them very difficult, and frequently meant ignoring their own needs in the interests of their children. Where children were injured, mothers feared being held irresponsible, although children's accidents were more likely to be as a result of their environment than individual conduct. They identified the tensions in the relationship between mothers and health visitors in terms of the balance between parental autonomy and state intervention:

> The health visitor personified the conflict between the two kinds of responsibility and the conflicting approaches of the state to securing the needs of children embodied in the Children Act [surveillance and intervention on part of state or non-intervention into family]. Called

---

[141] Michael Bloor and James McIntosh, 'Surveillance and Concealment: A Comparison of Techniques of Client Resistance in Therapeutic Communities and Health Visiting' in Sarah Cunningham-Burley and Neil P. McKeganey (eds.), *Readings in Medical Sociology*, Routledge: London, 1990, at pp. 163–4.

by health policy to befriend and court the household as her or his stair-way to success in reaching targets for health gain, at the same time the health visitor must observe the household as a potential minefield of danger to children. Not surprisingly, this paradoxical agenda creates conflicting roles, and generates dissatisfaction for both professional and parent. At the core of this conflict is the seemingly irresolvable dilemma of a professional friend who is an inspector in disguise.[142]

Whether the desired shift in the nature of the relationship between parent and professional to one of partnership in the delivery of child-centred healthcare services identified in chapter 2 is achieved, remains to be seen. The next chapter explores the case law when the tensions between professional and parent (in all cases doctors rather than midwives, nurses or health visitors) are taken to court for resolution. It will examine whether the law fosters the relationship between parent and professional in the joint endeavour of caring for children, respectful of their respective roles, functions and expertise.

---

[142] Debra Westlake and Maggie Pearson, 'Child Protection and Health Promotion: Whose Responsibility?' (1997) 19 JSWFL 139, at p. 153.

4

In the best interests of the child?

Introduction

As examined in the previous chapter, all parents have the legal obligation to secure treatment for everyday injuries and inevitable childhood illnesses yet some parents are confronted with a child whose medical condition presents a much more serious prognosis. Parents may have to take care of children with life-threatening conditions such as congenital heart problems, serious illnesses like leukaemia, or accidental injuries of such magnitude that without treatment they are life-threatening. Or, whilst not being life-threatening, the child's condition may mean extended dependency and require basic care, intensive nursing and therapeutic management such as is involved in the care of children with physical and mental disabilities.[1] Parents may be required to make decisions about treatment which alters appearance, with major ramifications for a child's life.[2] Parents of children with serious, severe or life-threatening illnesses or injuries have to navigate the healthcare system, negotiate with service providers and work in partnership with professionals with nursing and medical expertise to secure the best care for their child. In doing so, both parent and professional are confronted with uncertainty. For the professional there is uncertainty about the possibilities of medical science and the child's prognosis. For the parent there is uncertainty about their child's needs and welfare which may take them on an agonising journey through the emotions of hope, fear, worry and distress. In most cases, professionals and parents caring for a child with a serious, severe or life-threatening condition work together to determine

---

[1] The care of children with physical and mental disabilities is considered in chapter 6.

[2] Priscilla Alderson's study identifies how children's views about whether they should undergo orthopaedic surgery were influenced by the impact of their condition upon their lives and their judgment as to how surgery might make a difference: *Children's Consent to Surgery*, Open University Press: Buckingham, 1993.

which treatment is best for the child. Healthcare professionals are under a legal duty to use their skill and judgment to provide treatment in the best interests of the child, subject to the consent of the child's parent. It is their professional duty to work with parents, through a process of discussion and negotiation, to agree a treatment plan reflecting their parental and professional judgment of the best interests of the child. As with the minor treatment considered in chapter 3, parents are under a duty to consent to the medical treatment from the range of clinically indicated alternatives which, in their evaluation, is in the best interests of their child.

In a very small number of cases, when parental refusal of proposed medical treatment is believed to be putting the child at risk of significant harm, differences of opinion between parents and professionals may be resolved in the courtroom. These decisions are important not only for the outcome with regard to the individual child but, furthermore, because they establish the legal principles which govern the provision of treatment to all children and the roles of parents and professionals in caring for them. These cases will be analysed in this chapter, employing the theoretical perspective developed in chapter 1. In examining these cases it will be asked whether, when making the particularistic assessment of the interests of the child, sufficient consideration is given to the individual child – their personality, character and experiences – which when very young have to be identified by those caring for them. To what extent are understandings of the ideal child – a dependent, vulnerable, potential being in need of protection – employed in place of consideration of the child in question? Analysis of these cases also addresses whether consideration is given to the caring relationship between parent and child. Parents provide continuing care of their child through health, illness and recovery which contrasts with the episodic care provided by hospital staff and particularly by doctors who may 'take care of' rather than 'care for' the child. Parents will also be focused upon the needs of their child as an individual, whilst the focus of doctors is upon the medical problem presented by the child. Generally, as a result of their particular interest in their child, their experience of caring and their attentiveness to their child's needs, parents gain knowledge of their child as an individual which must inform assessment of the child's best interests. A presumption that the vulnerable child requires protection from his or her parents can result in failure to give weight to parental experience and interest in the needs and well-being of their child. The primary responsibility for the care of children lies with their parents, and factors which determine everyday life within the family, such as religious beliefs, or firmly held convictions about diet, exercise or medical treatment, must be explored, not simply dismissed, when decisions are made about the treatment of children with serious medical conditions. Furthermore, it is necessary to examine how parental assessment of their child's needs is influenced by the values and beliefs within their community which may contrast with professional and societal norms. However, parents are dependent upon those with expert knowledge and parental discharge of responsibility requires effective partnership with professionals:

> Sensing the child's best interests involves close observation, rational analysis, and also empathy . . . [It is] for the family and staff around the cot to try the hazardous task of unravelling the tangle, learning from one another about the child's best interests, developing their expertise through direct involvement.[3]

This dependency, the different roles and distinct contributions of parent and professional have to be recognised in reaching a decision about the best interests of the child.

In the cases considered in this chapter, the treatment being recommended by the medical profession as the best hope of curing the child is refused by their parents either because the treatment is contrary to firmly held religious convictions[4] or because the parents disagree with the doctor's assessment of which medical treatment or procedure is in the best interests of the child.[5] The case of conjoined twins, Jodie and Mary, raised different issues as the proposed surgery presented the best hope for Jodie with the inevitable death of Mary.[6] The court was required to address giving consent both to treatment refused by parents and to performing surgery upon a child which would result in her death. As a case concerning intervention to which parents were refusing their consent, it is appropriately considered in this chapter. In each of the cases considered, because of the potentially serious consequences for the child, it is right that the disagreement between parents and professionals was referred to court for resolution. However, it

---

[3] Priscilla Alderson, *Choosing for Children: Parents' Consent to Surgery*, Oxford University Press: Oxford, 1990, at p. 218.

[4] *Re S (a Minor) (Medical Treatment)* [1993] 1 FLR 376; *Re O (a Minor) (Medical Treatment)* [1993] 2 FLR 149; *Re R (Minor)* 15 BMLR 72 (web.lexis-nexis.com/professional/).

[5] *Re T (a Minor) (Wardship: Medical Treatment)* [1997] 1 WLR 242; *In re C (a Child) (HIV Testing)* [2000] 2 WLR 270; *Re MM (Medical Treatment)* [2000] 1 FLR 224.

[6] *Re A (Children) (Conjoined Twins: Surgical Separation)* [2001] 2 WLR 480. The aspects of this case concerned with the end of life are considered in chapter 5.

is argued that determination of the best interests of the child necessitates a more grounded analysis of the needs of the specific child, the parental and professional roles, the wider social, political, cultural or religious context and the support provided to parents in caring for the child.

The child as an individual

Decisions have to be made about the treatment and care of seriously ill children for whom treatment offers only a probability, and not a certainty, of cure but at the expense of pain, distress and the side-effects of treatment. In order to decide which of the treatments available, or whether the provision of any treatment, is in the best interests of the child, parents and the court have to consider carefully the medical evidence. But the treatment, procedure or surgery is being considered for a particular child. For cases decided under the Children Act 1989, section 3(1)(a) requires the court to give consideration to the wishes and feelings of the child concerned as far as they can be established and according to the child's age and understanding. Hearing from the child him- or herself would be helpful in considering his or her 'physical, emotional and educational needs' (s. 3(1)(b) Children Act 1989), the effect which the proposed course of action may have upon him or her (s. 3(1)(c) Children Act 1989), the child's characteristics (s. 3(1)(d) Children Act 1989) and the harm which the child has suffered or is at risk of suffering (s. 3(1)(e) Children Act 1989).

In some of these cases the children are very young. Yet, even very young children have experience of their condition, of pain and distress, feelings and preferences deserving of attention in assessing their best interests. The case of Re MM[7] was brought to court because of a difference of opinion between the child's parents and treating physicians about the course of treatment which should be administered to MM, a seven-year-old boy suffering from primary immunodeficiency (PID). The family were Russian, six months into their three-year stay in England. MM's parents wanted to continue with the treatment regime which he had received in Russia and to which they thought he would have to revert when they returned. In Russia, MM had been given immunostimulant therapy, administered monthly in order to stimulate his immune system, with small doses of immunoglobin (IG) when required. The treating physicians

---

[7] Re MM (Medical Treatment) [2000] 1 FLR 224.

wanted to administer replacement immunoglobin (IG) intravenously, the expectation being that this would be necessary for the rest of his life. The judgment catalogues the illnesses MM had suffered from and the impact of his immune deficiency upon his physical self, the consultations and treatment administered, but is dominated by expert medical opinion. Reference is made to MM's physical ability. We are told that, upon arrival in England, he explored the city, played football and went to school. His parents gave evidence to the effect that he had spent the weekend before an earlier court order was made, giving consent to aspiration of a bone abscess on his leg and the intravenous administration of antibiotics, running around, riding his bike and on a long walk. The judgment given by the court does not refer to this seven-year-old child's experience of his condition, his ability to cope with the different forms of treatment or his preferences as material to determination of which treatment was in the best interests of this particular child. Medical evidence can reveal which treatment is clinically indicated but not whether the proposed medical treatment (as opposed to a regime previously adopted or an alternative method) is in the best interests of the specific child. In their evidence, his parents expressed their own concerns and reasons for their preference for immunostimulant therapy but did not give an account of their understanding of their child's feelings, preferences or attitudes. As a seven-year-old child with a long-term condition, he could have been asked. Studies have shown how children with experience of illness frequently possess knowledge about their condition and a maturity of approach to it which adults do not expect.[8] Children can be asked about how they feel about their condition, the ways in which it limits them, their ability to tolerate treatment and their concerns about their state of health. Unless the child is heard, his or her own anxieties, feelings, fears, expectations and experiences expressed, it is easy to consider them according to the ideal of child: vulnerable, dependent, potential and in need of protection. In an example of dichotomous thinking, an understanding of children as *becoming* and not *being* persons has meant a failure within reported judgments to address the personality, or sense of self, of the child at all rather than careful consideration of the personality, or sense of self, of *the child*. The point is a simple one: judgments made about the best interests of the child have to be made with consideration of the needs of the individual child and not according to an ideal of child.

---

[8] Myra Bluebond-Langner, *The Private Worlds of Dying Children*, Princeton University Press: Princeton, 1978; *supra*, n. 2.

The refusal of consent by the parents in *Re S*,[9] *Re O*[10] and *Re R*,[11] determined by their religious beliefs, stood in opposition to the medical desire to
undertake treatment requiring the administration of blood. The judgments in these cases are dominated by clinical assessment, weighed against
parental beliefs, without any reference to the children whose treatment is
being considered. We learn nothing of the children, four-and-a-half-year-
old S, ten-month-old R and ten-day-old O. Whilst these children might be
'too young to express [their] wishes and feelings',[12] their best interests
cannot be determined without careful consideration of the individual child
by his or her parents and the professionals caring for them.

Eighteen-month-old C was likewise too young to give for himself a
rational, reasoned account of whether he wanted to undergo the proposed
liver transplant or not. The judges in *Re T*[13] attended to C's mother's view
that the transplant operation was not in his best interests. Whilst the Court
of Appeal rightly looked to considerations broader than medical assessment, including parental experience of the particular child, it is notable
that, apart from the reference to the pain and distress occasioned to C by his
initial operation which was a matter of concern for his mother, we learn
nothing more of C. We learn nothing of C's current state of health or his
ability to cope with medical intervention. There is no reference to his personality, character or spirit, all those aspects which make him a unique
individual and which are relevant to determination of his best interests.
Where children are too young to articulate for themselves their feelings and
experiences, they depend upon those caring for them to be attentive to their
unexpressed, but felt, needs.

Even younger were conjoined twins, Rosie Gracie and Gracie Rosie,
known for the purposes of the hearing as Mary and Jodie, who came to
national attention in the summer of 2000. The parents of the twins refused
their consent to separation surgery. In their opinion, the best interests of
their children lay in continuation of their permanent union which the
medical evidence suggested would last between a few months and a few
years before their simultaneous death due to heart failure resulting from the
strain upon Jodie's heart. All four judges assessed the proposed elective

[9] *Re S (a Minor) (Medical Treatment)* [1993] 1 FLR 376.
[10] *Re O (a Minor) (Medical Treatment)* [1993] 2 FLR 149.
[11] *Re R (Minor)* 15 BMLR 72 (web.lexis-nexis.com/professional/).   [12] *Ibid.* (Booth J).
[13] *Re T (a Minor) (Wardship: Medical Treatment)* [1997] 1 WLR 242, considered further at
    pp. 137–42.

separation surgery to be in the best interests of the stronger twin, Jodie. At the time of the hearing she was not thriving. Her blood gases were low, it was thought because her circulatory system was also supporting Mary, and it was predicted that this would ultimately result in heart failure and inevitable death. The operation carried for her a small risk of brain damage or death but would extend her life expectancy from a few months to normal. Jodie would require some reconstructive surgery. Immediately after separation, her pelvis would be broken to re-align her hips and legs, to create a bottom and construct an anus. It was accepted that further surgery might be required in the future[14] but it was considered that she would otherwise develop normally. Ward LJ noted, without comment, the evidence referring to literature to the effect that 'the separation is usually well accepted without any serious or other psychological effects on the survivor . . . it is unlikely that she will have any major psychological consequences from that separation'.[15] Robert Walker LJ agreed with the judge at first instance, Johnson J, that the surgery was also in Mary's best interests. In his opinion, her life would not only be of no benefit to her but continued life would be a distressing, harmful experience. This was because either she would be in pain, which would increase as Jodie became more mobile and dragged Mary around with her, or, alternatively, she could feel no pain but neither could she experience pleasure.[16] Ward LJ concluded otherwise in respect of Mary. The question which the court had to confront was: 'Is it in Mary's best interests that an operation be performed to separate her from Jodie when the certain consequence of that operation is that she will die? There is only one answer to that question. It is: "No, that it is not in her best interests."'[17] Having concluded that the paramount best interests of the children whose future was being determined by the court were in conflict, Ward LJ held that

---

[14] It was accepted that after separation surgery Jodie might have required further surgery to re-adjust the configuration of her pelvis if it spread as she grew, possibly surgery to correct a bend in her spine if one developed and surgery to construct a vagina. It was also accepted that if the surgery to construct an anus was unsuccessful she might have to use a colostomy bag, and, whilst it was expected that her bladder function would be preserved, if it was not she would have to use a urinary diversion bag.

[15] *Re A (Children) (Conjoined Twins: Surgical Separation)* [2001] 2 WLR 480, at p. 499. Her mother, in a later interview, explained that they had told Gracie that she had a sister who had died and took her to visit her grave but that she was, at the age of three, too young to be told the full circumstances. Rina Attard said, 'I want to make sure she never feels guilty about being the sister who lived.' Paul Harris, 'Amazing Gracie', *Daily Mail*, 8 July 2003.

[16] *Re A, ibid.*, at pp. 578–9.

[17] *Ibid.*, at p. 522. Brooke LJ agreed with Ward LJ on the determination of best interests and the course of action suggested by the least detrimental alternative.

the court had to choose the least detrimental alternative, which was that the twins should be separated.[18] Brooke LJ and Robert Walker LJ likewise gave consent.[19] Mary died moments after separation and was buried, Rosie Gracie Attard, on 19 January 2001. Jodie, Gracie Rosie Attard, survived.[20] Certainly, all four judges confronted with the duty to decide gave the legal principles careful scrutiny. They were also aware of the ethical issues and opposing moral opinions about the separation surgery and they acknowledged how extremely difficult the decision was for the parents who loved both their daughters. However, a 'thorough investigation of their plight' to which the babies had a right[21] demanded careful consideration of the distinct personalities, character and spirit of the children, connected to each other not only physically but also emotionally.

The judgment is littered with reference to the rights of the twin babies: Ward LJ refers to the right to life, Robert Walker LJ also to the rights to physical integrity ('right to a whole body over which the individual will, on reaching an age of understanding, have autonomy'), self-determination, bodily integrity and human dignity. As Michael Freeman has suggested, the list could be extended to include 'the right of Jodie to live with dignity, the right of Mary to die with dignity. Perhaps even the right of Mary to confer

---

18 Sabine Michalowski, 'Sanctity of Life – Are Some Lives More Sacred Than Others?' (2002) 22 *Legal Studies* 377, argues that the court took the wrong approach in balancing conflicting best interests. Assessment of the best interests of a child, she rightly identifies, is undertaken to justify a touching which, in the absence of consent, would amount to a civil and criminal battery. She argues that the conclusion that the operation was in Jodie's best interests justified the surgery. But, as the surgery was not in Mary's best interests, the question which then had to be answered was whether it could be lawfully performed even though it resulted in Mary's death. In comparison, Andrew Bainham, 'Resolving the Unresolvable: The Case of the Conjoined Twins' (2001) 60 CLJ 49–53, considers that the court took the right approach in balancing the interests of the twins.

19 Parents of conjoined twins, Natasha and Courtney Smith, born sharing a heart and liver, were reported to have agreed to separation surgery when the twins were strong enough. Prior to their birth the hospital had sought a declaration to clarify the legal position. The degree to which the heart was shared meant that the surgery could be seen as sacrificing one of the twins if either but not both were viable and surgery involved taking tissue from one twin and giving it to the other, raising different legal issues from those raised in the case of Jodie and Mary: Lorna Duckwort, 'Parents may face legal battle over surgery on twins who share a heart', *Independent*, 5 February 2002. Investigations after birth revealed that separation was not possible due to abnormalities with the shared heart and the twins both died: Rebecca Allison, 'Conjoined twins with shared heart die', *Guardian*, 18 May 2002.

20 Gracie is reported to have done extremely well. By the age of three she could walk and her physical and intellectual development had progressed normally: Martin Bashir, 'Living with the miracle of Gracie', *Sunday Times*, 3 August 2003.

21 Michael Freeman, 'Whose Life is it Anyway?' (2001) 9 Med Law Rev 259–80, at p. 279.

life upon her sister',[22] all of which would have to be balanced. It is notable that neither Ward LJ nor Robert Walker LJ undertook an analysis of the moral rights to which they referred to either guide or test their decision. This would, however, have been an abstract analysis when the concrete reality of life for the specific children, in the particular circumstances, needed to be considered.[23] Rather than talk in terms of rights, which are abstract, individualistic and competing, or about protection from unjust aggression,[24] the judgment would have been more convincing had the best interests of these children involved careful consideration of Mary and Jodie as distinctive, if physically (and perhaps emotionally and spiritually) joined persons. In their article which predates the case of Re A, Sally Sheldon and Stephen Wilkinson quote Edward Kiely, who operated on the Kuwaiti twins in 1995, expressing a degree of mystification and obvious fascination in the uncertainty surrounding the unity and separation in the physiological functioning of conjoined twins but in no doubt that 'their personalities are entirely different from the day that they are born'.[25]

The joined bodies of the twins – the judgment refers to the twins as connected, united, attached, interdependent – not only led the court to consider whether they were separate persons (which, it was emphasised, they were) but also directed the attention of the court to the babies as unique living beings to a greater extent than acknowledged in the previous cases. Beyond the medical prognosis for the girls with, or without, the surgery at issue, sketchy details are introduced of their state of being. In Mary's case, based upon the medical evidence, this is mainly in terms of a lack. Mary is described as being severely abnormal in her brain, heart and lung formation and functioning; Brooke LJ described her as having 'a useless brain, a useless heart and useless lungs'.[26] Mary is reported to have

---

[22] *Ibid.*, at p. 279.

[23] All three appeal court judges were of the view that the Human Rights Act 1998, which came into force before the surgery was performed, would not require a different answer from the court. Articles 2, 3 and 8 of the ECHR were mentioned.

[24] Ward LJ said: '[Mary] is alive because and only because, to put it bluntly, but nonetheless accurately, she sucks the lifeblood of Jodie and she sucks the lifeblood out of Jodie. She will survive only so long as Jodie survives. Jodie will not survive long because constitutionally she will not be able to cope. Mary's parasitic living will be the cause of Jodie's ceasing to live. If Jodie could speak, she would surely protest, "Stop it, Mary, you're killing me". Mary would have no answer to that.' *Re A (Children) (Conjoined Twins: Surgical Separation)* [2001] 2 WLR 480, at p. 530.

[25] Sally Sheldon and Stephen Wilkinson, 'Conjoined Twins: The Legality and Ethics of Sacrifice' [1997] 5 Med Law Rev 149–71, at p. 151, from an interview with Edward Kiely.

[26] *Re A (Children) (Conjoined Twins: Surgical Separation)* [2001] 2 WLR 480, at p. 545.

'primitive responses' and to be a 'hindrance to [Jodie's] instincts and development':

> Mary cannot cry. She has not the lungs to cry with. There is no way that can be remotely described as reliable by which those tending Mary can know even now whether she is hurting or in pain. When lightly touched or stroked her face contorts. When pinched there is the same reflex. But she cannot cry. So I asked, what would happen as the weeks went by and Jodie moved, tried to crawl, to turn over in her sleep, to sit up. Would she not, I asked, be pulling Mary with her? Linked together as they are, not simply by bone but by tissue, flesh and muscle, would not Mary hurt and be in pain? In pain but not able to cry. One very experienced doctor said she thought that was an horrendous scenario, as she put it, being dragged around and not being able to do anything about it. Accordingly, weighing up those considerations I conclude that the few months of Mary's life if not separated from her twin would not simply be worth nothing to her, they would be hurtful.[27]

In comparison Jodie was, according to the neonatologist who gave evidence before Johnson J: 'very sparkling really, wriggling, very alert, sucking on a dummy and using her upper limbs in an appropriate manner, very much a with it sort of baby'.[28] Ward LJ quoted from a report from the hospital written when the twins were twenty-three days old to the effect that Jodie 'appears to be a bright little girl achieving the expected developmental milestones'.

Commentators have rightly pointed to the assumptions about the self which were made by the judges of the Court of Appeal, assumptions which permeate English law. As Vanessa Munro has argued, the physically joined bodies of the conjoined twins confound the assumptions of abstraction, separation and individualism upon which the Court of Appeal proceeded. The relationship between the twins was conceived of as invasive, competing and harmful and what they shared, the bond between them, mentioned only in passing but not recognised as something intrinsic to their sense of self. Vanessa Munro draws upon feminist reconceptualisation of the concept of autonomy to argue for a relational approach which acknowledges relationship, connection and context. This approach, she suggests, would not have made the court's job any easier but, 'it can barely be disputed that affording legal credence to the connection thesis alongside the separation thesis

---

[27] *Ibid.*, at p. 507 (Ward LJ quoting from judgment of Johnson J).   [28] *Ibid.*, at p. 492.

would have presented a more comprehensive reflection of the realities of the dilemma from the experiential perspective of the legal agents involved'.[29] Nor, she suggests, would a relational approach, which more accurately reflected the experiences of the twins, necessarily have led to a different decision. It would have involved the acknowledgement of other factors centred upon the babies as persons with current interests, including, for example, their interests in each other's well-being.[30] The particular situation of the conjoined twins highlights the range of factors intrinsic to examination of the best interests of these babies which were not addressed in the reported judgments of the court. Ultimately, the conclusion may not be any different but it is vital that, when parents or the court determine the best interests of the child, careful consideration is given to the individual child as a living person with current, as well as future, interests.

The child situated within caring relationships

A consequence of determination of the best interests of the child without attentiveness to the needs of the specific child whose treatment is to be decided is that it provides the space for assumptions of childhood vulnerability, prompting a desire to protect the child. Newborn babies, young children, the sick, incapacitated and elderly infirm would not thrive, in some cases would not survive, without the care of those upon whom they depend. As Eva Feder Kittay has argued, dependency is inevitable in human society and it is a state we all have experience of, as dependents, and many as dependency workers.[31] To be dependent upon another does involve vulnerability. Dependents can be neglected or exploited and the functional work of meeting their needs can be discharged without a caring attitude. However, there are no issues of neglect, exploitation or lack of caring disposition in relation to any of the children whose treatment and care are under consideration in this chapter. The issue is a difference of opinion between those with responsibility for caring for the child about the best interests of the child. That is, there are different answers to the question of what, given their needs, is best for the child?

---

[29] Vanessa Munro, 'Square Pegs in Round Holes: The Dilemma of Conjoined Twins and Individual Rights' (2001) 10 *Social and Legal Studies* 459–82, at p. 478.   [30] *Ibid.*, at p. 479.

[31] Eva Feder Kittay, *Love's Labor: Essays on Women, Equality and Dependency*, Routledge: New York, 1999, at p. 1. 'Dependency worker' is the term which Kittay uses to describe those people, principally women, whose work (paid and unpaid) ensures the well-being of their 'charge'.

Appreciation of children's vulnerability where it co-exists with assumptions of parent and child as primarily separate, rather than as primarily connected, perceives the child as endangered by their parents. The inevitable response of the judiciary is to attempt to protect child from parent. Waite LJ in *Re T*, whilst recognising that the role of parents in caring for their child places them in the best position to make decisions about the child's medical treatment, expressed a deep-rooted scepticism about parental discharge of their responsibilities. The court, his Lordship said, needed to be alert to decisions 'prompted by scruple' or which are 'patently irreconcilable with principles of child health or welfare widely accepted by the generality of mankind'.[32] The cost of this fundamental distrust is a failure to see the history of caring, the connections between them and the particular interest which, generally, parents have in the well-being of their child:

> [P]arents are often the only adults able to have continuing knowledge of the child patient. Their knowledge is unique, not just in the amount of cumulative detail, but also in the quality . . . [M]ost parents identify very closely with their child, urgently longing for recovery yet for relief from painful treatment. [P]arents usually gain an intense awareness of their child's experiences and needs through feeling with the child.[33]

In *Re A* the court, as is often the case, adopted the role of protector of the babies from their parents which, as Vanessa Munro observes, was not only inconsistent with judicial pronouncements about the rights of the parents but had the effect of constructing the parents and their babies as in conflict. There is no scope in such an understanding for recognition of the connection between them and of the parents' love for them.[34] In her article responding to the case of conjoined twins, Jodie and Mary, Barbara Hewson notes that Ward LJ quoted Justice Scalia who expressed the opinion that the courts were in no better position to decide than 'nine people picked at random from the Kansas City telephone directory'.[35] If that is the case, she asks, why not let the parents make the decision? The particular interest which the parents have in their children's well-being may

---

[32] *Re T (a Minor) (Wardship: Medical Treatment)* [1997] 1 WLR 242, at p. 254.
[33] Priscilla Alderson, 'Consent to Children's Surgery and Intensive Medical Treatment' (1990) 17 *Journal of Law and Society* 52–65, at p. 61.   [34] *Supra.*, n. 29, at p. 467.
[35] *Re A (Children) (Conjoined Twins: Surgical Separation)* [2001] 2 WLR 480, at p. 487, Ward LJ quoting Justice Scalia in *Cruzan v Director, Missouri Department of Health* (1990) 110 S Ct 2841, at 2859.

put them in a better position to make the decision than the judiciary. And, Barbara Hewson suggests, when the court prefers the medical assessment to the decision of loving parents reached in accordance with their own value system, it is easy to understand that the parents would feel that this was a private matter upon which they ought to be able to decide.[36] In contrast, Michael Freeman argues that it was right that the decision was not taken by the parents: 'It was better for all concerned that this was a decision taken out of their hands and subjected to a principled reasoning.'[37] It is true to say that the effect of a court decision is that the parents, coping with the consequences, do not have to live with the fact that they made the decision (and inevitable self-doubt as to whether they did make the correct decision). And, whilst the judgment in *Re A* traverses the principles of English law venturing across family, medical, criminal and human rights law, it fails to engage with the parental perspective. This is the important point – not a debate over whether parents or judges should be the ultimate deciders, for decisions with serious consequences for the lives of others must be open to the possibility of independent scrutiny – but the question of which factors are to be considered in making the decision. In the case of the conjoined twins, that should have included respect for the views of the parents, through consideration of their shared past and hopes for the future, even if the physical condition of their babies limited their ability to care for their daughters.

There is nothing inherently uncaring about a decision that a child should not be given treatment or that treatment should be withheld or withdrawn. Indeed, parents may reach this difficult decision because they care[38] and parents who press for treatment to continue may be accused of putting their own inability to cope with the loss of their child above his or her needs.[39] In his written statement to the Bristol Royal Infirmary Inquiry, Jonathan Mallone, father of Josie, identified how 'doing the best for their child' may mean deciding to end treatment:

---

[36] Barbara Hewson, 'Killing Off Mary: Was the Court of Appeal Right?' (2001) 9 Med Law Rev 281–98, at p. 288.   [37] *Supra*, n. 21 at p. 279.

[38] As I have argued in relation to parental support for refusal of consent to continued treatment by teenagers in 'Because We Care? Children and Medical Treatment' in Sally Sheldon and Michael Thomson (eds.), *Feminist Perspectives on Health Care Law*, Cavendish: London, 1998, 97–114.

[39] Such criticism was levelled at the parents of Laura Davies (Angela Neustatter, 'Children: should their lives be in their own hands?', *Independent*, 3 October 1993, noted that Laura's parents had been attacked and received hate mail) and the father of Jaymee Bowen, considered in chapter 2.

> We decided to refuse further treatment. Nothing we had been told gave
> us any hope that there was a genuine chance of Josie surviving without
> being put through what we considered an unjustifiable amount of
> further suffering, and the risk of an even less dignified death. Joyce, the
> nurse, said that we mustn't feel that we'd given her a death sentence, but
> we both felt dreadfully guilty, even though we hoped that we were
> doing the right thing.[40]

Whilst parents of seriously ill children depend upon medical professionals
for their expertise in the diagnosis and treatment of their child, this dependency does not remove the responsibility of the parents for their child.
Episodes of medical treatment have to be understood as part of the care
parents provide for their children albeit, in this instance, in the context of
reliance upon medical expertise and technology. Parental decisions about
treatment are reached in the context of their continuing care for their child;
the focus of professionals is to respond to the specific medical problem. Eva
Feder Kittay distinguishes between the 'functionally specific' role of the
professional who takes an interventionist approach in responding to a
problem and the 'functionally diffuse' role of the parent whose care sus-
tains the child.[41] Parents who approach a particular treatment episode
within the context of previous treatment, their child's experience of their
condition and their hopes for the future may have a different opinion about
which course of treatment is in the best interests of the child from the professionals whose focus is upon a specific medical problem. This, I suggest, is
apparent at a simple level in the case of *Re MM*.[42] It is useful to consider the
different assessments of the best interests of the child from the perspective
of the continuing care provided by his parents and the episodic care delivered by the professionals. His parents wished him to receive the same treatment he had been provided with prior to their arrival in the UK and to
which they expected he would revert upon their return to Russia. They
were concerned that replacement IG therapy might not be available when
they returned to Russia or, if it was, that they would not be able to afford it.
From this perspective, to treat him differently whilst he was in the UK
might not only raise concerns about disrupting his ability to cope with the

---

[40] Written statement of Jonathan Mallone with regard to the treatment of his daughter, Josie, to the
Bristol Royal Infirmary Inquiry, at para. 42.

[41] *Supra*, n. 31, at p. 39. Eva Feder Kittay's work focuses upon the dependency work done by
women and presents an argument for the importance of acknowledging this if equality for
women is to be achieved. The roles of mothers, fathers and parents in taking care of children are
considered in chapter 1.   [42] *Re MM (Medical Treatment)* [2000] 1 FLR 224.

treatment he needed but also raise further questions about the consequences for his health of changing treatments.

In contrast to the abstraction of rights, responsibilities arising out of
relationships depend upon consideration of the needs of the dependent
child. This requires all who are involved in the care of the child to appreciate the contributions of others to assessment of the interests of the individual child, recognising that the experiences, perspectives and interaction
with the child will differ according to their caring role and the medical circumstances. It would not be unusual for parents to be more emotionally
involved and professionals to be more detached; for parents to place the
child's need for medical treatment within the context of a history and a
future and professionals to focus upon the insights gained through the
episodes of care provided. It should be recognised that nurses and mothers
will have insights gained as they care for a child which are different from the
views of doctors who take care of the child.

The meaning of caring for a child

One case stands out for an attempt to assess the best interests of the child
within the context of the care provided to the child by his mother. For this,
the judgment of the Court of Appeal in *Re T* has been subjected to critical
comment. The case concerned a boy, C, who was eighteen months old at
the time of the hearing. He had been born with a liver defect (biliary
atresia) for which he had undergone surgery when only three and a half
weeks old. This operation had failed to improve his condition but rather
had caused him pain and distress such that his parents resolved, having
obtained medical advice, that they would not put him through further
surgery. The medical view was that C required a liver transplant if he was to
live more than six months or a year. His parents (although, perhaps because
they were unmarried, the judgment focuses upon the opinion of C's
mother) refused consent to the transplant operation – major, complicated
surgery which would require life-time medication – believing that it was
not in his best interests. The court considered evidence from three consultants who all agreed that it was in his medical best interests to undergo a
transplant although they were divided in their views as to whether they
would be willing to perform the operation without parental consent. In the
Court of Appeal, Butler-Sloss LJ explained that the decision of the first
instance judge, Connell J, was flawed as he had concluded that the mother's

refusal of consent was unreasonable and had given consent on the basis of the medical evidence alone. The role of the court was to undertake an independent assessment of the welfare of the child, which included consideration and assessment of the views of the parents.[43] The court had to undertake a balancing exercise, assessing the relevance and weight of factors which would be considered by a reasonable parent. On the facts before them, this included the seriousness of the proposed operation, the benefits of major invasive surgery and post-operative treatment, the danger of short- and long-term failure, the possibility of further transplants, and C's life expectancy with and without the operation. Connell J had failed to balance the above factors or to give weight to the evidence of consultant paediatrician, Dr P.

The evidence of consultant paediatrician, Dr P, was highly influential with the Court of Appeal judges and it is worth considering his evidence in detail. Consistent with the other medical evidence, Dr P considered that the transplant operation was in C's best interests; however, he was not prepared to perform the operation against the wishes of C's mother. In his judgment, she was 'a loving and devoted mother and, given her professional background, an unusually well-informed parent'. In his opinion, 'her reluctance to submit her son to the operation was founded in love and care for him. She was to the best of her ability discharging her duty of trust to her child and her decision should be respected.'[44] Commitment of the child's carer to the procedure was, in his view, an important contributory factor to the success of the transplant operation. For the court to give consent and for the transplant to be performed against her judgment would have the

> effect of coercing, as Dr P put it, this mother into playing the crucial and irreplaceable part in the aftermath of major invasive surgery not just during the post-operative treatment of an 18-month-old baby but also throughout the childhood of her son. She would inevitably be the primary carer . . . and would be expected to care for him for many years through surgery and continuing treatment while she, on her present view, believed that this course was not right for her son. The total commitment of the caring parent, in Dr P's view, was essential to the success of the treatment.[45]

[43] *Re T (a Minor) (Wardship: Medical Treatment)* [1997] 1 WLR 242, at p. 250.
[44] *Ibid.*, at p. 246 (Butler-Sloss LJ quoting Dr P, consultant paediatrician).
[45] *Ibid.*, at p. 251 (Butler-Sloss LJ).

In his evidence, Dr P stressed his view that commitment of the primary carer to the child's treatment was material to the success of the transplant operation and thus C's mother's refusal, based in a genuine assessment of the best interests of the child she loved, should be respected. This evidence is indicative of an understanding of a carefully reached decision based in the mother's particular knowledge of her son arising from her care of him: she had made a decision about his quality of life given the short- and long-term consequences of major and risky surgery. This evidence reflects an appreciation that a court order against the 'present view' of the mother was not the appropriate way by which to proceed to securing the performance of major surgery upon a young child.

Butler-Sloss LJ then turned to consider the best interests of the child. Emphasising that the best interests of the child went beyond medical factors, Butler-Sloss LJ noted that the mother's conclusion was influenced by her experience of the pain and distress caused to him by his earlier, unsuccessful, operation. His mother appreciated that without the operation his life expectancy was short but had formed the view that it was not in his best interests to put him through further surgery. Consistent with the view of Dr P of the importance of the mother's commitment, Butler-Sloss LJ looked to the judgment of Lord Donaldson MR in *Re W*[46] who referred to consent having clinical value (as well as legal relevance) in ensuring commitment by the patient to treatment and suggested this was equally the case for the carer of a young child. In the attempt to recognise the caring relationship between mother and child, and the importance of the mother's views concerning the experiences of her child and his future quality of life, the judgment slips from the best interests of the child in relation to the prospect of major transplant surgery to the consequences for the mother:

> The alternative of the Court giving the consent and passing back the responsibility for the parental care to the mother and expecting her to provide the commitment to the child after the operation is carried out in the face of her opposition is in itself *fraught with danger for the child*. She will have to comply with the court order; return to this country and present the child to one of the hospitals. She will have to arrange to remain in this country for the foreseeable future. Will the father stay in country AB and work or come with her to England, giving up his job and having to seek another job? If he does not come she will have to manage unaided. How will the mother cope? Can her professionalism

---

[46] *Re W (a Minor) (Medical Treatment: Court's Jurisdiction)* [1992] 3 WLR 758.

overcome her view that her son should not be *subjected to this distress-ing procedure*? Will she break down? How will the child be affected by the *conflict* with which the mother may have to cope?[47]

All the factors, including the practicalities identified by Butler-Sloss LJ, pointed to the conclusion that the transplant operation was not in C's best interests. Dr P's evidence about the commitment of the mother to the treat-ment was reinterpreted in terms of uncertainty about the mother's com-mitment to her child and her willingness to care – emotionally and practically – for him. Consequently, the connection between mother and child was no longer understood as a nurturing, loving, protective one but one of danger to the child. The language of opposition, danger and conflict is apparent in the extract from Butler-Sloss LJ's judgment, quoted above, and is similarly employed by Waite LJ:

> [E]ven assuming that the operation proved wholly successful in surgi-cal terms – the child's subsequent development could be *injuriously* affected if his day to day care depended upon the commitment of a mother who had suffered the *turmoil* of having her child being *com-pelled* against her will to undergo, as a result of a *coercive* order from the court, a major operation against which her own medical and maternal judgment wholeheartedly *rebelled*.[48]

Discussion of the case in the media at the time variously referred to the parental rights to determine the best interests of the child, to refuse surgery for their child, to let their baby die and to choose. Critical comment on this case has focused upon the interests of the child as distinct from the interests of the mother. This was, perhaps, inevitable given the comment of Butler-Sloss LJ to the effect that '[t]his mother and this child are one for the purpose of this unusual case'.[49] In his response to this case, Andrew Bainham argues that the judgment demonstrates a failure to distinguish between C's interests and those of his mother, pointing out that the inter-ests of parent and child may clash and thus enormous care must be taken when considering the views of parents.[50] In a similar vein, Sabine Michalowski argues that courts should scrutinise carefully the decisions of parents and act as a check upon their decision to ensure that the interests of the child, and not those of the parents, prevail:

[47] *Re T (a Minor) (Wardship: Medical Treatment)* [1997] 1WLR 242, at p. 252, emphasis added.
[48] *Ibid.*, at p. 254, emphasis added.   [49] *Ibid.*, at p. 251.
[50] Andrew Bainham, 'Do Babies Have Rights?' (1997) 56 CLJ 48–50.

Even though parents are normally very committed to their children and society gives them the right to make important decisions on behalf of their children, it cannot be overlooked that parents have their own interests in decisions on life-saving treatment and are therefore not always impartial advocates for their children, but may be biased towards a promotion of their own values and interests.[51]

It is unclear upon what evidence this observation is made. The view expressed is contrary to the way in which parents talk about seeking to 'do their best' in their care for sick, injured and disabled children. It maintains a view of the parent as aggressor rather than an understanding of the connection between parent and child and the concern of parents to meet their child's needs, to care for and protect them.

To proceed from an understanding of the connection between parent and child provides a different starting point in assumptions about the self, relationships and caring. Marie Fox and Jean McHale, acknowledging the limits of rights discourse in relation to decisions relating to the healthcare of young children who are inevitably dependent upon others, see promise in the recognition of caring relationships by the Court of Appeal in *Re T*. However, they argue that greater clarity is required than is provided by the Court of Appeal upon the meaning of caring and the weight to be given to the views of carers when assessing best interests:

> [R]ooting the determination of the boundaries of treatment in an ethics of caring seems to us to be legitimate and to offer a more promising approach. Nevertheless, if a paradigm of caring is to function as a framework for deciding such cases the courts need to be explicit about what this means . . . Certainly, in cases involving young children, judicial guidance and clarification would be necessary as to the meaning of caring and the weight to be ascribed to the views of carers. In *Re T* itself, reference is made to the importance of caring without such articulation and there are unanswered questions as to why such stress was laid in this particular case on the part played by the 'caring parents'.[52]

The judgment of the Court of Appeal is to be welcomed for the attempt to acknowledge the role of C's mother and to recognise her expertise and

---

[51] Sabine Michalowski, 'Is it in the Best Interests of a Child to have a Life-Saving Liver Transplantation? *Re T (Wardship: Medical Treatment)*' (1997) 9 CFLQ 179–89, at p. 182.

[52] Marie Fox and Jean McHale, 'In Whose Best Interests?' (1997) 60 MLR 700–9, at p. 708.

interest in his well-being.[53] The relationship of care – the history of caring – is relevant to the extent that it provides insights into the best interests of the child. The Court was right to heed the concerns of C's mother about surgery given the pain and distress caused to C as a result of the earlier operation and consequential treatment, to recognise the ongoing responsibility of care and the reality that the task of caring for the child had been, and would continue to be, undertaken by his 'loving, caring mother'. However, raising practical problems in support of a conclusion that the Court should not consent to the operation had the opposite effect of undermining the connection between mother and child which had informed Dr P's opinion about his best interests. Furthermore, perceiving the mother and child as one resulted in a loss of recognition of the interests of the child. To appreciate mother and child as primarily connected but separate individuals permits a different understanding of the relationship between them, a relationship in which she has particular concern for her son and expertise in his needs. There are a lot of questions raised by the facts of this case which remain unanswered yet would be addressed by a focus upon the responsibilities of those caring for this child. The judgment is not clear as to the mother's views about liver transplant surgery for her son and her ability to care for him. An examination of the history of caring would address her concerns arising from nursing him through his first operation. As a parent of a seriously ill child, the mother was dependent upon the advice, information and support of professional carers and she appeared to be under pressure to consent to a complicated, risky procedure. Recognition that there are limits to the ability of caring parents should not be a reason that a child does not undergo a life-saving operation. Rather, it raises a host of questions which must be examined about the support provided to parents.

Parental beliefs and values

The state has an interest in the well-being of children and in ensuring the health of future generations of adults, whilst entrusting to parents the day-to-day upbringing of their child. Consequently, parents are at liberty to

---

[53] I suggest in chapter 3 that Butler-Sloss LJ more accurately identified the relevance of the views of the parents and the impact of treatment decisions upon the family in the subsequent case of *Donald Simms and Jonathan Simms v An NHS Trust and Secretary of State for Health; PA and JA v An NHS Trust and Secretary of State for Health* [2002] EWHC 2734.

raise their children according to their beliefs, values, preferences and priorities. The lives of children will thus be affected by parental choices on such matters as where they will live, where they will go to school and whether they engage in religious practices. Their everyday care will be affected by the religious views of their parents and by parental views on appropriate diet, the importance of exercise, and on alternative rather than traditional medicine. Whilst the minimum standards of parental care established in law are considered in chapter 3, the cases of treatment decisions concerning young children confront the issue of parental beliefs and the best interests of the child in relation to the healthcare of children.

Religious beliefs

The parents of the three children in *Re S*,[54] *Re O*[55] and *Re R*[56] were all Jehovah's Witnesses and refusing their consent to medical treatment in which the transfusion of blood was an essential element. S was a four-and-a-half-year-old boy who, just two weeks before the court hearing, had been diagnosed as suffering from T-cell leukaemia. Intensive chemotherapy offered a 50 per cent chance of cure. It involved four phases, extending over a period in excess of two years, including chemotherapy and radium treatment with 'powerful side-effects', and had to be supplemented with blood transfusions. The consultant paediatrician taking care of S described the steps which had been taken to modify treatment out of respect for his parents' views and how, if intensive treatment were to be provided, they would continue to modify the treatment but that intensive treatment could not be provided without the ability to give blood. The clinical view was that there was no alternative – either S received the intensive treatment or was merely given palliative care with no prospect of survival. R[57] was a ten-month-old baby girl suffering from B-cell lymphoblastic leukaemia. Blood products had been administered as an emergency measure when R was admitted to hospital. The local authority sought a specific issue order under s. 8 of the Children Act 1989 as she was likely to require more blood during the two years of her treatment.[58] Her parents, 'devoted to A and

---

[54] *Re S (a Minor) (Medical Treatment)* [1993] 1 FLR 376.
[55] *Re O (a Minor) (Medical Treatment)* [1993] 2 FLR 149.
[56] *Re R (Minor)* 15 BMLR 72 (web.lexis-nexis.com/professional/).   [57] *Ibid.*
[58] Both Johnson J in *Re O (A Minor) (Medical Treatment)* [1993] 2 FLR 149 and Booth J in *Re R (Minor)* 15 BMLR 72 (web.lexis-nexis.com/professional/) addressed the appropriate procedure for seeking consent to medical treatment from the court. Johnson J accepted the unanimous

inevitably distressed by the dilemma they were in, but . . . firm in their religious belief', were willing for the doctors to administer blood transfusions without their consent when her condition deteriorated to the stage where it could be considered emergency treatment for a life-threatening condition. The doctors treating her did not consider that this would enable them to treat her condition properly.[59] The case of *Re O (a Minor) (Medical Treatment)*[60] concerned a baby girl, J, born over twelve weeks premature weighing only 2lbs 13oz. As a consequence of her prematurity, she suffered from respiratory distress syndrome in which there is insufficient chemical in the lungs to ensure oxygen absorption. Premature babies such as J are given blood transfusions if their red blood cell levels fall, which they can do rapidly. J had previously received two transfusions of blood. Johnson J heard evidence from the consultant paediatrician who had exhausted all alternatives before applying to the court but was of the opinion that J's red blood cell count had fallen so low that her vital organs were in danger.

Thorpe J described S's father as a young man with sincerely held beliefs which left him with no choice but to refuse consent to the administration of blood products even if that resulted in the death of his son. In contrast, it was acknowledged that J's parents were faced with a dilemma as a result of the conflict between their beliefs and their daughter's medical needs:

> J's parents are members of the sect known as Jehovah's Witnesses. The parents are devout believers in that faith. They are also deeply committed and loving parents. They want whatever is best for J. They do not want J to die but, for them, physical death is not the end of life and in considering what is best for J they are torn, desperately, between their passionate desire to preserve J's earthly life whilst at the same time wanting to avoid causing her the damage in her greater life that, in their sincere view, would come to her were she to be transfused with blood or blood products. Their dilemma is awesome.[61]

Footnote 58(*cont.*)

    view of counsel that the appropriate procedure was provided by s. 100 of the Children Act 1989 by which the local authority can apply for leave to invoke the inherent jurisdiction of the High Court. Booth J thought that an application by the local authority under s. 8 of the Children Act 1989 for a specific issue order was appropriate, particularly in cases such as the one before her in which the parents were caring, loving, devoted and anxious to be involved in the care of their child but unable to agree to the specific treatment due to their religious beliefs. Both agreed that the application should be heard by a High Court judge and every effort should be made to ensure that it was an *inter partes* hearing.

[59] Anne Elton, Peter Honig, Arnon Bentovin, Jean Simons (1995) 310 BMJ 373–7.

[60] *Re O (A Minor) (Medical Treatment)* [1993] 2 FLR 149.   [61] *Ibid.*, at p. 150.

The parents' wishes were noted and medical evidence considered at greater length before, in all three cases, the court gave consent.[62] The judicial portrayal of the parental assessment of the best interests of their child ranged from unquestioned acceptance of the dictates of their faith, through an inability to address their child's best interests, to a conflict between religious beliefs and their desire to do the best for their child. In all three cases, the parents' decision to refuse the administration of blood products would appear to have been based solely upon their religious convictions – parental beliefs precluding wider assessment of the interests of the child.

In her analysis of these cases, Caroline Bridge notes the efforts of both the clinicians and the court to respect parental convictions even though this may involve administering treatment which is considered to be less effective, employing more invasive practices or results in deterioration in the health of the child:

> Whilst the court is prepared to compromise the child in all but the last resort in order to keep faith with the parental conviction and their perception of how welfare may best be enhanced, the effect of that compromise is further harm to the child. While clinicians dither about whether or when to seek legal intervention, knowing that invariably the court will order blood, the child's suffering continues, often with further physical deterioration.[63]

S's consultant detailed to the court the ways in which he had modified treatment in an effort to respect the views of S's parents. S's haemoglobin level had fallen below that point at which a transfusion would ordinarily be given, treatment had been administered which was not scientifically proven and the surgical insertion of a long line had been deferred with the consequence that, after frequent injections, S had become needle shy.[64] Whilst all other possible alternatives to blood had been tried, J's red blood cell levels had fallen to the point where the consultant paediatrician considered her vital organs to be at risk.[65] The order giving consent to the administration

---

[62] Jane Fortin argues that this conclusion is 'consistent with the state's positive obligation under article 2 of the ECHR, to preserve the life of a desperately ill child, as long as survival is not accompanied by considerable pain and impairment of his or her quality of life. Such arguments would counter a parent's claim that, by overriding his wishes, the court is infringing his right to respect for his family life under article 8, freedom of religion under article 9, and freedom from discrimination, under article 14': *Children's Rights and the Developing Law*, Reed Elsevier: London, 2003, at p. 324.

[63] Caroline Bridge, 'Religion, Culture and Conviction – the Medical Treatment of Young Children' (1999) 11 CFLQ 1–15, at p. 8.   [64] *Re S (a Minor) (Medical Treatment)* [1993] 1 FLR 376.

[65] *Re O (a Minor) (Medical Treatment)* [1993] 2 FLR 149.

of blood to R permitted doctors to do so without parental consent only in imminently life-threatening situations. In other circumstances, those caring for the child were required to consult the parents about alternatives and only administer blood without their consent if there was no reasonable alternative.[66]

In all three cases, the court was careful to limit their decision to the specific issue of the administration of blood products aware that the parents were loving and caring and, rather than neglecting their child, had reached a decision about his or her best interests according to their beliefs. The court in *Re S* addressed the question of the consequences for the future care of the child should blood products be administered contrary to the wishes of the parents:

> If this treatment is applied in the face of parental opposition what would be the difficulties and stresses for S in years to come – parented by parents who believe that his life was prolonged by an ungodly act? Well, that consideration seems to me one that has little foundation in reality. The reality seems to me to be that family reaction will recognise that the responsibility for consent was taken from them and, as a judicial act, absolves their conscience of responsibility.[67]

At the heart of the parental objections was a belief about the care of a child in this life to protect their future in the world beyond. Who authorised the administration of blood was not necessarily at issue nor was the question simply one of salving parental conscience. Whilst there was no reason to doubt that the parents would continue to care for their child, the infringement of their genuinely held beliefs about the wider best interests of their child should have been fully addressed. The parents in these cases were precluded from reaching a determination of the best interests of their child by their religious beliefs. Replacing their decision, the court failed to consider the best interests of the child fully, relying exclusively upon medical evidence.

Parents must go beyond their religious beliefs to weigh the various factors relevant to the determination of the best interests of their child and the court must undertake full consideration of the best interests of this particular child. This necessitates consideration of the medical evidence and includes, but is not confined to, the fact that the child has been born to parents (who as far as we know are loving, caring parents) adhering to the tenets of their chosen religion. The courts have, by invoking the weight of

[66] *Re R (Minor)* 15 BMLR 72 (web.lexis-nexis.com/professional/).   [67] *Supra,*n. 64, at p. 380.

the medical evidence, avoided interrogating the genuinely held beliefs of the Jehovah's Witness parents in these cases. A conceptual framework of relational responsibilities directs those responsible for the future medical treatment of the child to consider the child as an individual and not an extension of his or her parents or a medical object. For the parents this entails appreciating that their child, whilst being dependent upon their care, is an individual – both connected to them but separate from them. It requires consideration of the arguments based in the religious beliefs of the parents, to whom the individual child is connected and upon whom the child depends, in contrast to societal norms[68] and a general acceptance of the use of blood products. This goes beyond the history of parental care to an examination of the context of their decision and of the reasons for their beliefs.[69] This would require examination of the circumstances in which the administration of blood would be acceptable: two of the children had already received blood transfusions in an emergency and the parents of R were willing to consent if her condition became life-threatening. A further question to examine would be the support for, or pressure upon, the parents within the community in which they live.

Treatment decisions dictated by religious beliefs are not confined to the Jehovah's Witness example at issue in these cases. The beliefs of Christian Scientists that healing is achieved through belief in God rather than medical intervention clearly affect decisions about medical treatment, as do those of Orthodox Jews who believe that to fail to do everything possible to prevent death would result in punishment by God.[70] One of the factors

---

[68] On this point, I disagree with the approach of Holman J in the case of *An NHS Trust v MB*, which is considered in detail in chapter 5. The question before the court was whether artificial ventilation should be withdrawn from MB, a child with spinal muscular atrophy. His father was a practising Muslim and expressed the view that it was for God, not people, to decide when the time had come for a person to die. Holman J considered MB to be too young to have formed any religious beliefs himself and thus, whilst he respected the father's view, did not consider them in reaching his decision: *An NHS Trust v MB* [2006] EWHC 507 (Fam), at para. 50.

[69] Michael Freeman, *The Moral Status of Children: Essays on the Rights of the Child*, Martinus Nijhoff: Netherlands, 1997, at p. 139.

[70] *Supra*, n. 63, at p. 8; for this reason the parents of baby C, a sixteen-month-old girl with spinal muscular atrophy, could not agree to withholding of artificial ventilation from their daughter if she was unable to breathe unassisted: *Re C (a Minor) (Medical Treatment)* [1998] 1 FLR 384. In their affidavit, at p. 389, her parents explained: 'One of the principles fundamental to our religion is that life should always be preserved. Another is that someone of our faith cannot stand aside and watch a person die where their intervention could prevent that death. In such a case the person that stands by will subsequently be punished by God. Failing to resuscitate is equivalent to a situation such as this.'

upon which the parents of conjoined twins, Mary and Jodie, reached the
conclusion that the separation surgery was not in their best interests was
their religious beliefs. Their beliefs had led them to refuse to terminate the
pregnancy and to ask for as little intervention during labour as possible
such that labour commenced naturally at forty-two weeks and the twins
were delivered by caesarean section at the very last opportunity. The
parents could not sanction a course of action in which they would be con-
demning one of their babies to death:

> We cannot begin to accept or contemplate that one of our children
> should die to enable the other to survive. That is not God's will.
> Everyone has the right to life so why should we kill one of our daugh-
> ters to enable the other to survive.[71]

Whilst they understood both that the condition of the babies was very
serious and that the doctors were seeking to do their best for them, their
religious beliefs were one of the factors leading to their decision to refuse
the separation surgery:

> We cannot possibly agree to any surgery being undertaken that will kill
> one of our daughters. We have faith in God and are quite happy for
> God's will to decide what happens to our two young daughters.[72]

Ward LJ failed to address either the emotional or the religious aspects of
their decision. His response – pragmatic, rational and impersonal – was
that whilst he understood their despair at the prospect of treatment which
would end Mary's life, without surgery Jodie would also die. '[P]arents who
are placed on the horns of such a terrible dilemma simply have to choose
the lesser of their inevitable loss', which required them to accept that 'Mary
is lost to them anyway.'[73] Likewise, the influence of their beliefs upon their
decision is merely acknowledged by Robert Walker LJ:

> There are to my mind particularly strong reasons for having regard to
> the parents' views in this case, even if they have been, as the judge put it,
> 'overwhelmed by the circumstances that confront them'. They have sin-
> cerely held religious views, formed after discussion with a priest near
> the hospital, and now backed by the Archbishop of Westminster. Their
> views might be described as controversial but, unlike the objections to

---

[71] *Re A (Children) (Conjoined Twins: Surgical Separation)* [2001] 2 WLR 480, from parents' statement in Ward LJ's judgment, at p. 504.
[72] *Ibid.*, from parents' statement in Ward LJ's judgment, at p. 505.   [73] *Ibid.*, at pp. 528–9.

blood transfusion held by Jehovah's Witnesses, they are not obviously contrary to any view generally accepted by our society. Still less are their views contrary to those generally accepted in the remote community from which they have come to this country.[74]

The religious beliefs of the parents of Jodie and Mary were one of the factors upon which they made a decision about the best interests of their children but they did not preclude consideration of other factors. A further example is provided by the parents of Matthew Poynter who held strong spiritual beliefs that heart transplantation was unnatural and wrong, yet gave their consent. His mother explained that her spiritual beliefs would have been sufficient for her to refuse consent for herself but that the decision was for her son, not for her. As his father said: 'We agreed to the transplant because we thought it wrong to impose our views on Matthew.'[75] Responsibilities arise out of relationships and are determined by need and individual interpretation, including beliefs held about the way life should be lived and the values by which children should be raised. But, as the decisions of the Jehovah's Witness parents and of the parents of the conjoined twins reveal, interpretation of needs occurs within a social context which has to be examined.

Parental values

Non-religious beliefs, such as a refusal to use products tested on animals, a commitment to alternative medicine or to certain diets, will also affect healthcare and treatment decisions. As with the religious beliefs of parents, these values should not be summarily dismissed, rather they should be fully and openly examined. However, the unconventional beliefs of the parents in the case of *Re C (HIV Test)* were dismissed and treatment ordered according to mainstream medical opinion. The local authority had applied for a specific issue order that a baby girl should be tested to determine whether she was HIV positive.[76] This involved a blood test and, looking at

---

[74] *Ibid.*, at p. 577.

[75] *Poynter v Hillingdon Health Authority* 37 BMLR 192 (web.lexis-nexis.com/professional/), at p. 13, considered further in chapter 6.

[76] Reports to the British Paediatric Surveillance Unit between 1985 and the end of January 2001 found 1,101 children in the UK reported to have HIV, of whom 27 per cent were known to have died in that period. Amongst the older children were those who contracted HIV through the administration of drug products for haemophilia, although screening of donors and heat treatment of clotting-factor products means that transmission no longer occurs via this route. The most common route for transmission is from the child's mother. Office for National Statistics,

this in strict battery terms, Wilson J took the view that 'in terms of the need for the proposed directed intervention to be supported by active commitment by the parents in the long term, this case is at the end of the spectrum opposite to that in *In Re T (A Minor) (Wardship: Medical Treatment)* [1997] 1 WLR 242'.[77] Of course, the parental objection was not simply to the taking of blood from their daughter in order to test it.[78] Their objection was to the consequences of a positive test result for HIV which would inform the advice provided by doctors for the care of their daughter. The parents' 'vehement opposition' to the test arose from their beliefs about the efficacy of testing and their view that the orthodox aggressive treatment was positively harmful. C's mother had been tested as HIV positive some years before C's conception and, at the time of the hearing, remained in good health. After her own diagnosis, C's mother had researched HIV and AIDS, leading to her doubts about the dominant medical approach. C's parents argued that HIV was not a virus but 'oxidative stress on the cells of the body' which causes an increase in metabolism, breaks down the immune system and results from an unhealthy lifestyle. In support of this opinion, they pointed to the mother's lack of symptoms achieved, they considered, through maintaining a healthy lifestyle, keeping fit and complementary therapy. Or, they argued, if HIV is a virus it is not the only cause of AIDS; available tests were so inaccurate that they were sceptical of the result in relation to the mother and would be if the baby tested positive. Their position was that if their baby developed symptoms they would secure appropriate treatment but not on the basis that they arose from a virus as that would result in aggressive treatment which, in their view, would be harmful. Wilson J acknowledged the mother's right to deal with her status in the way she chose but was of the view that this right did not extend to her child. Rather, the approach of mainstream medicine had to be adopted. Wilson J gave consent to a blood test to determine whether the baby was

---

Footnote 76 (*cont.*)

    The Health of Children and Young People, March 2004, ch. 5, 'Infectious diseases', at p. 11, referring to R. Lynn, H. Kirkbride, J. Rahi and C. Verity, *British Paediatric Surveillance Unit 15th Annual Report, 2000/01*, RCPCH: London, 2001.

[77] *In re C (a Child) (HIV Testing)* [2000] 2 WLR 270, at p. 282.

[78] The risk of an infected mother passing the virus to her child is 25 per cent, reduced to about 2 per cent if antiretrovirals are taken during pregnancy, the baby is delivered by caesarean section and the baby is not breast-fed: Office for National Statistics, *supra*, n. 76 ch. 5, at p. 18. Of the 2,108 children reported born to HIV-infected mothers by the end of January 2001, 36 per cent were known to be HIV-infected and 41 per cent were known to be uninfected: at p. 18.

HIV positive.[79] This conclusion was reached with consideration of C's physical needs (s. 1(3)(b) Children Act 1989), her background, which meant the fact that her mother had the HIV virus (s. 1(3)(d) Children Act 1989), and the harm which she was at risk of suffering (s. 1(3)(e) Children Act 1989).

Despite focusing upon the single act of taking blood, Wilson J continued to suggest that, should the baby prove to be HIV positive, a future court may order monitoring, regular testing and drug therapy:[80] which, of course, would move the case along the spectrum to sit alongside *Re T*. Motivated by a desire to protect this child, Wilson J followed the views of orthodox medical practice, referring to the mother's evidence that she would talk to her daughter when she was older to enable her to make her own decision about whether to undergo a test as a 'hopeless programme for the baby's protection'.[81] Butler-Sloss LJ in the Court of Appeal, refusing permission to appeal against the order, characterised the issue as one of knowledge:

> Wilson J set out various Articles of the UN Convention on the Rights of the Child 1989. We do not in a sense need that. It is all encapsulated in s 1 of the Children Act, but it does give added strength to this most important of all points, that the parents' views, which are not the views of the majority, cannot stand against the right of the child to be properly cared for in every sense. This child has the right to have sensible and responsible people find out whether she is or is not HIV positive . . . [T]his child has her own rights. Those rights seem to me to be met at this stage by her being tested to see what her state of health is for the question of knowledge.[82]

The argument was that doctors needed to know the status of the child to avoid either over-treating or under-treating in the event of illness. This appears persuasive but the parental objection was to the validity of the knowledge gained by testing.

Demonstrating inconsistencies in judgment, or perhaps where the limits of legal intervention lie, the Court refused to order the mother to stop

---

[79] *In re C (A Child) (HIV Testing)* [2000] 2 WLR 270, at p. 281. The Court of Appeal refused permission to appeal: *Re C (HIV Test)* [1999] 2 FLR 1004, on grounds that an appeal stood no chance of success. The procedure for future cases is set out in *President's Direction: HIV Testing of Children* [2003] 1 FLR 1299.

[80] *In re C (a Child) (HIV Testing)* [2000] 2 WLR 270, at p. 281.   [81] *Ibid.*, at p. 282.

[82] *Re C (HIV Test)* [1999] 2 FLR 1004, at p. 1021.

breast-feeding. This was the one remaining possible route for transmission of the infection from mother to child. Interference with the decision to breast-feed was considered to be beyond the scope of the law: 'My belief is that the law cannot come between the baby and the breast.' Wilson J acknowledged the problem with enforcing such an order reminiscent of criticism of court intervention in pregnancy.[83] Such comment as there has been on this case seems agreed that the court made the right decision with regard to the blood test and should have ordered the mother to stop breast-feeding her daughter.[84] As it was, C's parents fled with C to Australia from the judgment of the English court.[85]

A focus upon the responsibilities of her parents and the healthcare professionals involved in her care may not have led to a different conclusion. It would, however, have resulted in a different judgment. First, it would have required the parents to confront their responsibilities to their daughter as a person. This focuses upon the child's needs, including her state of health. It would require her parents to consider whether the approach which they felt was appropriate for the management of the condition of the mother was also appropriate for the individual child. It would require examination of the relationship between those caring for the child, the responsibilities of her parents and of the professionals. Had the parents given open consideration to the views of the doctors? Had the doctors considered the arguments of the parents? Had they discussed the contribution and limits of alternative therapy, and a healthy lifestyle, to enhancement of well-being? Had they discussed the limits of the mainstream medical approach to treatment of HIV able to prolong life but not offer a cure within the context of inevitable side-effects? To what extent was the conclusion of the doctors as to her best interests influenced by the wider – public health – interest in knowing which individuals have the HIV virus? Given enduring discriminatory attitudes, had they discussed the particular difficulties of parenting

---

[83] *Re F (In Utero)* [1988] 2 All ER 193.

[84] Both Andrew Downie, '*Re C (HIV Test)*: The Limits of Parental Autonomy' (2000) 12 CFLQ 197–202 and S. I. Strong, 'Between the Baby and the Breast' (2000) 59 CLJ 259–63 agree that it was in C's best interests to be subjected to a blood test and argue that the court should have intervened to ensure that breast-feeding was discontinued.

[85] However, following her mother's death, the Australian authorities wished to administer anti-retroviral treatment. C and her father returned to England where she was made a ward of court which consequently makes all decisions relating to her upbringing, including those about her medical care: Clare Dyer, 'HIV Positive Girl made Ward of Court after Father Refuses to Allow her Treatment' (2002) 324 BMJ 1178.

a child who is, or may be, HIV positive or of being a parent who is HIV positive?

Supporting parents

The individualism of English law, focusing upon the best interests of the (ideal) child, means that the context of caring for the child is not addressed. Whilst we know that decisions to treat one child may mean that the resources are not available to care for another, decisions about what is in the best interests of the particular child are made unfettered by considerations of resources.[86] That is a different matter, however, from confronting the consequences of decisions to treat or to refuse consent to treatment of a child. As the legal framework originates with battery, with consent justifying touching which would, because it invades the boundaries of the body, otherwise amount to a criminal or civil battery, the focus of judgments is upon the invasive treatment. Parental concerns may extend, beyond that moment in time, to their previous experience of treatment and the future care of their child. Considerations of the journey for the child and his or her family through care might appear to be a matter for service provision and not relevant to determination of treatment decisions in relation to individual children. Yet, considerations of their future well-being clearly pose concerns for parents who perceive their child as a person, an individual now and not merely a potential adult.

Concerns of parents such as those voiced by Rina and Michaelangelo Attard about their ability to care for their daughter, Jodie, if surgery was performed should not simply be dismissed as they appeared to have been in that case. In addition to their religious convictions (considered above), given the facilities available on Gozo, they believed both that it would be very difficult for them to meet her needs and that life would be very difficult for her.[87] The management of the final stages of the pregnancy and the subsequent care of the twins was undertaken in Manchester under an arrangement which the Maltese Government had permitting their treatment by the NHS. At the time of the birth of the twins, Michaelangelo had been unemployed for six years and although Rina had been working her employment had been terminated once she became pregnant. There was a small hospital

---

[86] Failures to treat children due to lack of resources are considered in chapter 2.

[87] *Re A (Children) (Conjoined Twins: Surgical Separation)* [2001] 2 WLR 480, from parents' statement in Ward LJ's judgment, at p. 504.

near where they lived which provided emergency treatment but they did
not consider it offered the staff or facilities for treatment of a child with
serious ongoing healthcare needs. They did not have the money to return to
England for future treatment. Given their experience of life on the island,
they considered that life would be so difficult for her that, in order to
provide her with the best possible future, they would have to contemplate
leaving Jodie in England to be fostered or adopted if the surgery was performed. Ward LJ dismissed their concerns:

> Coping with a disabled child sadly inevitably casts a great burden on
> parents who have to struggle through those difficulties . . . They surely
> cannot so minimise Jodie's rights on the basis that the burden of possi-
> ble disadvantage for her and the burdens of caring for such a child for
> them can morally be said to outweigh her claim to the human dignity
> of independence which only cruel fate has denied her.[88]

He does nothing, in his judgment, to engage with their real concerns
grounded in their knowledge of the resources and services available to
them in their home country as well as the attitudes towards disability to
which she would be exposed. Robert Walker LJ acknowledges them but has
nothing to offer apart from a view that they are being pessimistic:

> Healthcare services (and, it may be, social security) are less readily
> available in that community and the parents are naturally concerned
> about what the future would hold. No one suggested that it was selfish
> or unreasonable that they should have concerns about their ability,
> either financially or personally, to care for Jodie at home, if there is a
> separation operation which Jodie alone survives . . . That is so, I think,
> even if they have taken what is on the medical evidence a rather pes-
> simistic view of the likely outcome for Jodie after elective surgery.[89]

Yet these are very real concerns, informed by their experiences, about their
ability to care for their child given her ongoing medical needs, the limitations of the healthcare service and attitudes towards disabled children in
their home country. The reality is that it is parents who have to care for
their child on a daily basis, meeting their needs twenty-four hours a day:
needs which go beyond the medical to the emotional well-being and happiness of their child. Unless these concerns are confronted, parents are aban-
doned to their responsibilities and unsupported in their caring. That is not

---

[88] *Ibid.*, at p. 528.   [89] *Ibid.*, at pp. 577–8.

to say that children should not receive treatment because health and social welfare services are inadequate. To the contrary, it is to demand that the inadequacies of these services are exposed and parents assisted to provide the best possible care for their child. It is to insist that the limitations of the care and support available to parents are properly explored, with the aim of finding creative solutions, not summarily dismissed. The responsibilities are not those of the parents alone. To discharge their responsibilities, parents depend upon the support, advice and care of professionals. The care which parents can provide depends upon the support provided to them within the context of prevailing attitudes. Determination of the best interests of the child requires consideration of the responsibilities of all.

Inadequacies of the current legal framework

In this chapter I have sought to identify the limitations of an approach to treatment decisions motivated by a well-meant, if misplaced, desire to protect the ideal, vulnerable child, which seeks to protect the child from his or her parents and fails to address the societal context in which parents assess the needs of their child. Retaining the best interests or welfare of the individual child as the principle for decision-making, I have argued for a conceptual framework of relational responsibilities to children. This requires a range of questions to be asked about the needs of the individual child whose treatment, care and future are in question, about the parental expertise gained through the experience of caring for their child, professional responsibilities towards the child and external factors which place limits upon abilities to care. The obligation imposed upon the judges to make hard choices is hindered, not helped, by the legal framework which, whilst sending them on a quest for the best interests of the child, forces judges to choose between the parents and the doctors. The search for the welfare of the child becomes an adversarial battle between conflicting interests overshadowing the shared endeavour of parents, professionals and the judges to do what is best for the child. The decision of parents to refuse consent to medical treatment has to be carefully explored. Discussion between parents and professionals might reveal a misapprehension on the part of the parents, for example, about the pain and suffering involved. Or the expertise of the parents gained from providing continuous care for their child, their focus on the child's needs and knowledge of him or her as an individual might reveal something to the professionals about the child's best interests.

Andrew Bainham points to the significance of reported cases as going beyond the consequences for the child whose future treatment is at issue to the understanding which healthcare professionals then have of what it is that the law requires of them in their treatment of children.[90] It is notable that only seven reported cases, resolving a difference of opinion between parent and professional and establishing the legal principles for children's healthcare decision-making, have been considered in this chapter. Parents and professionals caring for a child with serious or life-threatening illness more usually work together in the best interests of the child within the framework established by the case law. Thorpe J in *Re S*, considered above, noted the 'co-operative relationship' between the consultant and parents working together to care for the child in accordance with the parents' beliefs and stressed how important it was that this relationship was not 'jeopardised by these proceedings or their outcome'.[91] And Johnson J emphasised the 'mutual respect' between the consultant paediatrician and parents in *Re O*.[92] Legal proceedings, with opposed positions presented by legal representatives, one of which the judge chooses, threaten to damage the relationship between those caring. However, as happened in *Re MM*,[93] legal proceedings can change the position of one of the parties, after hearing the evidence, enabling them to reach an agreement, or permit the parties to gain a better understanding of each other's position. This was an issue upon which Wilson J reflected at length in *Re C*:

> A subject which never fails to intrigue me is the various extra functions of a hearing in the Family Division. The function often extends so much further than to reach a conclusion upon the issue raised. Sometimes the extra function is cathartic, so that parents who have to come to terms with a terrible reverse can at least feel for the rest of their lives that they did all that they could and that the judge listened empathetically . . .
>
> Here, too, there has been an extra function, new in my experience. One of the parents' complaints is that the local authority took proceedings before there had been sufficient discussion of the issues. I have to say that, in the light of the urgency of the subject, I do not find the complaint valid. At all events the hearing before me at times almost took the form of a long and intelligent discussion of the issues relating to the

---

[90] *Supra*, n. 50, at p. 50.   [91] *Re S (a Minor) (Medical Treatment)* [1993] 1 FLR 376.
[92] *Re O (a Minor) (Medical Treatment)* [1993] 2 FLR 149.
[93] *Re MM (Medical Treatment)* [2000] 1 FLR 224.

treatment of a baby between knowledgeable parents on the one hand and two top-flight consultants on the other. It was almost as if the rest of us were flies on the wall of the consulting rooms at Great Ormond Street Hospital and at St Mary's. Each doctor was questioned on behalf of the parents for about three hours; and the questions, both from Mr Horowitz on behalf of the mother and from the father himself, were admirable in every way. So also, as I have concluded, were the answers.[94]

The matter may have been one of urgency, but engaging in a long and intelligent discussion in the courtroom will not have hastened the occasion nor is it guaranteed to improve the relationship between the parties whilst resolving the conflict. As Wilson J identified, court proceedings can provide a forum in which issues are fully debated or assure the parties that difficult decisions have been reached after careful and full consideration. Yet, court proceedings are a stressful and currently an inevitably adversarial way of ensuring full, careful and considered decision-making between those who have different insights to bring to the decision. The law should be directed at supporting the parties to gain an understanding of the reasons for their differing opinions and to ensuring that the issue receives full and careful deliberation. As discussed further in chapter 7, the law has a role to play in creating the institutions and practices which support and foster a child-centred approach to decision-making in which the expertise of parents and professionals is recognised and exercised.

[94] *In re C (a Child) (HIV Testing)* [2000] 2 WLR 270, at p. 275.

5

The quality of life of severely disabled children

Introduction

Some parents of children with severe disabilities are confronted with the question whether it would be in their child's best interests for life-prolonging treatment to be withheld or withdrawn with the intention of ending their child's pain and suffering and ensuring a peaceful death. This chapter undertakes a full analysis of the law governing these difficult decisions which are, primarily, reached through agreement between parents and professionals. Two children feature very prominently in this chapter. Throughout, there is analysis of the role of the law in decisions about the future care of Charlotte Wyatt repeatedly referred, by her parents and the doctors taking care of her, to the High Court for determination, with occasional reference to the Court of Appeal. There is also specific consideration of the care of one child: David Glass, born with mental and physical disabilities, was twelve at the time of the hospital care which was the subject of legal proceedings and eighteen by the time the European Court of Human Rights (ECtHR) gave judgment. Central to all of the cases considered is the question of the quality of life of the child and whether it is morally correct for one person to form a judgment about another's quality of life. The litigation which has brought the predicament of these children and their parents into the public realm demonstrates the need to examine the responsibilities of parents and professionals for the care of children with severe disabilities within the wider context of attitudes to the disabled and the limits of medical science, technology and knowledge.

That Charlotte Wyatt survived her premature birth, heart surgery and first winter is due both to advances in medical technology and to the quality of nursing and parental care she received. Charlotte was born at Portsmouth Hospital on 21 October 2003 at twenty-six weeks' gestation, weighing approximately 1lb. She has numerous health problems, including severe respiratory failure, pulmonary hypertension, recurrent urinary tract infections, worsening kidney function and poor neurological function. The issue upon which the doctors and her parents have disagreed is whether it would be in Charlotte's best interests to be artificially ventilated in the event of a respiratory infection. In October 2004 and again in April 2005, Hedley J reached the conclusion that, should Charlotte's health deteriorate so that artificial ventilation was required, it would not be in her best interests to provide it. In a review in October 2005, the order was discharged. Wall LJ in the Court of Appeal expressed the view that it was inevitable that further life and death decisions would have to be made about her care, whilst her parents hoped to be able to take her home once her oxygen-dependency dropped to 30 per cent and a care package was agreed. In February 2006, Charlotte's health deteriorated as a consequence of an aggressive chest infection and the order was renewed. Her parents challenged the view of Hedley J that she was now on a 'downward rather than an upward trend'[1] and by April 2006 there were reports in the media that she had recovered sufficiently that she was expected soon to leave hospital.[2]

Whilst decisions about life-prolonging treatment previously arose in relation to children born with congenital abnormalities such as spina bifida, now they more frequently need to be made with regard to babies whose impairments are due to extreme prematurity or babies who suffered neurological damage at birth.[3] Discussions about treatment withdrawal or limitation occur in relation to up to 70 per cent of the babies who die in neonatal intensive care units.[4] Yet, there are very few reported cases arising from different evaluations by parents and professionals of the best interests of a child with severe disabilities. In the majority of cases, parents and professionals come to agree that the pain, suffering and prognosis for the child leave no other option than to withhold or withdraw treatment, enabling the child to die peacefully. The good practice guidelines of the Royal College of Paediatrics and Child Health, *Withholding or Withdrawing Life Sustaining Treatment in Children: A Framework for Practice*,[5] suggest that

---

[1] Andrew Davies, 'Judge rules that doctors must let ill baby die', *Daily Telegraph*, 25 February 2006. Charlotte's story is told from the perspective of her parents on the website http://charlottewyatt.blogspot.com.

[2] *Re Wyatt* [2006] EWHC 319, at para. 12; *Sunday Times*, 16 April 2006.

[3] Hazel E. McHaffie and Peter W. Fowlie, *Life, Death and Decisions: Doctors and Nurses Reflect on Neonatal Practice*, Hochland and Hochland: Cheshire, 1996, at p. 7.

[4] Royal College of Paediatrics and Child Health, *Withholding or Withdrawing Life Sustaining Treatment in Children: A Framework for Practice*, 2nd edn, 2004, at p. 14.   [5] *Ibid.*, at p. 34.

disagreement between parents and professionals may arise from a 'different understanding of the issues' and may be resolved with more time and discussion. The guidance advises that if parental evaluation is affected by uncertainty about medical advice the clinician should suggest that additional investigations are undertaken or that further medical opinion is sought. Furthermore, in the event of a difference of opinion, parents should be told that they can change clinician/consultant if that is feasible.

The early cases, *Re B*, *Re C* and *Re J* (1990), can be considered advisory cases in which the court was asked to determine the best interests of their ward and in doing so set out the legal principles governing their decision, rather than disputes arising from conflicting opinions held by parents and professionals. It is questionable whether *Re B*[6] is rightly considered here, although the legal principles established in that case have been applied in subsequent cases concerned with the provision of life-prolonging treatment to children. Although her parents and doctors had reached different conclusions as to whether an operation to remove an intestinal blockage was in Alexandra's (a baby with Down's Syndrome) best interests, the reason for involvement of the court was to clarify the legal duties of doctors and parents and the role of the court. The same function was performed by the court in relation to determination of the future treatment of sixteen-week-old C, born prematurely with congenital hydrocephalus and a poorly formed brain structure. C had been made a ward of court at birth as a result of concerns held by the local authority that her parents would be unable to care for her for reasons not connected to her disabilities.[7] The court had to decide upon her future treatment in the event that she developed an infection or illness. Her parents were represented but the judgment makes no mention of their views about her future care. Lord Donaldson MR described the parents of baby J, born prematurely at twenty-seven weeks' gestation with severe brain damage as a result of oxygen deprivation at birth, as being in an 'agonising dilemma', although there was 'no real difference of opinion' between his parents and doctors.[8] As J was a ward of court, it was for the court to decide whether it was in his best interests for ventilation to be withheld. In these cases there is a measure of agreement about future care but uncertainty regarding the legality of withholding treatment from the child. C's parents and doctors were agreed that it was in her best interests

---

[6] *Re B (a Minor) (Wardship: Medical Treatment)* [1981] 1 WLR 1421.
[7] *Re C (a Minor) (Wardship: Medical Treatment)* [1989] 3 WLR 240.
[8] *Re J (a Minor) (Wardship: Medical Treatment)* [1991] 2 WLR 140.

that artificial ventilation be withdrawn, sedation administered and loving care provided for what remained of her life.[9] C had been born prematurely and had brain damage as a result of meningitis. She was fed by tube and was being kept alive by artificial ventilation. Sir Stephen Brown P considered that the purpose of making C a ward was so that the court could take responsibility and 'relieve the parents in some measure of the grave responsibility' involved in the decision whether to discontinue artificial ventilation.

In contrast, clearly opposed evaluations of the best interests of the child were the reason for resort to judicial intervention in the remaining cases, *Re C*,[10] *Royal Wolverhampton Hospital NHS Trust v B*,[11] *A National Health Service Trust v D*,[12] Charlotte Wyatt, *Re L*[13] and, most recently, *Re MB*.[14] Sixteen-month-old C suffered from spinal muscular atrophy, a condition for which life expectancy is only one year. Her life was sustained by artificial ventilation and her parents and doctors were in agreement that ventilation should be discontinued to see if she could breathe independently. Her doctors were of the opinion that, if she could not breathe independently, it was not in her best interests to re-ventilate her. Whereas her parents, who were Orthodox Jews, wanted her to be re-ventilated. The court gave the order sought, replacing the parental decision reached according to their religious beliefs with one determined by the medical evidence.[15] In the *Royal Wolverhampton Hospital* case, the different views of the mother and the doctors caring for five-month-old E, who suffered from chronic lung disease resulting from prematurity, were held in the context of a breakdown of trust between them. Nineteen-month-old ID, the child whose future treatment was decided in *A National Health Service Trust v D*, had been born prematurely and consequently had neurological handicaps and severe developmental delay, problems with a number of organs, in addition to severe, chronic, irreversible and worsening lung disease. He had been

---

[9] *Re C (a Baby)* [1996] 2 FLR 43.

[10] *Re C (a Minor) (Medical Treatment)* [1998] 1 FLR 384.

[11] *Royal Wolverhampton Hospital NHS Trust v B*, 7 September 1999 (web.lexis-nexis.com/professional/).   [12] *A National Health Service Trust v D* [2000] 2 FLR 677.

[13] *Re L (Medical Treatment: Benefit)* [2004] EWHC 2713 (Fam).

[14] *An NHS Trust v MB* [2006] EWHC 507 (Fam).

[15] As with the cases concerning the children of Jehovah's Witnesses considered in chapter 4, the court did not examine their beliefs. The extract from the parents' affidavit, quoted in the judgment of the court, was to the effect that they believed that consequences would flow for the parents from failure to take all possible steps to preserve life rather than, as with Jehovah's Witnesses' refusal of blood products, for the child patient. That is a material difference and one which needs to be thoroughly examined.

ventilated soon after birth and continued to be ventilated for the first fifty days of life but had been cared for at home from the age of eight months, with occasional admissions to hospital for emergency treatment. The conflict in ID's case was rooted in a difference of opinion between his parents and doctors as to whether ID, who was terminally ill, had reached the point where artificial ventilation to save his life in the event of a respiratory or cardiac arrest or failure was no longer in his best interests. In *Re L* nine-month-old Luke Winston-Jones had spent all of his life in hospital. He had Edward's Syndrome, a genetic disorder, causing him to suffer from multiple heart defects, chronic respiratory failure, severe developmental delay, epilepsy, hypertonia and gastroesophageal reflux. The medical evidence was that his condition was incurable, and deteriorating, and only palliative treatment could be provided. His doctors and mother disagreed as to whether Luke should be aggressively treated with artificial ventilation other than continuous positive airways pressure or bag and mask. As with the parents of ID, his mother, whilst appreciating that his life expectancy was limited, did not consider that the time had come where his health had deteriorated to such an extent that he should be allowed to die.

This was also the position adopted by MB's mother in the most recent case at the time of writing. Eighteen-month-old MB had been born with the congenital condition, spinal muscular atrophy. His condition had been diagnosed when, at the age of seven weeks, his parents had become concerned about his development and sought medical advice. He had remained in hospital ever since. MB was suffering from the most severe type of spinal muscular atrophy, Type 1, a degenerative condition in which the voluntary muscles become increasingly weak with the consequence that artificial ventilation is inevitably required.[16] MB was dependent upon oxygen administered via a pipe into his lungs and fed through a tube inserted into his stomach. Although there was some disagreement, Holman J accepted for the purposes of his decision that MB had normal cognitive function, could see, hear, feel and was aware of his surroundings and of his family. His mother maintained that he could move his eyes and make small movements of his eyebrows, corners of his mouth, thumb and toes.

---

[16] Holman J explained that spinal muscular atrophy varies across a range of severity. Types 2 and 3 spinal muscular atrophy may not be apparent until the child is older and may result in only limited impairment so that sufferers can live normal lives. MB had the most severe degree of the most severe type of spinal muscular atrophy: *An NHS Trust v MB* [2006] EWHC 507, at paras. 3–5.

Holman J clearly felt the burden of having to determine whether artificial ventilation should be withdrawn from MB, a child with physical impairments but normal cognitive function, who was conscious, aware of his surroundings and responded to his family. Despite the unanimous opinion of fourteen consultants, including those involved in his care and independent experts, Holman J concluded that it was not currently in MB's best interests for ventilation to be discontinued. Much weight was placed upon MB's mother's evidence about the quality of his life in reaching the conclusion that it was not, at that time, in the best interests of this conscious child for artificial ventilation to be withdrawn, contrary to his parents' wishes, resulting in his immediate death.

The legal obligation rests with parents to give or withhold their consent to the provision, withholding or withdrawal of life-prolonging treatment according to their assessment of the best interests of their child in light of the medical evidence and other relevant factors. Where disagreements are referred to the court for resolution and the court agrees with the medical assessment, the declaration provided will give consent to the withholding or withdrawal of treatment. A declaration to that effect does not mean that treatment has to be withdrawn or withheld in the event of the specific situation covered by the declaration arising. The effect of a declaration from the court is to assure the doctors that they will be acting lawfully should they determine that withholding or withdrawal of treatment is clinically indicated given the prevailing medical condition of the child. The very important question which this raises of the refusal of judges to require a doctor to act contrary to their professional judgment is considered below.

This chapter analyses the decisions of the courts concerning the future care of children with severe impairments to argue that they demonstrate the limitations of an approach premised upon abstract individualism and conflict, dominated by a professional perception of the child with disabilities focused upon the functional limitations of the child. It is argued that decisions about life-prolonging treatment have to be made according to judgments about the quality of life of the child but that these judgments must be grounded in careful consideration of the child as an individual. The role of parents with caring responsibility for the child has to be recognised both in the vast majority of decisions in which agreement between parent and professional is reached on the wards and when disagreements are brought to court for resolution. Rather than abstract individualism and conflict, a conceptual framework of relational responsibilities would require careful consideration of the child with severe impairments as an individual, of the responsibilities of parents and professionals arising from their relationship with the child, and the wider context in which children with severe disabilities are cared for, including the possibilities and limitations of medical science, societal attitudes to disabilities and practical support for carers.

But first, the care treatment and case of David Glass are considered as illustrative of the range of issues raised by this body of case law. His story provides a good example of both the care provided by a mother to her disabled child and of a failure on the part of doctors during an episode of hospital treatment to have regard to her experiences of her son, gained as she cared for him. It shows how legal principles structure the relationship between parent and professional and, in this example, contributed to a breakdown in their partnership in circumstances of inevitable tension.

The story of one child: David Glass

David was born with severe physical and mental disabilities: he has cerebral palsy, hydrocephalus, epilepsy, curvature of the spine and a dislocated hip, limited sight and limited cognitive function. David smiles, laughs, uses facial expressions to indicate likes and dislikes and responds to those caring for him. He is cared for at home by his mother with the help of his sisters and aunts, with the assistance of community paediatricians and episodes of hospital care. At the age of twelve, he underwent a tonsillectomy in order to improve his ability to breathe. This resulted in an infection for which he was admitted to hospital a number of times in the following months during which time disagreements arose between his mother and the clinicians, the latter believing that David was dying so that aggressive treatment was not in his best interests, rather he should be treated in a way which would enable him to die with dignity. On one occasion, despite his mother's earlier refusal to consent to the administration of morphine to him, diamorphine (which in the alleviation of pain depresses respiratory function) was administered to him against her wishes and a 'Do Not Resuscitate' order (DNR) placed on his notes without her knowledge. The medical treatment thus involved both the provision, against his mother's wishes, of medication to alleviate distress which would have the effect of hastening death and the intention to withhold certain forms of resuscitation, without his mother's knowledge or consent. The meeting between family members and the Chief Executive at which the family were told that diamorphine would be administered was conducted in the presence of police. When Carol Glass then asserted that, if the hospital was correct and David was dying, she wished to take him home, she was told that she would be arrested if she attempted to do so and that the police would arrest any family member who tried to prevent the administration of diamorphine. Subsequently, the doctors agreed to reduce the dose on condition that the family made no attempts to resuscitate him. He was resuscitated by his mother, whilst other family members fought with the doctors who sought to prevent them (actions for which his aunts and uncle were charged, tried and imprisoned), and discharged later that day. The Medical Director of the Trust wrote to Carol Glass, explaining that the hospital would only be able to offer palliative care for David in the future so she would have to take him elsewhere for active treatment. Whilst all engaged in the activity of caring for him were genuinely acting in what they considered to be his best interests, the circumstances of David's care provide an example of spiralling distrust where there should be an effective partnership in a shared endeavour.

The ECtHR considered the compatibility with the European Convention on Human Rights and Fundamental Freedoms (ECHR) of the decisions of the doctors and hospital management caring for David.[17] Central to the case was the legal advice given to doctors caring for David that permission of the High Court was necessary if they were to treat against his mother's wishes but that no court had ever required doctors to treat contrary to their clinical judgment. This was in October 1998 and thus based upon the application of the principles stated by the Court of Appeal in *Re J* (1990), considered below. As a consequence of this advice, the doctors believed that the law permitted them to treat David, as they saw fit, contrary to his mother's wishes.

David and Carol Glass alleged that the actions of the hospital amounted to a breach of Articles 2 (right to life), 6 (right of access to court), 8 (right to

---

[17] *Glass v United Kingdom* [2004] 1 FLR 1019. The decisions of the doctors and hospital management had been considered in the English courts in judicial review proceedings, *R v Portsmouth Hospitals NHS Trust, ex parte Glass* 50 BMLR 269 (web.lexis-nexis.com/professional/) and *R v Portsmouth Hospitals NHS Trust, ex parte Glass* [1999] 2 FLR 905. Carol Glass had sought judicial review of the decision of the Trust in relation to David's future care – that he was regarded as terminally ill and if admitted in the future would be provided with palliative care but not life-prolonging treatment. These cases affirm, if there was any doubt, that different evaluations of the best interests of the child upon a specific issue should be decided by a Family Division judge as a specific issue order or in the exercise of the court's inherent jurisdiction.

respect for family and private life), 13 (right to an effective remedy), and 14 (not to be discriminated against in the enjoyment of Convention rights) of the ECHR. The complaint that the actions of the hospital amounted to a breach of their Article 8 rights was held admissible, with the remainder rejected as manifestly unfounded.[18] The European Court of Human Rights decided that the actions of the doctors in administering diamorphine without the consent of his mother or the court was an interference with David's rights under Article 8 of the ECHR – his right to respect for his private life and specifically his right to physical integrity.[19] Although the doctors had acted with a legitimate aim (in accordance with their clinical judgment of David's best interests), administration of diamorphine against his mother's wishes without seeking consent from the court was not necessary in a democratic society.[20] The doctors knew that his mother was opposed to the administration of morphine and could have applied to court at that stage or by an emergency application at the point at which administration of diamorphine was, in their view, in David's best interests. Consequently, the view of the European Court of Human Rights was that English law places with parents the power to make decisions about the healthcare of their child, with involvement of the court in cases of disagreement with professionals and, as such, is compatible with the Convention. The majority did not consider it necessary to determine whether putting a DNR on his notes without his mother's knowledge was an interference with David's Article 8 rights.[21] Nor did the majority find it necessary to determine whether his mother's Article 8 rights had been interfered with. Was not the administration of medication to her son, contrary to her objection, an interference with her right to family and private life not justified by any of the exceptions in Article 8(2)?

Whilst the European Court of Human Rights emphasised the role of parents, rather than doctors, as decision-makers, with the intervention of the courts in instances of irreconcilable dispute, the court did not address the issue underlying the way in which the doctors wished to treat David, which was their perception of his quality of life. It is both notable and shocking that, after being told that David was dying, his family revived him

---

[18] ECHR, *Decision as to the Admissibility of Application no. 61827/00 by David and Carol Glass against the United Kingdom*, 18 March 2003, (2003) 37 EHRR CD66.

[19] *Glass v United Kingdom* [2004] 1 FLR 1019, at para. 70.   [20] *Ibid.*, at paras. 77–83.

[21] Judge Casadevall dissented, considering the DNR to be an aggravating factor exacerbating the distress of Carol Glass.

by stroking him and whispering to him and he recovered sufficiently to be discharged later that day. Was it the case that his disabilities coloured the doctors' views of his quality of life and thus whether to treat (with treatment – for an infection following a tonsillectomy – which would unquestionably have been provided to a child without those disabilities)?[22] As his mother, Carol Glass, commented:

> What the doctor couldn't understand was that David is not a handicapped child. He is a child with handicaps. It got to the stage where it was out of my hands and the doctors seemed to think his life was not worth saving. But I knew David, and I knew he wasn't dying.[23]

Finding there to have been a breach of David's Article 8 right did amount to an acknowledgement of David, a child with severe mental, physical and learning disabilities, as an individual with rights, in this instance the right to 'physical integrity'. The decision confirms that the bodies of all children are entitled to protection from interference without consent (because of their physical integrity) although, as they lack the capacity to decide for themselves (mental integrity), consent is sought from parents or the court. This is an important acknowledgement of the minimum guarantees available to children in relation to their healthcare – treating children as equal to adults in the protections afforded to them by convention rights. It reveals, however, the conceptualisation of rights within the ECHR as based upon respect for autonomy and protection of the individual from non-consensual interference. This is a limited formulisation of rights which cannot address the dependency of a disabled (or young) child upon their parent who cares for them. Further, there is no scope for acknowledgement of the dependency of the child's parents upon healthcare professionals upon whom they have to rely to take care of their sick, injured or disabled child. And decisions about children remain isolated from the context in which they occur, for example, political decisions about the limits of support for disabled children and their families[24] and societal attitudes towards disability.

---

[22] A. R. Maclean, 'The Human Rights Act and the Individual's Right to Treatment' (2000) 4 *Medical Law International* 245–76, at p. 268.

[23] Carol Glass quoted in E. Day, 'Do Not Resuscitate – and don't bother consulting the family', *Sunday Telegraph*, 14 March 2004.

[24] Antje Pedain, 'Doctors, Parents, and the Courts: Legitimising Restrictions on the Continued Provision of Lifespan Maximising Treatments for Severely Handicapped, Non-Dying Babies' (2005) 17 CFLQ 535–44.

At the same time, the case, care and treatment of David Glass provide a clear example of the limitations of the existing legal framework. They also reveal how consideration of the child as an individual situated in a caring relationship, whose quality of life is dependent upon his family, whose ability to care is affected by external factors beyond their control (such as the support available to them and discriminatory attitudes), would have provided a more thorough and grounded assessment. The understanding of the law upon which the doctors proceeded meant that treatment decisions were made by doctors caring for a child at a time of crisis rather than by, and to the exclusion of, his mother who had knowledge of her son gained through the years of caring for him twenty-four hours a day. Despite the small glimmer offered by the (exceptional) case of *Re MB*, the majority of the decisions of the English courts since, most notably the ongoing saga of the care of Charlotte Wyatt, do nothing to counter the view that the court will be more convinced by medical opinion than by the experience and knowledge of parents. As Barbara Hewson observes, in her analysis of the judgment of the ECtHR, 'What would have happened if the doctors had sought judicial authorisation to override Mrs Glass's wishes? Judges are unlikely to prefer maternal instinct to medical opinion in these situations. Such deference to doctors is potentially a problem, as the most conscientious doctor can sometimes be wrong.'[25] The legal rights of the ECHR were thus placed within the existing framework of English law and the case represents a missed opportunity to challenge the limits of both. Consequently, despite the ECtHR decision reiterating that the legal duty in relation to decisions about the healthcare of their children rests with their parents, the position remains one of potential conflict in which medical opinion generally takes precedence when disagreements arrive in court.

Children, including those with severe disabilities such as David Glass, are entrusted to the care of their parents, with the greatest responsibility often falling, as with Carol Glass, upon their mothers with support from their families and (some, often inadequate) support from the state. Although David's quality of life is heavily dependent upon the care provided by his mother, with the assistance of his aunts and sisters, his treatment highlights the dependency of his mother upon the care, support and attitudes of others. We have no evidence upon which to comment upon the practical support which David's mother receives from the state on a daily

[25] Barbara Hewson, 'When Maternal Instinct Outweighs Medical Opinion' (2004) 154 NLJ 522–3.

basis as she meets his needs twenty-four hours a day. However, the hospital care provided to him does raise the question of the attitudes of the doctors towards the quality of life of a child with severe disabilities in contrast to the experiences of his mother who provided the majority of his care. David's mother considered that the decision to administer diamorphine to him was a judgment about David's quality of life as 'a pointless continuation of a burdensome existence'.[26] Adrienne Asch has argued that medical professionals adopt the perspective of an able adult in their assessment of the quality of life of people with disabilities and, from that position, make prejudicial judgments about them. She argues that medical professionals need to confront their ambivalences about people with disabilities through learning of their experiences from those living with disabilities.[27] The same point is made by Phil Fennell in his commentary on the *Glass* case:

> If a wholly clinician-based approach to best interests and quality of life is adopted, there is a danger of imposing the subjectivity of a healthy, highly educated case-hardened medical practitioner without looking at what the person himself would or might want, or those who know (and love) the patient think he would want.[28]

This is not to suggest that professionals do not have legitimate opinions worthy of consideration by the court. Of course they do. It is to emphasise the importance of a thorough examination of the best interests of the child which includes consideration of the views of those caring for the child:

> Since it is impossibly hard for an able-bodied person to appreciate what value David gets from his life then surely we should accept the view of the person best placed to judge – which in this case is his mother.[29]

As Carol Glass herself commented: 'I was angry for David because I knew him best and I needed to stick up for him. I needed to give him a voice.'[30] In the provision of care which is attentive to their particular needs, parents will develop knowledge of their child as an individual with personal integrity, that is, 'the countless aspects of each personality [which] interrelate and

---

[26] Antje Pedain, 'Terminating Care' [2004] CLJ 306–9, at p. 309.
[27] Adrienne Asch, 'Distracted by Disability' (1998) 7 *Cambridge Quarterly of Healthcare Ethics* 77–87.
[28] Phil Fennell, 'Withdrawal of Life Sustaining Treatment for a Child without Parental Consent' (2000) 8 Med Law Rev 125, at pp. 126–7, commentary on Court of Appeal judgment.
[29] *Supra*, n. 22, at p. 270.   [30] *Supra*, n. 23.

integrate to form each unique whole'.[31] Further, through the 'functionally diffuse' care parents provide to sustain their child, they gain expertise in their child's needs, ability to cope with his or her condition and quality of life. Both aspects may inform their judgment about treatment and have to be examined alongside medical opinion.

Andrew Bainham points to the significance of reported cases as going beyond the consequences for the child whose future treatment is at issue to the understanding which healthcare professionals then have of what it is that the law requires of them in their treatment of children.[32] It is notable that this observation, made in relation to the Court of Appeal judgment in Re T,[33] could have been a comment upon the actions of the doctors and hospital management with regard to the care of David Glass. Legal advice which reflected a partial account of the law, failing to distinguish between previous case law and the situation confronting the hospital, resulted in hospital care which failed to respect the role of David's mother in healthcare decision-making or to secure a thorough assessment of David's best interests. It has been argued that the care provided to children is affected by perceptions of what children are – vulnerable, dependent and in need of protection. It is suggested that the care provided to children with disabilities may be affected by prejudiced perceptions about their lives. Unless these understandings are confronted and alternative accounts provided by those who care for them are heard, considered and explored, decisions made about their treatment will reflect and reinforce them. Therein lie the limits of the rights analysis taken by the ECtHR and the potential difference of a responsibilities approach.

The responsibility of deciding about life-prolonging treatment

There are very few reported cases in which the court decides about withholding or withdrawing life-prolonging treatment from a child. Far more decisions are taken together by parents and professionals on the ward. Anonymity means that we have, until the recent cases of David Glass, Charlotte Wyatt and Luke Winston-Jones, known very little about the parents, children and families at the centre of these cases. It is therefore instructive to consider the study by Hazel McHaffie et al. of the reflections of parents of children from

---

[31] Priscilla Alderson, 'Researching Children's Rights to Integrity' in Berry Mayall (ed.), *Children's Childhoods: Observed and Experienced*, Falmer Press: London, 1994, 45–62, at p. 47.
[32] Andrew Bainham, 'Do Babies Have Rights?' (1997) 56 CLJ 48–50, at p. 50.
[33] *Re T (a Minor) (Wardship: Medical Treatment)* [1997] 1 WLR 242, considered in chapter 4.

whom treatment was withheld or withdrawn to inform the conceptual framework for decision-making through responsibilities.

This study of parents of children from whom treatment was withheld or withdrawn during infancy identified that whilst 'there is widespread agreement that this should be a shared commitment, the balance of responsibility has not been spelled out'.[34] The generally accepted understanding amongst parents that it was their responsibility as the child's parents to be *involved* in treatment decisions contrasted with the view held by professionals that parents should not take *ultimate responsibility* for the decision because it was too great a burden to bear.[35] The majority of parents in their study did consider that they had made the decision: others who did not, wished that they had. The authors caution against rigid guidelines and protocols given that individual needs differ, whilst concluding that 'parents ought to be given the *opportunity* to accept responsibility for decision-making, although the fact that a significant number declined to do so indicates that they should not be *obliged* to make the ultimate decision themselves'.[36] This is reflected in the Royal College of Paediatrics and Child Health guidelines which state that it is the responsibility of the treating team to determine *the extent* to which the parents want to take responsibility.[37]

Hazel McHaffie points to 'the critical issue', which is equally critical for the way in which the law deals with disputes about treatment limitation, which is that 'the parents need to be *personally persuaded* that this course of action is the best for their child':[38]

> These are crucial decisions with which the parents will have to live for the rest of their days, and they should be based on deep beliefs, not spur-of-the-moment choices.
>
>> What's important is that you can live with your decision, at the end of the day, in the longer term. And that's the really difficult bit . . . Much as it's sad for the baby who dies, it's the people who are left who have to come to terms with that. So their wishes and views have to be important.
>> (P50: mother of baby with congenital anomalies)[39]

---

[34] Hazel E. McHaffie in association with Peter W. Fowlie, Robert Hume, Ian A. Laing, David J. Lloyd and Andrew J. Lyon, *Crucial Decisions at the Beginning of Life: Parents' Experiences of Treatment Withdrawal from Infants*, Radcliffe Medical Press: Abingdon, 2001, at p. 3.

[35] *Ibid.*, at p. 396. 97 per cent of doctors and 94 per cent of nurses considered that parents should not take ultimate responsibility.   [36] *Ibid.*, at p. 409, emphasis added.

[37] *Supra*, n. 4, at para. 3.1.1.   [38] *Supra*, n. 34, at p. 397.

[39] *Ibid.*, at p. 383, quoting one of the mothers in their study.

The researchers identified that parents weighed up suffering and the prospect of a poor quality of life in determining whether treatment should be withheld or withdrawn from their child whereas the doctors weighed up the chances of survival, given technical and prognostic medical factors, and the consequences of treatment against future pain and impairment.[40] One concern in the reported cases, occasionally articulated, is that the emotional attachment of parents to their child may mean that parents are unable to grasp the reality of the child's condition or will seek for the child to be kept alive in their own interests at the expense of pain and suffering for the child. Yet, as this study shows, parents with responsibility for a child with severe impairments do take the decision that further treatment is not in the best interests of their child.

> [T]he parents whom we studied give a clear message: limits should be set to what is attempted in our efforts to save the lives of imperilled infants . . . In general, they want everything done to cure their child's problems and they are supportive of technological interventions which may save the lives of their children, but they fear severe impairments, and they regret the imposition of prolonged pain and suffering in cases where the prognosis is bleak. They do not view as a kindness an aggressive fight which results in children surviving with devastating impairments, enduring protracted dying processes, or suffering without any prospect of future benefit.[41]

Parents in the study were reluctant to offer advice to other parents as they appreciated that circumstances and individuals differed. The advice they gave was put in general terms, focused upon ensuring that this difficult decision was reached in a way with which parents felt comfortable. They highlighted the need to get as much information and advice as possible, to ask for things to be done in a way which felt right to them, not to be pressurised into making premature decisions, to decide as a couple and, once they made a decision, not to dwell upon whether it was the right one. All parents placed the interests of their child at the centre of their decision and doubts were expressed by parents who were not entirely convinced that they had been right in agreeing to treatment limitation. Parents whose child died following treatment limitation were able to separate the (careful, informed, shared) process of decision-making from the (desperately sad) outcome. They quote one father: 'This is not a decision I ever want to be fully at peace with.'[42]

---

[40] *Ibid.*, at p. 394.   [41] *Ibid.*, at p. 393.   [42] *Ibid.*, at p. 397.

From this study we can see the central importance of the partnership between parents and healthcare professionals, respectful of the distinct contribution of the other, in caring for a child and in reaching a decision to limit treatment. It highlights the particular role of parents arising from their relationship with the child and their focus upon the needs of their child. Importantly, this study of parents of children from whom treatment had been withheld or withdrawn reveals the importance of reaching what feels like the right decision at the right time. Ending treatment too soon leaves parents doubting whether they did all they could for their child; continuing treatment too long causes unnecessary pain and suffering for the child.

Best interests: intolerable life?

Until the Court of Appeal consideration of Charlotte Wyatt's future treatment, the approach to the application of the best interests principle to treatment limitation decisions was as determined by the Court of Appeal in *Re J* (1990), drawing upon the judgments of Templeman LJ and Dunn LJ in the earlier case of *Re B*.[43] Lord Donaldson MR held that the court was required to perform a balancing exercise. The court had to start not with 'what might have been, but what is' and with a presumption in favour of prolonging life in weighing up the pain and suffering and quality of life if life is prolonged, and the pain and suffering caused by the treatment, from the point of view of the child.[44] In the same case, Taylor LJ stressed that treatment should only be withdrawn or withheld if, from the perspective of the child, the child's continued life would be intolerable.[45] Where the child had sustained injuries in an accident, their awareness of their limitations might be a material factor to their quality of life. For all children, the extent to which treatment would, as with ventilation, worsen their condition whilst sustaining life would have to be considered. Taylor LJ, in his judgment, established a high threshold for the low quality of life which a child must be determined to have before treatment may be withheld or withdrawn in their best interests: he pointed to the need for the circumstances to be 'extreme'. The relationship between best interests and intolerability of life was directly addressed by Hedley J in his consideration of the question whether Charlotte should be artificially

---

[43] *Re J (a Minor) (Wardship: Medical Treatment)* [1991] 2 WLR 140; *Re B (a Minor) (Wardship: Medical Treatment)* [1981] 1 WLR 1421.   [44] *Ibid.*, at pp. 147–9.   [45] *Ibid.*, at p. 158.

ventilated in the event of a respiratory infection and his approach was the subject of appeal. Hedley J explained that he understood that it was his duty to assess whether ventilation in the event of a respiratory infection was in Charlotte's best interests, that the concept of best interests should be given a wide interpretation but (having quoted from Lord Donaldson MR and Taylor LJ in *Re J*) that 'the concept of "intolerable to that child" should not be seen as a gloss on, much less a supplementary test to, best interests. It is a valuable guide in the search for best interests in this kind of case.'[46] This approach was approved by Wall LJ, giving the judgment of the Court of Appeal (sitting with Laws LJ and Lloyd LJ), noting that the focus upon intolerability arose from *ex tempore* dicta in *Re B* which were adopted by Taylor LJ alone in *Re J*.[47] From that single judgment of the appeal court we now have the clearest statement of the principles to be applied in judicial determination of whether life-prolonging treatment should be provided, withheld or withdrawn. These principles are that:[48]

1. It has to be decided which course of action is in the best interests of the child, in which the welfare of the child is paramount and determined from the assumed perspective of the child (*Re J*);
2. Best interests are given a wide definition including medical, social and other factors (*Re A*);
3. There is a strong, but not irrebuttable, presumption in favour of prolonging life (*Re J*);
4. Determination of best interests must balance the relevant factors (*Re J*), which may be achieved though a balance sheet of certain and possible benefits and disadvantages (*Re A*).

Wall LJ stressed that determination of best interests requires careful consideration of the facts of the individual case. Hence, it was not helpful to attempt to identify a list of relevant criteria, for that may prove unnecessarily limiting in a future case. Intolerability of life was not, however, entirely irrelevant: it was, as Hedley J had employed it, a guide in the assessment of best interests in cases concerning treatment limitation.

In October 2004, Hedley J had weighed up Charlotte's interest in dying peacefully in her parents' arms as opposed to a death whilst undergoing

[46] *Portsmouth NHS Trust v Wyatt and Wyatt, Southampton NHS Trust Intervening* [2004] EWHC 2247, at para. 24.
[47] *Wyatt and another v Portsmouth Hospital NHS and another* [2005] EWCA Civ 1181, at para. 76.
[48] *Ibid.*, at para. 87.

invasive and painful aggressive medical intervention; the medical evidence that she was unlikely to live for another year; that if she did develop a respiratory infection in that time it might result in her death even with mechanical ventilation or she might recover to her present condition; that her sensory abilities were key to determination of her interaction with others; and evidence that she could not see, hear or respond, that she did experience pain and it might be that she was unable to experience pleasure.[49] Hedley J concluded that Charlotte's best interests, at that time, were not in the provision of artificial ventilation in the event of a respiratory infection but in her comfort, ensuring that she was given high-quality care and love in her life and security and love when the time of her death came. With her improvement, the balance shifted such that in October 2005 artificial ventilation would, in certain circumstances, be in her best interests. In the unusual circumstances of Charlotte Wyatt's case, discussed below, Hedley J considered once again that artificial ventilation was no longer in her best interests when she developed an aggressive chest infection six months later.

Sanctity and quality of life

The Official Solicitor in *Re J* had put to the court that English law must respect the sanctity of life, which meant that there were no circumstances in which the court would be justified in withholding consent to treatment which might enable a child to survive a life-threatening condition whatever the pain and suffering involved and the quality of life enjoyed. Their Lordships rejected this 'absolutist' approach, Lord Donaldson MR concluding that 'in the end there will be cases in which the answer must be that it is not in the interests of the child to subject it to treatment which will cause increased suffering and produce no commensurate benefit, giving the fullest possible weight to the child's, and mankind's, desire to survive'.[50] The alternative was put in terms of the quality of life of the child, the Official Solicitor presenting the position outlined above that treatment should only be withheld where the life of the child would be intolerable.

Whether the court must apply the principle of respect for sanctity of life or determine whether the child's quality of life with the treatment would be intolerable was directly addressed by the Court of Appeal in the case of the

---

[49] *Supra*, n. 46, at paras. 27–39.
[50] *Re J (a Minor) (Wardship: Medical Treatment)* [1991] 2 WLR 140, at p. 150.

conjoined twins, Jodie and Mary.[51] Ward LJ adopted the distinction between vitalism, sanctity of life and Quality of life drawn by John Keown in a published article responding to the decision of the House of Lords in relation to the treatment of Tony Bland.[52] John Keown argues that vitalism refers to an approach which prohibits the shortening of human life and requires human life to be preserved irrespective of the pain, suffering or cost. Thus, the 'absolutist' approach of counsel in *Re J* was vitalism, not sanctity of life. Whereas, he argues, respect for sanctity or inviolability of life prohibits the intentional ending of life by either act or omission. Here he uses intention to mean purpose, so that the administration of treatment to relieve pain which has the effect of shortening life (double effect) and withholding treatment because it is not worthwhile 'either because it offers no reasonable hope of benefit or because, even though it does, the expected benefit would be outweighed by burdens which the treatment would impose'[53] are both consistent with respect for sanctity of life. In John Keown's analysis, the focus is upon the contribution of the treatment, whether it is 'worthwhile' given the treatment's 'benefits and burdens' to the patient. What he considers ethically and legally unacceptable is assessment of the patient's Quality of life because, he argues, that requires assessment of the '*worthwhileness of the patient's life*'.[54] To engage in this process 'denies the ineliminable value of each patient and engages in discriminatory judgments, posited on fundamentally arbitrary criteria such as physical or mental disability, about whose lives are "worthwhile" and whose are not. The arbitrariness is highlighted when it is asked which disabilities, and to which degree, are supposed to make life not worth living?'[55]

Whilst it is absolutely essential that decisions about the provision of life-prolonging treatment to children with severe disabilities are not discriminatory judgments founded on arbitrary criteria, the approach proposed by John Keown and adopted by Ward LJ in *Re A* – that the question is whether the treatment is worthwhile – is problematic. John Harris goes as far as to suggest it is 'astonishing': '[t]he treatment is worthwhile if it contributes to

---

[51] *Re A (Children) (Conjoined Twins: Surgical Separation)* [2001] 2 WLR 480. This case is also considered in chapter 4.

[52] In which the court considered the legality of withdrawing artificial nutrition and hydration from Tony Bland who was in a persistent vegetative state as a consequence of the injuries which he sustained in the Hillsborough Football Stadium disaster: *Airedale NHS Trust v Bland* [1993] AC 789; John Keown, 'Restoring Intellectual Shape to the Law After *Bland*' (1997) 113 LQR 481–503.

[53] Keown, *Ibid.*, at p. 485, suggesting that he is using a narrow concept of intention.

[54] *Ibid.*, at pp. 486–7, emphasis added.   [55] *Ibid.*, at p. 487.

the continuance of a worthwhile life, a life the continuance of which is a benefit to the individual whose life it is, not otherwise'.[56] As John Harris points out, the purpose of medical treatment is to enhance the quality of life or to extend life. Assessments of the *quality* of life can, but do not have to, involve judgments about the *worthwhileness* of life. Every life does have 'equal inherent value' whilst involving different degrees of, for example, health, well-being, pain, suffering and pleasure. Consideration of the worthwhileness of the treatment results in a focus upon the medical possibilities. Judgments *are* then being made about the patient's quality of life but from the narrow perspective of the improvements which can be brought to it by the medical procedure under consideration. The contribution of the medical treatment is relevant to the quality of life that the child will then experience, whether the medical treatment can improve the child's condition, alleviate pain and suffering or, alternatively, increases suffering in efforts to sustain life. But, it demands no consideration of the person who is the potential recipient of the treatment beyond its impact upon their physical well-being. It demands no consideration of the recipient as a person whose best interests extend beyond the medical.

In *Re A*, Ward LJ adopted John Keown's distinctions between vitalism, sanctity and Quality of life to assess whether the surgical separation of the conjoined twins was worthwhile treatment alongside assessment of the best interests of each. In the remainder of the cases, the judiciary express respect for the sanctity of life but determine whether the provision of life-prolonging treatment is in the best interests of the child through assessment of their quality of life. Respect for the sanctity of life functions to create a presumption in favour of providing treatment which will prolong life against which judges consider the quality of the child's life extended by the treatment, aware that the treatment may result in pain and suffering to the detriment of quality of life. Hedley J, considering Charlotte's best interests, expressed the view that central to her quality of life was her capacity to experience pain, pleasure, human contact and love. He further acknowledged the subjectivity of quality of life assessments and that '[t]hose who have cared for a disabled child often have different perceptions of "quality of life" and "intolerability" to those who have not'.[57] In her response to the judgments

---

[56] John Harris, 'Human Beings, Persons and Conjoined Twins: An Ethical Analysis of the Judgment in *Re A*' (2001) 9 Med Law Rev 221–36, at p. 225.

[57] *Portsmouth NHS Trust v Wyatt and Wyatt, Southampton NHS Trust Intervening* [2004] EWHC 2247, at paras. 30–1.

of Hedley J in relation to the future ventilation of Charlotte Wyatt, Margot Brazier identifies the different perspectives upon her quality of life held by her parents and doctors:

> The evidence in a sense depicted different babies. The parents described a daughter, a child who was terribly ill but still, in their view, a child whose continued life is worth living. The doctors (in the main) presented a picture of an infant in the ante-room of death for whom prolonging the process of her death could result in nothing but suffering.[58]

Parents who have been caring for their child will be uniquely positioned to provide insights into the quality of life of their child and, as considered below, can make an enormous contribution to the care which enhances their child's quality of life. The parental relationship with the child is different from that between professional and child. Doctors have to balance the needs of all their patients as they work to cure or, if that is not possible, to improve quality of life and alleviate pain and suffering, applying their professional knowledge and skills to the medical problems of the individual. Doctors, in particular, come and go, taking care of the child through directions issued to others. In contrast, the full attention of parents is likely to be directed to the needs and well-being of their child as an individual and they will often spend far more time with their child than can the doctors. This is still the case even if the child's disabilities limit the ability of the parents to participate in the practical activity of caring for their child and, through interaction, to gain insights into the child's quality of life. Parents, like those of ID, who care for their child at home, will have many more opportunities to assess the overall quality of life of their child. That those caring for the child have particular insights into the child's quality of life was appreciated by the paediatrician who reported to the court in *Re C*. His report detailing C's condition, prognosis and recommendations for her future care concluded that any decisions should be made with reference to 'the opinions of the local nurses and carers . . . for they know her well, show great love for her, and have a feeling for her needs that an outsider cannot have'.[59]

We are not used to hearing evidence about the personality of young children, and those who may be in a position to have appreciated the child as an

---

[58] Margot Brazier, 'An Intractable Dispute: When Parents and Professionals Disagree' (2005) 13 Med Law Rev 412–18, at p. 414.
[59] *Re C (a Minor) (Wardship: Medical Treatment)* [1989] 3 WLR 240, at p. 245.

individual – whether parents or others caring for the child – have often not been asked. A focus upon responsibilities derived out of relationships would require full investigation of the individuality of the child in assessment of quality of life and, hence, best interests. A full and proper assessment of the quality of life from the perspective of the child has to involve careful consideration not only of the medical evidence but of the child as an individual, which, given their age and condition, is reliant upon interrogation of those caring for him or her. Judgments of the quality of life do not have to be judgments about the worth of the child's life nor of the value of the child's life but should be based upon the child's living experience.

John Keown rightly identifies the link between conceptions of personhood and judgments of the quality of life. He argues that the judiciary had adopted a 'dualistic' approach, distinguishing between the 'body' and the 'person': that because Tony Bland had lost his capacity for rational thought he was no longer considered a human being with any interests.[60] The point is made in chapter 1 that although young and disabled children enjoy legal personhood, they do not fulfil the criteria traditionally required for qualification for moral personhood. In contrast, Eva Feder Kittay's conceptualisation of personhood is outlined in chapter 1, focusing upon the relationship between individuals and the ability to have an impact upon the lives of others even when the capacity for rational, reasoned argument is absent. To respect the personhood of another thus conceived requires a willingness to appreciate their individuality through attention to the smallest detail:

> It requires an openness to experience it. In one who can scarcely move a muscle, a glint in the eye at the strain of familiar music establishes personhood. A slight upturn of the lip in a profoundly and multiply disabled individual when a favourite caregiver comes along, or a look of joy in response to the scent of a perfume – all these established personhood.[61]

A reading of the judgment of Holman J in the case of *Re MB*, in comparison with the other cases considered in this chapter, is notable for

---

[60] Keown, *supra*, n. 52, at pp. 493–4, quoting, for example, Sir Stephen Brown P: 'This spirit has left him and all that remains is the shell of his body . . . [which is] kept functioning as a biological unit': *Airedale NHS Trust v Bland* [1993] AC 789, at p. 804.

[61] Eva Feder Kittay, 'When Caring is Just and Justice is Caring: Justice and Mental Retardation' in Eva Feder Kittay and Ellen K. Feder (eds.), *The Subject of Care: Feminist Perspectives on Dependency*, Rowman and Littlefield Lanham, 2002, 257–76, at p. 266.

recognition of the personhood of the child from whom doctors wished to withdraw ventilation. This results, I suggest, from the evidence of his parents presented to the court in the form of written statements, oral evidence, photographs and a video of their child. Echoing the quote from Eva Feder Kittay above, his mother's evidence identifies how, through awareness of the smallest response, the personhood of the child can be experienced:

> The mother says that M does indeed show pain or distress by frowns and by tears. She says that he similarly displays pleasure to her by his eyebrows going up slightly rather than going down, and she can see the merest movement upwards of the side of his lips as if he is trying to smile. She says that his eyes fix on her and will follow her until, because he cannot move his head, he cannot see her any more. She says that when his brother and sister are there, which they very frequently are, he shows recognition of them and his eyebrows and the corner of his mouth will move slightly upwards. If she touches his thumb it will move. She is convinced that he sees, hears and takes in certain TV and DVD programmes and music on CDs . . . He has his favourites and will turn his eyes away and nod off if bored. His brother and sister sing to him and play Round and Round the Garden to which, she believes, he reacts positively and with pleasure.[62]

Through recognition of his family members, having and communicating preferences (for *Shark Tale* and *Shrek* and against *Eastenders* and the news[63]), through the smallest of responses, and experiencing and expressing pleasure, MB's personhood is apparent. Holman J noted that MB was a conscious human being, assumed to have 'normal, age appropriate cognition and power of thought; and normal, age appropriate capacity for moods and emotions, and the capacity to feel pleasure from the stimuli he may receive', although his experiences were more limited than those of a normal child of his age. His Lordship accepted that MB could see, hear, feel, touch and gain pleasure from media and from his relationships with his parents and siblings.[64] His mother's account of MB's personhood and the pleasures in his life weighed heavily against the detached, objective, impersonal medical evidence. This detail about MB's quality of life, dependent upon his relationships with his family, meant Holman J was unable to give

---

[62] *An NHS Trust v MB* [2006] EWHC 507 (Fam), at para. 16.
[63] Paul Harris, 'Doctors say my son is doomed. But he smiles, he cries, and he deserves to live', *Daily Mail*, 9 March 2006.   [64] *Supra*, n. 62, at paras. 63–9.

consent to withdrawal of life-prolonging treatment. This was achieved with respect to a child who was believed not to have any cognitive impairment. The same recognition of the personhood of the child should be considered, and can be appreciated, in children with impaired mental functioning.

It is easy to allege that parents will present their own interests: either that the child should be allowed to die to relieve them of the burden of care or that the child should be provided with treatment because they have not yet reconciled themselves to his or her death. A focus upon responsibility avoids this because it demands consideration of a range of questions, asked of all of those involved in the care of the child, about the child as an individual to inform assessment of their quality of life. It is notable that the judgments in Charlotte's case detail the view of the medical professionals and experts about her prognosis and her parents' hopes but there is no evidence presented of the views of the nurses, upon whom she depended for much of her care, of her quality of life. A focus upon responsibilities would require parents, doctors and nurses to consider the individual child from the perspectives of all involved in caring, enabling each to arrive at a fuller picture of the quality of life of the child and providing more comprehensive evidence upon which the judge could decide in the event of a dispute. After all, 'deciding on behalf of another human being, especially one who has just embarked on life, what constitutes an acceptable quality of life, is an awesome responsibility. It is right that much agonising goes into every such decision.'[65]

Caring: a shared endeavour?

It has been argued elsewhere that a rights-based approach would ensure that the child's interests are considered. Jane Fortin, for example, suggests that rights can usefully be employed in treatment limitation decisions:

> Whilst it may be difficult to cast every legal principle relevant to children in a rights-based mould, the case-law involving desperately ill and dying neonates and infants seems a particularly appropriate vehicle for doing so. Such cases not only raise questions about the existence of a child's right to die, as opposed to a right to live, but also test the balance between the rights of children, parents and doctors, when involved in conflicts about life-sustaining medical treatment.[66]

[65] *Supra*, n. 3, at p. 107.
[66] Jane Fortin, '*Re C (Medical Treatment)*: A Baby's Right to Die' (1998) 10 CFLQ 411.

In this quote, arguing that a rights-based approach would ensure consideration of all the relevant interests and the relevant interests of all, two aspects of the nature of rights discourse which may prove to conceal rather than to illuminate the relevant issues in decisions about life-prolonging treatment are apparent. The first is that a number of conflicting rights are inevitably at issue – the right to respect for dignity,[67] the right of the child to life,[68] the right of the child to a dignified death, the 'right to choose a course of action which will fail to avert death'[69] – and which will ultimately prevail is dependent upon the values of the decision-maker. Secondly, approaching difficult decisions about ending life-prolonging treatment through a framework of rights constructs the situation as one of conflict between the child, his or her parents and healthcare professionals; whereas the dilemma is how to resolve a difference of opinion between parents and professionals all of whom are seeking to ensure, as best they possibly can, that the interests of the child are met. These are difficult life or death decisions made not about separate individuals threatening harm through their pursuit of self-interest but arising from different perspectives from different positions about what is best for the child. It is of note that, whilst there is often passing reference to moral rights, the courts have not yet employed rights to assist in determination or to test their conclusions. The simple reason may be given that the relevant legal principle is the welfare principle, not the rights of the child or parental rights. Alternatively, it could be that this particular dilemma is not best approached through universal, abstract, individualistic, conflicting rights discourse.

What is currently not properly explored within these cases but would be in an approach which focused upon responsibilities arising out of relationships is the distinct contributions of doctors, nurses and parents to the care of the child. This would involve both consideration of the history of practices of caring – which will differ, for example, if the child's condition

---

[67] *Portsmouth NHS Trust v Wyatt and Wyatt, Southampton NHS Trust Intervening* [2004] EWHC 2247, at para. 27 (Hedley J).

[68] Recognised by Article 6 of the United Nations Convention on the Rights of the Child, 1989: 'States Parties recognise that every child has the inherent right to life', and by Article 2 of the ECHR.

[69] *Re J (a Minor) (Wardship: Medical Treatment)* [1991] 2 WLR 140, at p. 147 (Lord Donaldson MR): 'What is in issue in these cases is not a right to impose death, but a right to choose a course of action which will fail to avert death. The choice is that of the patient, if of full age and capacity, the choice is that of the parents or court if, by reason of his age, the child cannot make the choice and it is a choice which must be made solely *on behalf of* the child and in what the court or parents conscientiously believe to be his best interests.'

means that they have never left hospital or if they have been cared for at home – and examination of the different roles of parents and professionals arising out of their relationship with the child.

It is important not to assume that all cases involving children with severe disabilities are the same but, rather, to examine fully the views of all those involved in the care of the child. In this respect, the case of *A National Health Service Trust v D* is particularly troubling. It reveals the need for judicial examination to extend beyond the medical evidence to parental care, most particularly in those instances where the child is cared for at home. At the time of the application to the court, terminally ill ID was nineteen months old and had been cared for at home by his parents with the assistance of community healthcare professionals, and occasional admissions to hospital, for almost a year. The question before the court was whether his condition had deteriorated to the point where further life-prolonging artificial ventilation was not in his best interests. The court considered evidence from a consultant in paediatric intensive care who wrote his report upon the basis of an examination of ID, four days after his admission to hospital with a fever, the hospital records and medical notes. This evidence appears to have been more persuasive to the court than that of the community healthcare providers who supported his parents in their care of him (his parents did not themselves give evidence).[70] Although the application was prompted by an episode of hospital treatment, ID had recovered sufficiently from that crisis to return home. Medical opinion was that mechanical ventilation might provide short-term relief but would be painful and distressing and would lead to further intensive care where ID would eventually die, denying him a dignified and peaceful death. His parents did not agree that his condition had deteriorated to the point where ventilation should be withheld. They pointed to his current state of health, the developmental progress he had made and to the intimate bond between them which he demonstrated in his recognition of them and pleasure at being with them. The paediatric therapist, occupational therapist, home visitor, lead nurse in neonatal home care and speech and language therapist, with whom his parents worked to provide his daily care, supported his parents' evaluation. Yet, Cazalet J gave a declaration to the effect that it would be lawful to withhold mechanical ventilation unless the doctor in charge considered it to be clinically appropriate. Where, as in *A National*

---

[70] *A National Health Service Trust v D* [2000] 2 FLR 677.

Health Service Trust v D, the child is cared for at home, by his parents, with the assistance of community services and periodic hospitalisation in response to episodes requiring medical treatment, the parents will become experts in the condition of their child and their knowledge needs to be given as careful consideration as the medical evidence.

This is not to argue for the simple shift of power from doctors to parents in these cases, rather that the views, knowledge and experience of all contributing to the care of the child have to be considered in order to determine where the best interests of the child lie. In many of these cases, the children have never left hospital or have done so for very small periods of time. Despite this, the child's parents may well have spent much time with their child, caring for them and attending to their needs. As Holman J acknowledged with regard to assessment of MB's best interests:

> The views and opinions of both the doctors *and* the parents must be carefully considered. Where, as in this case, the parents spend a great deal of time with their child, their views may have particular value because they know the patient and how he reacts so well; although the court needs to be mindful that the views of any parents may, very understandably, be coloured by their own emotion or sentiment.[71]

Holman J considered evidence from the consultants taking care of MB, a senior sister who provided the court with details of the 'one-to-one nursing care which is given to M round the clock, 24 hours a day and 7 days a week',[72] expert witnesses and his parents. The doctors were unanimous that withdrawal of ventilation was in MB's best interests. The nursing staff were divided according, it was suggested by the senior sister, to their experience of caring for children with spinal muscular atrophy. His mother had spent more time with MB than any other, focused upon meeting his needs as a child as opposed to his medical care. The court was shown a video taken by his mother which showed that M was able to move his thumbs, very slightly but discernibly, and wiggle his feet at the request of his mother.[73] The consultants taking care of M were adamant that they had not witnessed such responses. But they could not argue with the video evidence.

Whilst the role of the consultant is to 'take care of' the child, focusing upon those aspects of the child within their speciality, much of the ongoing

---

[71] *An NHS Trust v MB* [2006] EWHC 507, at para. 16.   [72] *Ibid.*, at para. 27.
[73] *Ibid.*, at para. 43. At a very practical level, parents, in future cases, would be well advised to consider providing video evidence to the court.

'caring for' will be done by junior doctors, nurses or parents responding to the needs of the individual child. In contrast to the general neglect to examine the contribution of parental care, the quality of paediatric care provided is frequently commended by the court. The quality of care was addressed most directly in the case of baby C in response to adverse comment in the media about her treatment. First, it was suggested that she should undergo a shunt operation to relieve pressure on her brain – an operation which had already been performed. Secondly, following from the misleading wording of Ward J in the High Court who gave an order permitting the hospital to 'treat the minor to die', there was critical comment reported in the press that C was being treated in a way which would bring about her death.[74] Lord Donaldson MR, in the Court of Appeal, countered this criticism, expressing the opinion that C had received 'the finest and most caring medical and nursing attention which this country has to offer'.[75] The professor who reported to the court on her condition, prognosis and his opinion about C's future care noted that '[s]he is receiving outstandingly devoted care . . . which could not be replicated in many children's units, or in many homes'.[76]

In addition to the distinct roles of parents and professionals with respect to the activity of care, parental attachment to the child contrasts with professional detachment. The emotional attachment of parent to child was acknowledged by Bodey J in *Royal Wolverhampton Hospital NHS Trust v B:*

> Their [the parents'] wishes and views are of the greatest importance. E is their child. Theirs is the heartbreak. Theirs is the responsibility for her, if she were able to live through and survive. That they wish to take on that responsibility is of the greatest credit and importance, and the court must accord their views much weight.[77]

However, rather than explore the consequences of emotional attachment it is assumed to have a detrimental effect upon the ability of parents to decide, leaving others better placed to determine where the interests of the

---

[74] For example by the organisation Life: David Cross, 'Judge allows brain-injury baby to die', *The Times*, 17 April 1989.

[75] *Re C (a Minor) (Wardship: Medical Treatment)* [1989] 3 WLR 240, at p. 243.

[76] *Ibid.*, at p. 245. C died on 25 May 1989, *Guardian*, 26 May 1989.

[77] *Royal Wolverhampton Hospital NHS Trust v B*, 7 September 1999 (web.lexis-nexis.com/professional/), at p. 4.

child lie.[78] In contrast, Priscilla Alderson argues that the emotional attachment of parent to child can enhance the quality of decisions made with regard to their future care:

> [A]n essential part of caring for sick children is for adults to respect and learn from the child's feelings through their own feeling reactions. Such empathy might be dismissed as unscientific and unreliable. Emotions of anxiety, compassion, and hope might be regarded as disqualifications, preventing parents from being sufficiently calm and rational to be able to make informed judgments. Yet parents' distress indicates emotional as well as rational understanding . . .; both are essential in truly informed proxy consent.[79]

A proper examination of parental views would have to explore the 'intuitive feelings'[80] of parents who know their child best whilst considering whether that means that hopes have blinded them to reality or whether the parents are, by virtue of their attachment to the child, 'overly-optimistic' about the improvements their child has made.[81]

Parents and professionals: tensions and dependency

Most parents will appreciate the support of professionals in the period after the birth of a child and their advice in relation to specific health needs which occasionally arise. Being a parent of a child with severe disabilities means greater dependency upon services and professionals to meet the medical, nursing and developmental needs of their child, whether their child is cared for at home or in hospital. In most instances parents and professionals work together, each appreciating the contribution of the other, in the shared endeavour of caring for the child. In his October 2005 judgment in Charlotte Wyatt's case, Hedley J stressed that it is the responsibility of doctors to work in partnership with the child's parents.[82]

---

[78] As cautioned by Holman J in the above quote: *An NHS Trust v MB* [2006] EWHC 507 (Fam), at para. 16. Lord Donaldson MR observed that having to decide whether treatment should be withheld or withdrawn 'is an awesome responsibility and only made easier for [judges] than for parents to the extent that judges are able to approach it with greater detachment and less emotional involvement': *Re C (a Minor) (Wardship: Medical Treatment)* [1989] 3 WLR 240, at p. 242.

[79] Priscilla Alderson, 'Consent to Children's Surgery and Intensive Medical Treatment' (1990) 17 *Journal of Law and Society* 52–65, at p. 61.

[80] *Portsmouth NHS Trust v Wyatt and Wyatt, Southampton NHS Trust Intervening* [2004] EWHC 2247.

[81] *A National Health Service Trust v D* [2000] 2 FLR 677.

[82] *Re Wyatt* [2005] EWHC 2293 (Fam), at para. 29.

Where parents and professionals hold different opinions about the future care of the child which they are unable to resolve, the partnership between parents and professionals is threatened. Yet, the dependency of parents upon the professionals caring for their child continues. The judgments of the court concerned with the care of Charlotte Wyatt became increasingly critical of the way in which her parents responded in the circumstances of tension caused by their disagreement with the treating doctors about their daughter's best interests in the event of a life-threatening crisis. In his first reported judgment, in October 2004, Hedley J recognised the dignity of Charlotte's parents, their commitment to her and their generosity in recognising the quality of care she had received even in the face of a difference of opinion regarding the provision of life-prolonging medical treatment.[83] Charlotte's parents continued to have a good relationship with the consultant paediatrician caring for her, despite holding different opinions about ventilation, and continued to 'give a public and unequivocal acknowledgment of the outstanding care' she received.[84] However, the dispute between her parents and the hospital was a cause of stress to the staff and meant that, for a while, Charlotte's father was accompanied by a member of security when visiting his daughter. The deteriorating relationship between her parents and the hospital was a factor in the decision that the declaration should be continued on the grounds that a legal conflict in the event of a future crisis was not in Charlotte's best interests.[85] Yet, Hedley J also stressed that if the medical crisis did occur and the doctors had to decide whether to withhold invasive treatment, despite the fractured relationship between them and her parents, any decision had to be reached in close consultation. Six months later, at which point Charlotte's health had improved sufficiently for the order to be discharged, Hedley J set out at length criticisms of the behaviour of her parents.[86] Rather than be critical of her parents, analysis could more productively have focused upon the respective roles of parent and professional and the relationships between Charlotte, her parents and the doctors, contrasting the emotional attachment of her parents focused upon the needs of their child

---

[83] *Portsmouth NHS Trust v Wyatt and Wyatt, Southampton NHS Trust Intervening* [2004] EWHC 2247 (7 October 2004), at para. 42.   [84] *Supra*, n. 82, at para. 10.

[85] *Wyatt v Portsmouth NHS Trust and Wyatt (By her Guardian) (No. 3)* [2005] EWHC 693 (Fam), at paras. 18–21.   [86] *Re Wyatt* [2005] EWHC 2293 (Fam), at paras. 18–26.

and the detached opinion of the doctors for whom she was one child of a number in their care.

The tension between the mother of Luke Winston-Jones, who had 'consistently and resolutely helped her son fight for his life', and the doctors caring for him was similarly noted by the court. Butler-Sloss P told his mother that, as the issue of Luke's future treatment had now been determined by the court, she should 'go back to pick up her child and to help to care for him', 'turn over a new leaf', 'move forward' and accept that his future care was to be determined by the clinical judgment of the doctors.[87] It was the duty of the mother, Butler-Sloss P stressed, 'for the sake of L, to reduce those areas of conflict to a minimum, and to listen to what is proposed by those who have a great deal of medical and nursing experience'.[88] Surely, it was even more so the duty of the hospital and its doctors, given their professional responsibilities to the child and the inevitable dependency of his mother upon the care they provided, to reduce conflict, appreciating her emotional attachment to, and focus upon, her child?

Sharing the responsibility, referring to court

Some parents of children born with severe disabilities may not be able to take care of their child or may press for continued treatment against all the evidence of extreme pain and suffering and it is necessary to explore fully the reasons for their stance. In addition to the professional responsibility to work with parents is the responsibility to ensure that appropriate cases (not every case) are referred to court for judicial consideration. This must not be confined to cases where doctors disagree with the parents' decision but must also include obtaining guidance in new situations: after all, these are life and death decisions. A comparison of the care of John Pearson and Baby Alexandra highlights the responsibilities of parents, doctors (hospitals) and the court in this regard. Both babies were born in 1981 and questions about their care ended up in court because of attitudes towards the abilities and quality of life of people with Down's

---

[87] *Re L (Medical Treatment: Benefit)* [2004] EWHC 2713 (Fam), at para. 31.

[88] *Ibid.*, at para. 32. Luke died three weeks later in November 2004. His mother claimed that doctors treating him had withheld treatment and failed to comply with the order of the court. The Coroner found that Luke had died from cardiac failure as a result of his condition: Russell Jenkins, 'Staff were right to let boy die, mother told', *The Times*, 10 May 2005.

Syndrome which would not be generally held today,[89] and were not uniformly held at the time.[90]

John Pearson was rejected by his parents at birth. Upon being informed that her baby was 'healthy apart from the awful handicap that presented itself in the form of Down's syndrome', his mother became distraught, telling her husband 'I don't want it, duck', and expressed concerns as to the effect which caring for him would have upon the family. Dr Arthur ordered 'nursing care only' and the administration of a sedative and, three days later, John Pearson died. Dr Arthur was charged with his murder, a charge which was amended to attempted murder for which he was acquitted by the jury.

According to the judgment of Templeman LJ in the Court of Appeal, the parents of Baby Alexandra, born with Down's Syndrome and an intestinal blockage, with 'great sorrow', refused consent to surgery in the 'genuine belie[f]' that it was in her best interests.[91] Alexandra's parents appear to have held a similar view of Down's Syndrome to that articulated in Farquharson J's summing up in *R v Arthur*, although they stressed that they had refused consent in the child's interests and not because of the burden which would be imposed upon them.[92] The view of the local authority that they would be able to arrange for Alexandra's adoption, and that she would be able to lead a happy life, contrasted with Farquharson J's opinion that John Pearson faced the prospect of a life in institutionalised care. The court gave consent to the performance of the surgery upon their ward. The point is not to condemn John Pearson's

---

[89] It is to be hoped that the description given by Farquharson J of Down's Syndrome would not be repeated by a judge today: 'We are dealing with severely handicapped children, but particularly with a mongol, a Down's syndrome child. Any child who is a mongol is faced with the most appalling handicap. It is true, apparently, that mongols vary to some degree in their handicaps. Some mongols grow up and lead affectionate lives, even if they never do, and never can, become normal, because Down's Syndrome is a state that is irreversible.' *R v Arthur* 12 BMLR 1 (web.lexis-nexis.com/professional/), at p. 4. The difference between the understanding of the abilities of children with Down's Syndrome in 1981 and 2005 was acknowledged by Wall LJ in *Wyatt and another v Portsmouth Hospital NHS and another* [2005] EWCA Civ 1181, at para. 67. Janet Read and Luke Clements focus upon the cases of John Pearson and Baby Alexandra to examine changing attitudes towards disability: 'Demonstrably Awful: The Right to Life and the Selective Non-Treatment of Disabled Babies and Young Children' (2004) 31 *Journal of Law and Society* 482–509.

[90] Ian Kennedy, *Treat Me Right: Essays in Medical Law and Ethics*, Clarendon Press: Oxford, 1988, at pp. 156–7.

[91] *Re B (a Minor) (Wardship: Medical Treatment)* [1981] 1 WLR 1421, at pp. 1422–3.

[92] *Ibid.*, at p. 1423.

parents; they were uncertain about their ability to care for a child, who was not the baby they had anticipated, within the context of negative attitudes widely held within society about disability and the lack of support given to parents. The point is to highlight these attitudes, the need of parents for support and the responsibility of professionals to provide initial care, information and advice, to direct parents to sources of support for the future and to ensure that decisions are not made which condemn a child to death without full and proper examination. Ian Kennedy refers to a survey of consultant paediatricians and paediatric surgeons carried out in November 1981, none of whom would have given an otherwise healthy baby with Down's Syndrome, whose parents had rejected him or her, sedation and nursing care only as had Dr Arthur. Ninety per cent of those who responded said that they would provide the same care for the child as for any other.[93] A few months after the court case and surgery, Alexandra was returned to the care of her parents,[94] a fate denied John Pearson, demonstrating the potential value of thorough judicial investigation of life and death decisions in relation to disabled children.

Responsibility of the court

In *Re J* (1992), Lord Donaldson MR expressed the opinion that he was unable to imagine any situation in which the court would require a doctor to treat contrary to their clinical opinion of the best interests of the child.[95] For the court to require a practitioner to act contrary to his duty to his patient would, he thought, be an abuse of power. That duty 'is to treat the patient in accordance with his own best clinical judgment, notwithstanding that other practitioners who are not called upon to treat the patient may have formed a quite different judgment or that the court, acting on expert evidence, may disagree with him'.[96] *Re J* (1992), which has been described as an attempt by parents to force doctors to treat contrary to their professional judgment, was concerned with an appeal against an interim injunction granted by Waite J to the effect that, in the period prior to the hearing,

---

[93] *Supra*, n. 90, at pp. 157–8.

[94] Michael Freeman, 'Do Children Have the Right Not to Be Born?' in *The Moral Status of Children: Essays on the Rights of the Child*, Martinus Nijhoff: Netherlands, 1997, at p. 171.

[95] *Re J (a Minor) (Child in Care: Medical Treatment)* [1992] 3 WLR 507, at p. 516. This view was put into effect in *Re C (a Minor) (Medical Treatment)* [1998] 1 FLR 384; *A National Health Service Trust v D* [2000] 2 FLR 677.   [96] *Re J, ibid.*, at p. 516 (Lord Donaldson MR).

if J should suffer a life-threatening event he should be treated, including with artificial ventilation, so far as possible to prolong his life.[97] At the time of the application, J was sixteen months old and had been severely brain damaged in a fall when he was one month old. His parents had divorced and J was cared for by foster parents. His mother supported the view of the local authority that artificial ventilation should be provided in the event of a future life-threatening event (his father did not know what was best for their son) and the interim injunction was granted to ensure that attempts be made to prolong his life in the event that be necessary prior to the full hearing on the issue.[98]

The role of the courts was clarified by Lord Woolf MR in *Glass*, who stated that the courts would not interfere with clinical judgment *where this can be avoided* and stressed that the refusal of the court to dictate treatment to clinicians was *subject to the power of the court to decide in the child's best interests, taking fully into account the attitude of medical practitioners*.[99] Soon after, in *Royal Wolverhampton Hospital NHS Trust v B*,[100] counsel were agreed that the court could not order treatment of a child overriding the opinions of the clinicians responsible for her. This was accepted by the court in the belief that it was important that E was cared for by professionals confident in their ability to treat her according to their judgment of what was best for her. More recently, in *Re MB*, Holman J sought to follow this position whilst distinguishing the conclusion in the case before him. He refused to give a declaration giving consent to withdrawal of ventilation but merely stated his conclusion that the provision of nursing and medical care which was necessary as a consequence of continued ventilation was in MB's best interests because, he said, he could not make a declaration to that effect.[101] If the court cannot so order, what is the purpose of an application for an order of the court in the event of a difference of opinion between parents and professionals?

The purpose of an application to court for a declaration giving consent to the provision, withholding or withdrawal of treatment from a child must be to provide an independent assessment of the conflicting conclusions as to the best interests of the child. As A. R. Maclean has argued, courts do not order doctors to treat, they authorise treatment. A declaration merely states that withholding or withdrawal of treatment is lawful or unlawful. The

[97] *Ibid.*   [98] *Ibid.*   [99] *R v Portsmouth Hospitals NHS Trust, ex parte Glass* [1999] 2 FLR 905.
[100] *Royal Wolverhampton Hospital NHS Trust v B*, 7 September 1999 (web.lexis-nexis.com/professional/).   [101] *An NHS Trust v MB* [2006] EWHC 507 (Fam), at paras. 89–90.

negotiation process, discussion about the treatment options and interests of the child, has to continue. For a court to declare that withholding or withdrawal of treatment from a child is unlawful does not amount to directing an individual clinician to provide a particular treatment or to provide any treatment but, if it is contrary to their conscience, to refer the child to another clinician.[102] However, a conceptual framework of relational responsibility, ensuring a full exploration of the situation, would avoid the dichotomy: win/lose, withhold treatment/treat, doctor's opinion/parent's views. It would avoid creating a conflict between those involved in caring for the child but, rather, focus upon ensuring a full examination of the reasons for their views to inform a decision about the best interests of the child (which are, it must be emphasised, more than merely medical interests). It would focus upon ensuring all options have been considered in the care of the child, asking what efforts have been made to secure other medical opinions. It would move away from the polarisation of give/withhold this particular treatment, ensuring that all treatment options are before the court. The court has a vital role to play in providing an independent review of the judgment of parents reached in consultation with the child's doctors and, inevitably, through discussion with other family members.

A further aspect of the role of the court in making decisions about the future care of children with severe impairments has been highlighted by the litigation concerning the care of Charlotte Wyatt. It is common, in giving an order that it is lawful to withhold life-prolonging treatment contrary to the evaluation of the child's parents, for the judge to emphasise that the order is permissive, that the parties should know that they can return to court should circumstances alter or if there is new evidence and for arrangements to be made to review the decision. Previously, this does not appear to have occurred, presumably either because the child has died soon after the order in circumstances envisaged by the order or because the parties have been able to agree on the future care of the child. The unexpected survival of Charlotte and the inability of her parents and the hospital to reach agreement on her best interests, particularly on the question whether she should receive invasive artificial ventilation in the event of a respiratory infection, have already resulted in judicial involvement in decisions about her care over a period in excess of eighteen months.

---

[102] *Supra*, n. 22, at p. 271.

Hedley J has considered the specific issue of whether it would be lawful to withhold artificial ventilation if her condition deteriorated to require mechanical ventilation to prolong her life on five occasions[103] and the Court of Appeal twice.[104] Further, in November 2004, Hedley J made an order permitting the administration of diamorphine to relieve the pain of a fractured femur (due to brittle bones), her parents having refused, fearing that it would depress her breathing, and in December 2004 made declarations giving directions in relation to palliative care.[105]

As Wall LJ stated, generally once the court has determined the best interests of the child, whether in relation to the provision of treatment or the withdrawal/withholding of treatment, the matter is decided. The treatment is provided, withdrawn or the circumstances prompting the application occur and treatment is withheld. The treatment of a child should, his Lordship stressed, be agreed between the child's parents and the treating clinicians, it was 'not the function of the court to oversee the treatment plan for a gravely ill child'.[106] Where the expected medical crisis does not occur and the parents and professionals continue to disagree, it appears that is the very role of the court. However, it is my contention that a focus upon relational responsibilities would work to secure greater understanding between parents and professionals of the reasons for their views and further work to support and foster the relationship between them in their shared endeavour, rather than as currently, undermine it and require them to adopt positions of conflict.

The care of severely disabled children

These are desperate cases: seriously ill children with complex needs, parents anxious to ensure that they do the best for their child dependent

[103] *Portsmouth NHS Trust v Wyatt and Wyatt, Southampton NHS Trust Intervening* [2004] EWHC 2247 (7 October 2004); *Portsmouth Hospitals NHS Trust v Wyatt and others* [2005] EWHC 117 (Fam) (28 January 2005); *Wyatt v Portsmouth NHS Trust and Wyatt (By her Guardian) (No. 3)* [2005] EWHC 693 (Fam) (21 April 2005); *Re Wyatt* [2005] EWHC 2293 (Fam) (21 October 2005); *Re Wyatt* [2006] EWHC 319 (23 February 2006).

[104] Unreported [2005] EWCA Civ 185 (9 February 2005); *Wyatt and another v Portsmouth Hospital NHS and another* [2005] EWCA Civ 1181 (12 October 2005).

[105] Details of the unreported cases are set out in the Court of Appeal judgment *Wyatt and another v Portsmouth Hospital NHS and another* [2005] EWCA Civ 1181, at paras. 17–25. There were also orders granting anonymity to expert witnesses (13 September 2004) and forbidding identification of expert witnesses in the media (16 September 2004), later extended to all experts who gave evidence with regard to her care.

[106] *Wyatt and another v Portsmouth Hospital NHS and another* [2005] EWCA Civ 1181 (12 October 2005), at para. 117.

upon professionals working at the margins of medical possibilities and the court with ultimate responsibility for deciding about the life and death of a loved child. As Priscilla Alderson et al. found in their study of parents of babies in neonatal intensive care: 'these babies are very highly valued, loved, and grieved for; if withholding treatment is reluctantly considered, the primary concern is the best interests of the baby'.[107] David Wolfe, opening argument in one of the Charlotte Wyatt cases, said that, 'a society is measured by the way it treats its most disabled members'.[108] The law can be measured by the extent to which it fosters the relationship between those working together to care for a child with severe disabilities and supports them to do their best for the child. It is my contention that, despite its efforts, it currently does not measure up very well.

The current legal framework polarises the positions of those confronted with life and death decisions about children in their care. It need not do so. In their study of doctors and nurses in neonatal intensive care units, Hazel McHaffie and Peter Fowlie found that:

> There was some reluctance expressed about going along the route of appealing to an outside agent if it meant that legal powers overtook medical responsibility, since so much emphasis was placed on trust and continuing negotiation. To call in legal advice and have parents over-ruled by someone else ran the risk of breaking down this special relationship irretrievably.[109]

The decision must be made by the parents based upon information, advice and with the support of professionals. Whether the decision is that treatment should be provided or withheld, both parents and professionals have to be satisfied that they have done the best for the child from their own perspective and with understanding of the position of the other. Parents have to feel supported by professionals to feel that they have done the best possible in meeting the needs of their child which may, when appropriate, include the decision that no further treatment should be provided.

In the event of an intractable difference of opinion, the court must make an independent assessment. Currently, the judge is placed in the unenviable position of being forced to choose between two genuinely held positions which have to be presented as in opposition to each other: doctors

---

[107] Priscilla Alderson, Joanna Hawthorn and Margaret Killen, 'The Participation Rights of Premature Babies' (2005) 13 *International Journal of Children's Rights* 31–50, at p. 39.
[108] *Wyatt v Portsmouth NHS Trust and Wyatt (By her Guardian) (No.3)* [2005] EWHC 693 (Fam), at para. 1.   [109] *Supra*, n. 3, at p. 203.

concerned at 'the extent to which [the child] is exposed to discomfort, distress or pain, coupled with [their] inability to communicate the extent . . . of that discomfort, distress or pain and inability ever to seek help to reduce discomfort, distress or pain'[110] and parents appreciating that whilst many of the pleasures of life may be denied to their child, he or she maintains 'a core of pleasure, including what is probably the single most important source of pleasure and emotion to a small child, his relationship with his parents and family'.[111] For a child to be allowed to die, following the order of a court, in circumstances in which the child's parents do not agree that it is in the best interests of their child must leave the parents with uncertainty about whether they did all they could to protect their child at a time when they most need the support of those who shared with them the journey through their child's life and death.

The decision to withhold or withdraw treatment from a child with severe disabilities must be reached with full consideration of the relevant factors, including a focus upon the child as an individual, the respective insights provided by the impartial clinical view of those who provided intermittent care in response to episodes of crisis and the partial view of those who continuously cared, attentive to the needs of the child. In the present composition, it is 'extremely difficult for laws to take account of all the fine nuances attending these real life tragedies'.[112] The legal framework polarises positions, condensing the views of parent and professional as in opposition, one of which must prevail. This is too simplistic for such complex decisions which need to involve full examination of the responsibilities of all involved in caring for the child.

---

[110] *An NHS Trust v MB* [2006] EWHC 507 (Fam), at para. 70.
[111] *Ibid.*, at para. 69.   [112] *Supra.*, n. 3, at p. 51.

6

Obligations and caring responsibilities

Introduction

The previous three chapters have considered decision-making responsibility in relation to the health and well-being of children. It has been argued that healthcare decisions should be approached through a conceptual framework of relational responsibilities. The responsibilities of both parent and healthcare professional arise out of their relationship with the child, are determined both by social expectation and by individual interpretation but, importantly, differ depending upon the needs of the child. A central element of the relationships between professionals, parents and the child is dependency, the nature of which differs. Sick or injured children, children with complex needs and children with disabilities are dependent upon their parents to meet their needs according to their age, state of health or impairments. They also depend upon healthcare professionals to work together in a team with the child's parents to meet their health needs. Parents, primarily responsible for and emotionally attached to their child, depend upon healthcare professionals to take care of their child, using their skills and expertise. The vulnerability that this reliance brings is clearly apparent in the evidence given by parents to the Bristol Royal Infirmary Inquiry where parents articulated their feelings of being let down by professionals to whom they had entrusted the care of their child, which meant that they felt that they, in turn, had let down their child. This web of dependency, reliance and trust is not acknowledged by laws premised upon selfish individualism.

The purpose of this chapter is, through examination of cases from the law of negligence concerned with the provision of healthcare, to expose the caring responsibilities of parents and thereby highlight the dependency of children upon their parents and the nature of the dependency of parents and their child upon healthcare professionals. Consideration is first given to the response of the law to 'wrongful conception' cases in which damages are sought for the cost of raising a child who would not have been born but for negligence of the healthcare professional in the provision of sterilisation treatment or advice. The legal principles, which are equally applicable to wrongful birth claims where the pregnancy would not have been continued but for the negligence alleged,[1] determine the obligations of the professional but do not require the *needs* of the child or their family to be considered. Children have to be cared for and, as we know, the primary responsibility for doing so rests with their parents, a responsibility principally undertaken by their mothers.

By way of a case study, the care of children with cerebral palsy is considered through the lens of the case law in which it is alleged that the child's disabilities were caused by professional negligence during pregnancy or birth. These cases are rarely given academic attention as unexceptional examples of the application of the principles of breach and causation to determine professional obligations. The legal principles are applied to determine whether the loss lies where it falls (upon the child and his or her family) or whether breach of obligation requires monetary reparation. The unspoken stories of these cases, and the reason why they are extremely important, are devastating injuries to children at the time of their birth leaving them with complex needs and long-term dependency upon their parents to meet those needs. However, the abilities of parents to meet those needs are affected by factors beyond their control such as the support and resources available to them, environmental obstacles and discriminatory attitudes.

In a small number of cases, the harm caused to parents resulting from negligent care provided to their child has been recognised. The success of these relational claims amounts to limited recognition of the web of relationships between parent, child and professionals. More generally, it is argued, assumptions of individualism prevail. As a consequence, the connection between parents and their children is not recognised and the presumption of the vulnerability of children to their parents persists. Cases concerning allegations of negligence in the provision of information about treatment likewise centre upon determination of the obligations imposed upon professionals. Yet, the particular nature of the relationship, in which parents depend upon healthcare professionals to provide them with

---

[1] *Groom and Selby* [2001] EWCA Civ 1522, at para. 18 (Brooke LJ).

information and advice about their child's health, is not acknowledged. This is a relationship of dependency through which parents seek to fulfil their responsibilities to their child. Yet, within the law, the duties of health-care professional to provide information and advice are no different from those of the financial adviser who advises them with respect to their investments or the surveyor upon the basis of whose report they decide to purchase a house.

The overall purpose of this chapter is to highlight the caring needs of children, the caring relationship between parents and children and the dependency of parents upon healthcare professionals. Through examination of these discrete aspects of law, all of which apply the legal principles to determine the obligations of healthcare professionals, the argument builds through the following stages. Children need to be cared for. The primary responsibility falls upon parents who generally seek to do their best to meet their child's needs although their abilities to do so are affected by political, cultural and societal factors. Furthermore, in order to meet their child's needs, parents depend upon healthcare professionals for information, advice and support and to use their professional skills in taking care of the child. The law of obligations establishes the minimum owed by one individual to another. A conceptual framework of relational responsibilities would ensure, in the determination of these obligations, recognition of the responsibilities arising out of relationships and their inherent dependencies. As a consequence, the law would foster the relationship between parent and professional and support them to work together to meet the needs of the child.

Caring for children: the cost of wrongful conception/birth

The 'wrongful conception' cases reveal very starkly the limits of professional obligations, a consequence of which is that the responsibility for the care of children is placed firmly within the realm of the family. In these cases, actions are brought by parents alleging negligence in the provision of failed contraceptive advice or treatment followed by a pregnancy. These might be public-policy-driven decisions, with the odds stacked high against the parents. The spectre of adoption, or even abortion, is never far away. The joys of children, particularly as they would be understood by adults who have unsuccessfully tried to conceive, are measured against the sleep deprivation of the early years and the door-slamming responses of

teenagers. The costs claimed, of raising a child, are considered dispropor-
tionate to the careless performance of a minor, elective procedure. There is
an unarticulated sense that it is inappropriate for scarce NHS resources to
be filtered away from treatment to pay for private education and skiing
holidays. Alternatively, these cases could be understood as determined by
the application of legal principle: the three-stage test, assumptions of
responsibility and distributive, rather than corrective, justice.[2] Either way
there is a failure to explore, within these cases, the full costs of caring for
children, whether healthy or not; that is, the needs of the family unexpect-
edly confronted with the burden of responsibility.

The starting point for the modern law is the House of Lords decision in
McFarlane v Tayside Health Board,[3] in which the majority held that damages
were recoverable for physical harm to the mother arising from the pain and
suffering of pregnancy, labour and confinement and any consequential
financial loss (medical expenses, clothes, equipment and loss of earnings if
incurred).[4] To the majority, the cost of raising the child was pure economic
loss (the father's claim was for such loss and 'it would be absurd to distinguish between the claims of the father and mother'[5]). As such, damages were
not recoverable for want of a duty of care: although a relationship of proxi-
mity existed, it was not just, fair and reasonable to impose a duty.[6] Parental
rights were noted in passing without appearing to assist in determination of
the issue of liability.[7] These included 'the right . . . to make decisions on
family planning' and 'the right to care for an initially unwanted child',
respected as aspects of parental 'rights of personal autonomy'.[8] As Nicky

---

[2] *McFarlane v Tayside Health Board* [1999] 3 WLR 1301, at pp. 977–8 (Lord Steyn).

[3] *Ibid.* Although there were a number of cases in the preceding years, this was the first occasion
upon which the question was considered by the House of Lords. The decision provides a comprehensive account of earlier cases, the way these claims are dealt with in other jurisdictions and
the principles ordinarily applicable in economic loss cases.

[4] On which point, Lord Millett dissented. He allowed a sum, in the region of £5,000, for loss of
freedom to limit the size of their family.   [5] *Supra.*, n. 2, Lord Steyn at p. 975.

[6] Followed in *AD v East Kent Community NHS Trust* [2002] EWCA Civ 1872. The child's mother
had become pregnant whilst detained on a mixed psychiatric ward under s. 3 of the Mental
Health Act 1983. The child, who was healthy, was being raised by her grandmother.

[7] In *Greenfield v Flather* [2001] EWCA Civ 113, loss of earnings incurred when the mother gave up
work to care for a healthy child, born after the injectable contraceptive was administered
without first confirming that she was not pregnant, were not recoverable. The Court of Appeal
also considered argument based upon Article 8 of the ECHR and held that it did not impose a
positive obligation upon the state to provide financial support to parents to enable one to stay at
home and thus did not impose an obligation upon the state to award damages to achieve this.

[8] *Supra.*, n. 2, Lord Steyn at p. 976.

Priaulx argues, these rights are invoked in a construction of the issue as one of parental choices in relation to reproductive autonomy rather than as one of needs.[9] As a tort case, their Lordships also recognised the obligations at issue – those of the defendant to 'make reparation' for any breach of duty and those of parents to maintain their child[10] – in a case about responsibility, dependency and needs.

Mr and Mrs McFarlane had decided that their family, of four children, was complete. They had moved to a larger house and Mrs McFarlane had returned to work to enable them to pay the mortgage. Mr McFarlane underwent a vasectomy and, six months later, was negligently advised by the consultant that his sperm count was nil. Mrs McFarlane subsequently became pregnant and gave birth to a daughter, their fifth child. Their Lordships approached the harm of 'wrongful conception' (beyond the physical effects of pregnancy) as pure economic loss and thus beyond recovery. It was possible to reach this conclusion given an abstract appreciation of the impact upon the family of a further, a fifth, healthy and cherished child and a conceptualisation of the responsibilities of parenthood as purely financial. The consequences of the birth of a further child upon all the family – mother, father and existing children – were not acknowledged. In her analysis of the judgment, Nicky Priaulx argues that the House of Lords in *McFarlane* failed to appreciate that the birth of a planned-against child results in a loss of reproductive autonomy and alters the couple's life plans as they take on the 'inescapable parenting obligations, including financial, social and psychological implications'.[11] The birth of a further child has practical, as well as material, consequences for the whole family. Joanne Conaghan suggests that beyond the bodily invasion of pregnancy, the court should have recognised the 'disruption of relations already formed and the involuntariness of the relations that result'.[12] The supposition that 'fellow travellers on the London Underground'[13] would be of the view that the cost of bringing up a healthy and loved, if planned-against,

---

[9] Nicky Priaulx, 'That's One Heck of an "Unruly Horse"! Riding Roughshod over Autonomy in Wrongful Conception' (2004) 12 *Feminist Legal Studies* 317–31, at p. 330.

[10] *Supra.*, n. 2, Lord Clyde at p. 995.

[11] Nicky Priaulx, 'Joy to the World! A (Healthy) Child is Born! Reconceptualizing "Harm" in Wrongful Conception' (2004) 13 *Social and Legal Studies* 5–26, at p. 7.

[12] Joanne Conaghan, 'Tort Law and Feminist Critique' (2003) 56 *Current Legal Problems*, M. D. A. Freeman (ed.), Oxford University Press: Oxford, 2003, at p. 193. In this article, Joanne Conaghan criticises the analysis of Christian Wittig in 'Physical Damage in Negligence' (2002) 61 CLJ 189, who argues that there was a socially constructed harm.

[13] *Supra.*, n. 2, Lord Steyn at p. 977.

child was the responsibility of the (individual) family and not of the profes-sional (collective) was a moral judgment reached through abstract analysis.

Lord Steyn, in *McFarlane*, noted counsel's concession that the conclu-sion might be different if the child was born with serious disabilities. This issue was inevitably soon considered by the courts in the case of *Parkinson v St James and Seacroft University Hospital NHS Trust*.[14] Mrs Parkinson underwent a sterilisation operation, which was negligently performed, after which she fell pregnant with her fifth child. She was advised during pregnancy that the child might be born with disabilities and she gave birth to a son who had behavioural problems. Commencing her judgment with reference to the right to bodily integrity incorporating both the positive right to physical autonomy and the negative right to protection from inva-sion infringed by a planned-against pregnancy, Hale LJ in the Court of Appeal did appreciate that the responsibilities of parenthood went beyond the financial. Her Ladyship gave a full account of the physical and psycho-logical changes and autonomy-limiting consequences of pregnancy and recognised that: 'Parental responsibility is not simply or even primarily a financial responsibility. The primary responsibility is to care for the child. The labour does not stop when the child is born.'[15] In addition to financial responsibility for the child is '[t]he obligation to provide or make accept-able and safe arrangements for the child's care and supervision . . . 24 hours a day, 7 days a week, all year round, until the child becomes old enough to take care of himself'.[16] Hale LJ recognised that the costs of raising a child are merely one aspect of the responsibility of caring for the child.[17]

The Court of Appeal held that damages were recoverable for the cost of providing for the child's special needs and care attributable to his disabili-ties but, in the shadow of *McFarlane*, not for the ordinary costs of upbring-ing. Hale LJ considered that a duty of care was owed to the claimant, the question was whether the damage was too remote: this was to be deter-mined by the principle of 'deemed equilibrium', a process that involved balancing the benefits and burdens.[18] Her Ladyship expressed the opinion that a disabled child brings the same pleasure and advantages as a non-disabled child but that a disabled child needs extra care, incurring addi-tional costs which were recoverable: 'The difference between a normal and

[14] *Parkinson v St James and Seacroft University Hospital NHS Trust* [2001] EWCA Civ 530.
[15] *Ibid.*, at para. 70.   [16] *Ibid.*, at para. 71.   [17] *Ibid.*, at para. 72.
[18] Subsequently, in *Rees* (below), Lords Steyn and Millett held that this was not the interpretation to be given to the earlier case of *McFarlane*.

a disabled child is primarily in the extra care that they need, although this may bring with it extra expenditure.'[19]

The same conclusion was reached in the wrongful birth cases of *Rand and another v East Dorset HA*,[20] *Gaynor and another v Warrington HA and another*,[21] *Lee v Taunton and Somerset NHS Trust*,[22] *Groom and Selby*[23] and *Hardman v Amin*.[24] In *Gaynor*, Hale LJ noted that the responsibilities of parents to children, particularly children with disabilities, do not end with the child's eighteenth birthday. Alluding back to *McFarlane*, Henriques J in *Hardman v Amin* expressed the opinion that:

> If the commuters on the underground were asked whether the costs of bringing up Daniel (which are attributable to his disability) should fall on the claimant or the rest of the family, or the state, or the defendant, I am satisfied that the very substantial majority, having regard to the particular circumstances of this case, would say that the expense should fall on the wrongdoer.

To award compensation for the additional cost of caring for the child incurred in meeting the need arising from his severe disabilities would 'permit the Hardmans, as a family unit independent of the state, to meet Daniel's needs'.

In a further variation, a seven-strong panel of Law Lords considered a claim for damages brought in respect of the birth of a healthy child to a mother with severe visual impairment after the failure of a sterilisation which she had undergone in the belief that her impairment rendered her unfit for parenthood. [25] The minority followed the approach of the Court of Appeal in *Parkinson*, understanding *McFarlane* to be an exception to the compensatory principle. The additional costs of raising the child incurred as a consequence of the mother's impairment were recoverable, enabling, Lord Hope said, 'a parent who has special needs to provide her child with as normal a life as possible'.[26] The majority of four, Lords Bingham, Nicholls, Millett and Scott, followed the approach adopted by Lord Millett in

---

[19] *Supra.*, n. 14, para. 94. Brooke LJ reached the same conclusion by employing a 'battery of tests': para. 50.

[20] *Rand and another v East Dorset HA* [2000] Lloyd's Rep Med 181 QBD (web.lexis-nexis.com/professional/).

[21] *Gaynor and another v Warrington HA and another*, 9 March 2000 (web.lexis-nexis.com/professional/).   [22] *Lee v Taunton and Somerset NHS Trust* [2001] 1 FLR 419.

[23] *Groom and Selby* [2001] EWCA Civ 1522.

[24] *Hardman v Amin* 59 BMLR 58 (web.lexis-nexis.com/professional/).

[25] *Rees v Darlington Memorial Hospital NHS Trust* [2003] UKHL 52.   [26] *Ibid.*, at para. 62.

McFarlane in their understanding of the harm suffered by Ms Rees for which a conventional award, suggested as £15,000, was recoverable. According to Lord Bingham, this was the lost 'opportunity to live her life in the way that she wished and planned'[27] whilst Lord Millett expressed her loss in terms of 'the right to limit the size of their family'.[28] Whilst this approach may cautiously be welcomed for demonstrating a willingness to acknowledge different types of harm within law, it would appear to have been arrived at with little appreciation of the reality of the harm or loss incurred. The claim was understood as one of a loss of choice and not one of caring responsibilities incurred.

Only Hale LJ in *Parkinson* directly acknowledged that the consequences of a planned-against pregnancy are greater for mothers than for fathers not only because they carry the child but because the greater burden of the responsibility of caring usually falls upon mothers. Someone has to care for the child. The facts of the cases themselves reveal that it is the child's mother who is primarily responsible for meeting the needs of the child and that this responsibility goes beyond the financial. In *Parkinson*, the family of six were living in a two-bedroomed house. Mrs Parkinson intended to return to work, enabling the family to move to a larger house. Three months before the birth of the child, Mr Parkinson left the family home as 'the pregnancy [had] placed an intolerable strain on the marriage',[29] leaving the burden of caring for the child, and the management of his needs alongside those of her other children, with his mother (whilst Mr Parkinson retained both the status as father and parental responsibility in law for his child). This was likewise the case in the wrongful birth case of *Lee v Taunton*[30] in which Toulson J further observed that the child's mother received 'minimal professional service support' in meeting the complex needs of her son (his father had left the family home earlier in the year).

In *Rees*, it was noted that the additional costs of raising Anthony due to his mother's visual impairment were unknown (the matter being before the court as a preliminary issue). Without examining this, the court was left to imagine the impact of the birth of a child after a failed sterilisation and appeared to assume that the consequences upon the family of a planned

---

[27] *Ibid.*, at para. 8.
[28] *Ibid.*, at para. 123, 'an important aspect of human dignity, which is increasingly being regarded as an important human right which should be protected by law'.
[29] *Supra.*, n. 14, at para. 6.   [30] *Supra*, n. 22.

against pregnancy were minimal. For example, Lord Steyn in *Rees* speculated as to the impact upon the health of the mother of a fifth child in comparison with the consequences of the birth of a child following a failed sterilisation upon a mother with impairments:

> If one were to add that the lady with four children was poor, but the lady with a disability was rich – what then? It would simply emphasise the perception that the rule was not operating fairly. One can add to the example by making comparisons between possible family circumstances of the different mothers. Assume the mother with four children had no support from husband, mother or siblings, and then compare her with the person who is disabled, but who has a husband, siblings and a mother all willing to help. I think ordinary people would feel uncomfortable about the thought that it was simply the disability which made a difference.[31]

In the cases where damages are sought for the cost of raising a plannedagainst child born following negligence in the performance of a sterilisation operation, in the provision of information with regard to the sterility of the couple or pre-natal testing, liabilities have been determined according to imagined consequences, with a preference for individual parental obligation over professional obligation. The traveller journeying with judges on the London Underground may be more convinced of the responsibility to families caring for a planned-against child or a child born with negligently undetected disabilities if there is a full examination of their needs. Abstract determinations of competing obligations have to be replaced with consideration of the needs of the individual child, with reference to caring practices and in the context of social norms of family life.

Making amends, taking responsibility and caring for children with disabilities

Making amends

An example of the benefits of financial reparation, and the limits of the law of negligence, is provided by the response of the law to children born with cerebral palsy. Affecting over 1,300 children born each year,[32] cerebral palsy

---

[31] *Supra.*, n. 25, at para. 54.
[32] *Making Amends: A Consultation Paper setting out Proposals for Reforming the Approach to Clinical Negligence in the NHS*, a report by the Chief Medical Officer, Department of Health, June 2003, ch. 2, para. 51.

is the result of failure of a part of the brain to develop either before birth or in early childhood. This may be a consequence of an inherited disorder, infection during pregnancy, a blocked blood vessel, complications during labour,[33] extreme prematurity, illness just after birth or an infection such as meningitis.[34] The term 'cerebral palsy' describes the physical disabilities which result from damage to the brain.[35] The disabilities, which range from mild to severe, are classified according to the movement disorders – spastic (muscles are stiff and weak which can affect control of movements); athetoid (loss of control over posture which can result in unwanted movements); ataxic (which can affect balance) – and according to the limbs affected – quadriplegia (all four limbs), diplegia (legs more than arms), hemiplegia (one side of the body).[36] Cerebral palsy may be confined to physical disabilities or the child may also suffer with learning difficulties, epilepsy, and sensory or behavioural impairments.[37]

Cerebral palsy can be very mild such that the child is able to live a normal life with their condition. At the other end of the range, it can be very severe with a profound impact upon the child and their family. Children with disabilities are inevitably dependent upon others to meet their needs if they are to survive and to thrive. The hope, the expectation, is that the parents of a child born with disabilities will care for him or her.[38] As expressed by Roger Gottlieb, a philosopher and father of a daughter with developmental delay and physical problems: 'The much more extreme dependence of those with disabilities goes on forever, cannot be commodified to anything like the extent to that of normal children, and is much more extreme in any case.'[39] In a society which provides limited support and services, parents

---

[33] As with the disabilities of David Glass whose treatment is considered in chapter 5. Although antenatal monitoring had revealed some brain damage, his condition was complicated by an episode of oxygen deprivation at and after his birth, arising from negligence in respect of which compensatory damages were paid by the Health Authority: *R v Portsmouth Hospitals NHS Trust, ex parte Glass* 50 BMLR 269.   [34] See www.scope.org.uk.

[35] *Supra.*, n. 32, ch. 2, para. 39.   [36] See www.scope.org.uk.

[37] *Supra.*, n. 32, ch. 2 para. 42.

[38] According to the Department of Health, there are approximately 700,000 disabled children in Great Britain, the majority of whom live at home: Department of Health, *National Service Framework for Children, Young People and Maternity Services*, Standard 8, October 2004, para. 2.1, referencing Department for Work and Pensions, *Family Resources Survey* 2002–3, 2004. The NSF uses the term 'disabled' to include children with learning disabilities, autistic spectrum disorders, sensory impairments, physical impairments and emotional/behavioural disorders (para. 1.5).

[39] Roger S. Gottlieb, 'The Tasks of Embodied Love: Moral Problems in Caring for Children with Disabilities' (2002) 17 *Hypatia* 225–36, at p. 227.

may resort to negligence litigation in a search for the means of securing assistance in caring for their child and providing them with the best possible quality of life.

According to the Chief Medical Officer's Report, *Making Amends*, between 1998 and 2001 the National Health Service Litigation Authority (NHSLA) received 400-500 claims annually relating to cerebral palsy, that is, where it is alleged that cerebral palsy was caused by oxygen deprivation due to negligence in the care provided during or related to birth.[40] Damages were awarded in around a third of the cases which had been considered by NHSLA by September 2002 (between 135 and 180 a year). Fewer than 4 per cent went to trial (about ten a year).[41] *Making Amends* reports that in 2002/03, 5 per cent of successful medical negligence cases were due to birth-related brain damage but that these cases accounted for 60 per cent of the costs.[42]

These cases are merely examples of the application of the principles of negligence which serve to illuminate the assumptions and values underpinning legal obligations in the context of healthcare. The relationship between the parties – healthcare professional and child suffering injuries during delivery – means that there is no doubt that a duty of care is owed. Hence, the focus is upon the facts and questions of breach of duty and causation and, where liability is established, assessing the compensation to be paid. Despite the fact that in many of these cases it is accepted that the child was without disability shortly before birth, the application of the principles of breach of duty of care[43] or difficulties in establishing causation[44] may lead to the conclusion that there is no liability. Irrespective of the context in which the harm occurred or the needs of the victim, if the facts support the conclusion that the defendant took reasonable care, the loss lies where it falls – upon the child with the disabilities and his or her parents with the task of meeting the needs of their child. If the act or omission

---

[40] *Supra.*, n. 32, ch. 2, para. 51. The incidence of cerebral palsy considered to be due to oxygen deprivation at birth is estimated to be between 3 per cent and 20 per cent: ch. 2, para. 47.

[41] *Ibid.*, ch. 2, para. 52.   [42] *Ibid.*, ch. 2, para. 43.

[43] *DA v North East London Stategic Health Authority* [2005] EWHC 950 (QB); *French v Thames Valley Strategic Health Authority* [2005] EWHC 459 (QB); *Sheldon-Green v Coventry HA* [2004] All ER (D) 288; *Morris v Blackpool Victoria Hospital NHS Trust* [2004] EWCA Civ 1294; *Smithers v Taunton and Somerset NHS Trust* [2004] EWHC 1179; *Martin v Norfolk and Norwich Healthcare NHS Trust*, 25 January 2001 (web.lexis-nexis.com/professional/); *Julien and another v East London and City Health Authority*, 10 November 2000 (web.lexis-nexis.com/professional/).

[44] *Smith v West Yorkshire HA*, 27 May 2004 (web.lexis-nexis.com/professional/).

demonstrated a want of reasonable care,[45] financial reparation is paid, according to established heads of liability.[46] Clearly, a damages award will make a difference to the ability of parents to care for their child, given the limits of social services and support for meeting their needs. As Silber J acknowledged in *Smith v West Yorkshire HA*, having concluded that neither breach nor causation had been established against the defendants in respect of oxygen deprivation causing Thomas, at time of the litigation aged thirteen, to be born with quadriplegic cerebral palsy:

> Anybody who heard the evidence in this case could not fail to be greatly saddened by the devastating injuries sustained by Thomas. His grandmother, Mrs Squires, with her husband have devoted themselves to bringing him up. Undoubtedly, Thomas' life would be greatly assisted by the fruits of success in the present litigation. My task, however, is to apply legal principles, which lead to my conclusion that Thomas is unable to show that the medical staff at the hospital were negligent or that even if they were negligent, that this negligence caused his devastating injuries. [47]

Leslie Bender has argued that because of the values upon which the tort system is based, legal responsibility is understood as monetary obligation, reparation or making amends.[48] An understanding of responsibility as the provision of money results in a failure to explore fully the nature of taking responsibility which, she suggests, in the context of the family involves taking care:

> People responsible for the care of children understand that responsibility to and for those children involves a great deal more than money. Money might buy some of the things children need, but it cannot figure out what they need at any given time or in any given context or plan how to provide for those needs. Money doesn't listen to children,

---

[45] *Kingsberry v Greater Manchester Strategic Health Authority* [2005] EWHC 2253 (QB); *Holsgrove v South West London Strategic Health Authority* [2004] EWHC 501 (QB); *Macey v Warwickshire HA* [2004] EWHC 1198 (QB); *Nyarko (a Minor by Her Mother and Litigation Friend Owusu) v Newham Primary Care Trust* [2003] EWHC 1687; *Simms v Birmingham Health Authority* 58 BMLR 66 (web.lexis-nexis.com/professional/); *Milkhu v North West Hospitals NHS Trust* [2003] EWHC 94 (QB); *Reynolds v North Tyneside Health Authority*, 20 May 2002 (web.lexis-nexis.com/professional/).

[46] *Gentleman v North Essex Health Authority*, 27 June 2001 (web.lexis-nexis.com/professional/); *Page v Plymouth Hospitals NHS Trust* [2004] EWHC 1154.

[47] *Smith v West Yorkshire HA*, 27 May 2004, at para. 236 (web.lexis-nexis.com/professional/).

[48] Leslie Bender, 'Frontier of Legal Thought III: Feminist (Re)Torts: Thoughts on the Liability Crisis, Mass Torts, Power and Responsibilities' (1990) *Duke Law Journal* 848–912, at p. 876.

soothe their fears, show them affection, teach them values, or socialize them. People must take interpersonal responsibility for these activities – the planning, organization, and forethought, the time and emotional sharing, and attention to needs and contexts.[49]

Children with severe disabilities need to be cared for.

Caring for children with disabilities

In denying liability, and thus in judgments which inevitably focus upon the child's birth as the event in relation to which negligence is alleged, the judiciary frequently applaud the wonderful care provided to these children by their parents and families. In *Smithers v Taunton and Somerset NHS Trust*, Cox J commented that:

> As a result of his disabilities Lewis requires, and will for the rest of his life continue to require, help with every aspect of his daily living. He is therefore totally dependent upon his parents for all activities. The fact that Lewis has continued to maintain a good standard of health and to avoid infections or other complications, despite these severe disabilities, is mainly due to the devoted care and attention provided by his family, who deserve in consequence the highest praise.[50]

Concluding that there had been no breach of duty and thus there was no liability in respect of the damage sustained at birth by seventeen-year-old Christopher who had 'cerebral palsy with three-limbed spasticity, spastic quadriplegia, acquired microcephaly, learning difficulties and epilepsy', Rix LJ remarked:

> Finally, as Silber J did at the close of his judgment, I would express my own sense of sorrow for Christopher and his parents at the outcome, for all that the facts of the case and legal principle have mandated my conclusion. Not every tragic case of injury arises out of negligence. The judge said that he had read with admiration the statements of Christopher's parents which demonstrated the very impressive way in which they and their other children have helped Christopher; and I can join in those sentiments.[51]

---

[49] *Ibid.*, at pp. 900–1.
[50] *Smithers v Taunton and Somerset NHS Trust* [2004] EWHC 1179, at paras. 2 and 55.
[51] *Morris v Blackpool Victoria Hospital NHS Trust* [2004] EWCA Civ 1294, at para. 90.

As noted above, the hope, the expectation, is that children with severe disabilities will be cared for by their parents with the assistance of community services. Studies of parents of children with disabilities, although not confined to children with cerebral palsy, provide insights into practices of caring. Their accounts of the care provided are consistent with, whilst going far beyond, the accounts relayed in the judgments of the courts (often without comment). In practice, the functionally diffuse work of caring,[52] twenty-four hours a day seven days a week, primarily falls upon mothers.[53] Mothers, more than fathers, undertake the tasks of everyday care: the practical aspects of personal care, the emotional support of their children and the management of the family. Their role is described by Janet Read and Luke Clements as that of 'jugglers and mediators who balance out the interests of different individuals within the household' and between their family and service providers.[54] A greater proportion of families with disabled children than families generally are single-parent families, which both has implications for the financial well-being of the family and results in a lack of support, as mothers in two-parent families identified their partner as the greatest source of support.[55] Fathers who continue to work report having to take time off or refuse overtime with consequences for career progression (and hence family income) and other children within the family often provide some care for their disabled sibling or help their parent.[56] The increased costs of caring for a disabled child, coupled with limitations upon the abilities of parents to earn, places families in financial hardship, limiting the quality of life of families. Families with disabled children are less likely to own items such as a washing machine, freezer, refrigerator, central heating, telephone or car than the population generally – items which all contribute to the standard of life of the family and to an easing of the burden of the work involved in caring.[57] Their child's behavioural, social or communication difficulties may make trips out which are required (e.g. to the shops) or which families without disabled children take for granted (e.g. to the park) difficult, even if other obstacles, 'transport problems, an inaccessible built environment, a restricted budget, the need to transport equipment and parental fatigue' can be overcome.[58]

---

[52] Eva Feder Kittay, *Love's Labor: Essays on Women, Equality and Dependency,* Routledge: New York, 1999, at p. 39.

[53] Janet Read and Luke Clements, *Disabled Children and the Law,* Jessica Kingsley: London, 2002, at p. 29.   [54] *Ibid.,* at pp. 29–30.   [55] *Ibid.,* at p. 30.   [56] *Ibid.,* at p. 31.

[57] *Ibid.,* at pp. 34–5.   [58] *Ibid.,* at p. 32.

Parents have also reported the stress caused by having to 'negotiate and fight' for the services which their children require: 'Provision which parents regard as suited to their own and their children's needs is often simply not available or is provided inconsistently.'[59] The services available have been criticised by parents for appearing to be designed to meet the interests of providers and not the needs of users.[60]

In addition to acute health services, the health needs of children with severe disabilities will entail the use of primary care services and may involve physiotherapy, speech and language therapy, community nursing services, rehabilitation and respite care. However, care for the health and well-being of their child may mean mothers continuing to provide personal care (bathing, washing, feeding, toileting, moving), meeting dietary requirements, administering medication, physiotherapy, assisting with communication, supervising and stimulating their child – day and night.[61] In assessing the damages payable to Edward Parry, Penry-Davey J noted the additional care provided to him by his mother as a consequence of his disability so that as well as being his mother full-time, she had become 'in effect a specialist carer, a carer trainer, a physiotherapist and a speech and language trainer', effectively a full-time job 'to which she has devoted herself with love, care and skill'.[62]

Determination of the obligations owed to children with severe disabilities through a framework which considers responsibilities to them would centre attention upon their needs. Given that the primary responsibility for caring rests with parents, it is necessary to examine their experiences in order to determine what is needed to provide their child with an acceptable quality of life. Whilst the specific needs of children and families will differ in terms of assistance and services required, we can gain a better understanding of the experiences of children and their families through personal accounts[63] and through studies of families caring for children with severe disabilities.[64] Three themes emerge: the need to recognise the child as an

[59] *Ibid.*, at p. 35.
[60] A point made about children's services generally in chapter 2. The standards for children with severe disabilities and complex needs set out in the *National Service Framework for Children, Young People and Maternity Services* are also noted in chapter 2 where it is suggested that attainment of the standards could amount to a noticeable improvement in the quality of life of children and their families.   [61] *Supra*, n. 53, at pp. 31–2.
[62] *Parry v North West Surrey HA*, 29 November 1999 (web.lexis-nexis.com/professional/), at p. 7.
[63] Julia Hollander, 'Why is there no one to help us?' *Guardian*, 28 May 2003.
[64] Barbara Dobson, Sue Middleton and Alan Beardsworth, *The Impact of Childhood Disability on Family Life*, Joseph Rowntree Foundation: York, 2001; *No Ordinary Life*, Mencap: London, 2001;

individual person, the relationship of responsibility of parent for child and the dependency of parents upon professionals.

The child as a person

Parents with responsibility for the daily care of a child with severe disabilities in the study carried out by Barbara Dobson, Sue Middleton and Alan Beardsworth[65] revealed that although they appreciated their child as an individual, others, including professionals, did not appear to be able to see beyond their child's disability. Many parents felt that the presence of their disabled child meant that they were no longer treated as a normal family. People stared when they went out but appeared not to see a mother and child but only the child's disability. They explained how professionals prodded and poked at their child, made assessments of them and asked intimate questions about them, but appeared to fail to see beyond the child's condition to a child who was valued, by people who cared about him or her, as an individual.[66] As Julia Hollander said of her daughter: 'And innocent little Immie . . . She wasn't allowed to be herself; she was a clinical phenomenon with all the generalising, sentimental terms to describe it.'[67] In the case law, the inabilities of the child are fully described. For example, Cox J described the inabilities of four-year-old Lewis, who had 'dystonic athetoid quadriplegic cerebral palsy with microcephaly, severe learning difficulties and cortical visual impairment':[68]

> He is, as a result, profoundly disabled. He is unable to sit unaided, to stand or to make any useful, functional movement. When lying supine he is unable to roll over. Although he is fed by mouth he can neither chew nor swallow well. With great care and skill his mother has managed to feed him without aspiration pneumonia developing and he has had few chest infections. He is registered as blind, although he can recognise light and dark, and he has normal hearing. He also suffers from epilepsy, which is controlled by medication, and he takes additional medication to help with involuntary muscle spasms. He is unable to reach out and grasp toys and he shows no interest in things placed in his hand. He is quite unable to communicate or to express his

Brian Lamb and Sarah Layzell, *Disabled in Britain: Behind Closed Doors, The Carers' Experience*, Scope: London, 1995; Bryony Beresford, *Expert Opinions: A National Survey of Parents Caring for a Severely Disabled Child*, Policy Press: Bristol, 1995; Bryony Beresford, *Positively Parents: Caring for a Severely Disabled Child*, Social Policy Research Unit, HMSO: London, 1994.

[65] Dobson, et al. *ibid.*   [66] *Ibid.*, at pp. 28–9.   [67] *Supra.*, n. 63.

[68] *Smithers v Taunton and Somerset NHS Trust* [2004] EWHC 1179, at para. 1.

needs. At present Lewis is cared for at home by his parents, whose first
child, Ellen, is a normal and healthy daughter, now aged six. As a result
of his disabilities Lewis requires, and will for the rest of his life continue
to require, help with every aspect of his daily living. He is therefore
totally dependent upon his parents for all activities.[69]

This may be a consequence of an examination of the disabilities for which
compensation is sought. However, in such a description, the child is lost
behind his disabilities.

For whom they are responsible

Barbara Dobson et al. noted how many of the parents in their study felt
'overwhelmed by the responsibility'[70] and alone in their endeavour of
caring for their child. Whilst parents made no distinction between being a
parent and the care they provided, they felt that professionals treated them
as carers, ignoring the emotional bond between parent and child. Julia
Hollander expressed how she felt after she was told of the diagnosis in relation to her daughter: 'Having entered the clinic as a parent, I came out a
"carer". The intimacy of motherhood, the joy of that responsibility, had
been removed. It seemed I now had to provide a care based on duty, not
love.'[71] Yet, the expertise which parents gained through the care they provided for their child was not recognised:

> Parents resented this cavalier attitude and were angry and frustrated at
> how professionals ignored their knowledge and the fact that they pro-
> vided the bulk of the day-to-day care for their child when it suited
> them, but would not afford them the same rights as a carer.[72]

The practices and experiences of parents caring for children with severe
disabilities must inform understanding of the needs of those taking
responsibility for caring. In his assessment of the heads of liability under
which damages were to be awarded to Alexander Stephens, Buxton J
demonstrated understanding of the purpose of care assistance. This was to
take the burden of the physical work of attending to Alexander from his
parents:

> He is entitled to have parents who are not exhausted simply by the
> physical effort of looking after him. He is entitled to have intercourse
> with his parents and his family which bears some resemblance to the

---

[69] *Ibid.*, at para. 2.   [70] *Dobson* et al., *supra*, n. 64, at p. 31.   [71] *Supra*, n. 63.
[72] Dobson et al., *supra*, n. 64, at p. 30.

relations that an unhandicapped child would have with his family, rather than his main or only connection with them being when they are assisting his purely physical functions.[73]

In assessing what was required to enable Alexander and his parents to live as normal a life as possible, Buxton J appreciated that Alexander was a child whose needs meant that care assistance was required to enable his parents to care for him as parents:

> The care and attention that Alexander requires is care and attention to enable him to live some resemblance of a normal life and for instance to enable him to perform functions performed unaided by any normal 7-year-old, like communication with the outside world or going to the lavatory. When a parent gives attention to a normal child of that age he or she does not do so in order to enable that child to communicate, but rather simply to engage in communication with the child. Similarly, the attention paid to a normal child does not extend to helping them to perform every bodily function. What Alexander's parents look for, and what Alexander needs from them, is something like the attention that a normal child can expect from his parents.[74]

Parental dependency upon professionals

The study carried out by Barbara Dobson et al. of 273 parents with responsibility for daily care of a child with severe disabilities revealed that, due to the additional costs of caring for a child with a severe disability, they were financially unable to provide their children with a reasonable quality of life.[75] It was not just money that was short – so too was practical and emotional support. Parents expressed dissatisfaction with services which were organised with little consideration of the needs of their child or which provided an inadequate level of care.[76] Furthermore, parents had to re-assess their 'life plans and aspirations', such as career ambitions, holiday or retirement plans: '[a] few parents were angry because it was not their child's condition per se that brought about these changes but rather the lack of appropriate practical help'.[77] In other words, it was not their child's disability which was experienced as the problem, rather it was the lack of support

---

[73] *Stephens v Doncaster HA*, 16 June 1995 (web.lexis-nexis.com/professional/), Buxton J at p. .9.
[74] *Ibid.*, at p. 13.   [75] Dobson et al., *Supra*, n. 64, at p. 24.
[76] The anxiety caused to the parents of six-year-old Joshua Neale by the inadequacy of the arrangements for night-time care was acknowledged in *Neale v Queen Mary's Sidcup NHS Trust* [2003] EWHC 1471 (QB).   [77] Dobson et al., *supra*, n. 64, at p. 32.

available to them. And, as recognised in the *National Service Framework for Children, Young People and Maternity Services*, reflecting the findings of the study by Barbara Dobson et al., societal discrimination and material obstacles within the environment affected the ability of parents to provide a normal life for their child:[78]

> It is not only disabled children's impairments that determine their quality of life, but also poverty, negative attitudes and a disabling environment, for example, unequal access to education, healthcare, leisure activities, transport and housing.[79]

Bryony Beresford's study of twenty parents caring for a severely disabled child makes the powerful yet simple point that the reason parents continue to care for their child is because they love them. Consequently, the focus of support provided to children with severe disabilities and their families should be upon sustaining the quality of the parent–child relationship.[80]

Taking responsibility

In *Making Amends* the Chief Medical Officer recommended putting tort law at the margins of response to medical injuries with the introduction of an NHS Redress Scheme. Recognising that those injured may want other outcomes beyond compensation in monetary terms, the recommendations sought to meet the *needs* of NHS patients by responding with what those injured by medical care want.[81] This may include an investigation, the provision of an explanation as to what went wrong and the steps taken to ensure that it will not occur in the future, and the development and delivery of a care package. Compensation should be paid if there were 'serious

---

[78] *Ibid.,* at p. 35.

[79] Department of Health, *National Service Framework for Children, Young People and Maternity Services,* Standard 8, October 2004, at para. 2.3.

[80] Bryony Beresford suggests that these should include: child-focused support (with sleeping, behaviour, eating, treatment and therapy); parent-focused support (through respite care, schooling and child-minding); financial and practical support (for example, housework); opportunities such as for access to employment; and emotional support: Beresford, *Positively Parents, supra,* n. 64, at p. 113.

[81] *Supra.,* n. 32, at p. 119 (initially for hospital and community healthcare); in the understanding that claimants are seeking 'a thorough investigation leading to explanations, apologies and assurances that action has been taken by the health service to prevent repetition. They also want the means to rectify the harm, either through further treatment or care or financial recompense': ch. 4, para. 17.

shortcomings in care', harm could not have been avoided and the outcome is not the result of progression of illness.[82]

Making Amends took a broader view, than does common law tort, of obligations to children with severe neurological disabilities and their families. It notes the context of harm caused by doctors – that the NHS is a caring organisation where patients (pregnant woman and their newborn babies) expect to be taken care of. If, instead, harm is caused, the responsibility of the organisation is to care. Fault is no longer the central issue, taking responsibility is.

> [F]or those injured by NHS treatment it can be argued that the NHS itself should be under an obligation to put right the damage caused. Although money is now the traditional response, a comprehensive care package (i.e. 'non-financial compensation'), promptly provided and efficiently delivered, is an obvious alternative. The NHS would often need to put together such a package of care from a variety of private sources. However, the obligation to organise *high quality care*, rather than simply pay the money, could lead to a *better understanding of*, and a *sense of responsibility for*, the long-term effects of a medical injury on patients. This in turn could provide an incentive to initiating measures to prevent recurrences of the problem.[83]

The proposals specifically extended the NHS Redress Scheme to include severely neurologically impaired babies, including those with cerebral palsy. The proposed criteria were that the child must have been born in NHS care, have a severe neurological impairment related to, or resulting from, birth and the claim is made within eight years of birth.[84] The severity and cause of the child's condition would be reviewed by a panel of experts and a package of care provided depending upon the child's 'ability to perform the activities of daily living'. This could include a managed care package, monthly payments to cover the costs of additional care not provided through the package, periodic lump sum payments to cover the cost of adaptations to the home and for equipment as required, and compensation for pain, suffering and loss of amenity up to £50,000.[85]

In its current form, the NHS Redress Bill will not extend to children with severe neurological injuries. The Bill provides for the Secretary of State to issue regulations establishing a redress scheme covering personal injury or

---

[82] *Ibid.*, at p. 120 – recommending a pilot based upon the *Bolam* standard of care but with consideration given to a test, and consequences, with a lower threshold.

[83] *Ibid.*, ch. 4, para. 33, emphasis added.   [84] *Ibid.*, at p. 121.   [85] *Ibid.*, at p. 121.

death resulting from a breach of duty in relation to diagnosis or care and treatment provided by a healthcare professional in the delivery of hospital services.[86] The Bill requires regulations to make provision for financial compensation and explanations as to what went wrong and to permit redress in the form of a contract for remedial care.[87] Within the scheme there may be an upper limit set for financial compensation but, if there is no such upper limit, one must be set for compensation for pain and suffering.[88] The procedure for initiating proceedings, investigation and decisions about claims, and the form and content of settlements will be set out in regulations. Where an agreement is reached, there must be a waiver of the right to bring court proceedings in respect of the breach of duty.[89] The Bill seeks to provide for all aspects of the remedies sought by patients harmed in the delivery of NHS care, by making provision for an explanation and ensuring that lessons are learnt from mistakes and action taken in response, but it is envisaged that it will apply only to claims with a low monetary value, with an upper limit of £20,000.[90] Children born with severe neurological injuries as a consequence of oxygen deprivation at birth will therefore be beyond the scope of the scheme.

Statistics given in *Making Amends* reveal that only in the region of 135–80 families of children with cerebral palsy receive damages through the NHSLA each year, yet over 1,300 children are born each year with cerebral palsy. Whether the healthcare professional was in breach of their duty and caused the harm or not, the needs of the child and the responsibilities of their parents to meet those needs are the same. Recognising children with severe neurological disabilities as individuals, the responsibility taken by their parents and their dependency upon professionals and services as they care does not have enormous cost implications. But it could make a real difference to the lives of children and their families as society grapples with the further question of the responsibility of society to take care of all children with severe neurological disabilities and their families.[91] The

---

[86] NHS Redress Bill 2004, cl. 1.   [87] *Ibid.* cl. 3.   [88] *Ibid.* cl. 3(5).   [89] *Ibid.* cl. 6(3).

[90] Department of Health, *NHS Redress: Statement of Policy*, 2005, at para. 36.

[91] Plans to introduce an NHS Redress Scheme for severely neurologically impaired babies have been dropped. Rather, the intention is to develop better public services for disabled children and their families, initially through the standards set in the *National Service Framework for Children, Young People and Maternity Services*. The Spastics Society (now Scope) suggest that a no-fault compensation scheme for disabled people would not provide a 'quick fix'. They argue that the only way to achieve equitable and adequate support is through a comprehensive disability income scheme: Brian Lamb and Richard Percival, *Paying for Disability, No Fault Compensation, Panacea or Pandora's Box?* Spastics Society, London, 1992, at p. 26.

current position is that, unless negligence can be established, the responsi-bility to meet the child's needs rests with their parents alone. If negligence is established, the obligation can be discharged through monetary compen-sation. The reality of caring for a child with severe disabilities remains a private obligation.

Responsibilities arise out of relationships. Parents of children living at home with disabilities undertake a long-term commitment to care for their child and to meet their needs as best they can. Their ability to do so is influenced by the support provided and the extent to which responsibilities to individual children with particular needs are understood to be a respon-sibility of society to support those families to have as near as normal a life as possible.

Duties of care?

Relationship of care?

The relationship between parent and child and implicitly the dependency of parents upon the healthcare professionals taking care of their child have been recognised in law where courts have found that a duty is owed to a mother who has suffered psychiatric harm as a consequence of physical harm caused to her child by negligent medical care. In *Tredget*,[92] a duty was owed in respect of the psychiatric harm suffered by the mother due to neg-ligence in her care which resulted in her baby's severe asphyxiation and death forty-eight hours later. In *Farrell*,[93] Tracy Farrell's son, Karol, suffered brain damage due to negligence during birth for which liability was admit-ted and a settlement reached when he was eight years old. The hospital admitted negligence in relation to her antenatal care, the emergency cae-sarean which was performed without pre-medication and the failure to administer antibiotics with the result that she developed an infection. A further question arose as to whether the health authority owed the mother a duty of care in relation to psychiatric harm suffered due to the trauma of the labour and delivery. Due to the circumstances of his birth, Tracy Farrell did not see Karol before he was transferred the next day. It was only upon her arrival at the same hospital that evening that she saw her son, was told that he was not expected to live and that, if he did, he would be severely

[92] *Tredget and Tredget v Bexley HA* [1994] 5 Med LR 178.
[93] *Farrell v Merton, Sutton and Wandsworth HA* 57 BMLR 158 (web.lexis-nexis.com/professional/).

disabled. Steele J considered her to be a primary victim (a patient of the defendant whose psychiatric harm was caused by a breach of duty to her, rather than a relational claimant harmed as a consequence of the breach of duty to her son), with the trauma of her son's birth continuing until the following day when she realised that he had sustained severe brain damage. The judge noted her system of coping, her (in my view entirely understandable) mistrust in the ability of doctors to care for her child and all-encompassing focus upon her child. In a comment which is revealing of the responsibility upon her for meeting her son's needs and for protecting him, Steele J observed that the 'strain of continual care for Karol, her obsessive cleaning and inability to "let go" and share his care with others is part of the illness (quite apart from the inability to fund appropriate care until after the settlement of his case)'.[94] In *Walters*,[95] the hospital had failed to diagnose that Ceri Walter's son, Elliot, was suffering from acute hepatitis. She had been woken in the early hours of the morning by the sound of her son fitting. Later that morning she was told that it was unlikely that he had suffered any harm as a result of the fitting but that the hospital wished to transfer him for a liver transplant. Upon arrival, she was told that he had suffered serious brain damage and that there was only a 50 per cent chance that he would survive the transplant operation. After a further scan, the consultant told her that her son would have no quality of life and the claimant and her husband agreed to the termination of life support. The Court of Appeal upheld the finding of the court of first instance that she was a secondary victim who had suffered a foreseeable recognised psychiatric illness, pathological grief reaction, arising from the horrifying 'drawn-out experience' of the negligent treatment of her son.[96]

In these cases there was admitted negligence on the part of the professionals caring for the child in circumstances where the child's mother was closely involved in the event, such that interests of mother and child could be clearly understood as 'congruent'. In *JD (FC) v East Berkshire Community NHS Trust and others and two other actions (FC)*,[97] the House of Lords was asked to determine whether a duty was owed to the child's parents in circumstances where it was considered that there might be a conflict between the interests of the parent and their child. On assumed

[94] *Ibid.*, at p. 8.
[95] *North Glamorgan NHS Trust v Walters* [2002] EWCA Civ 1792.   [96] *Ibid.*, at para. 34.
[97] *JD (FC) v East Berkshire Community NHS Trust and others and two other actions (FC)* [2005] UKHL 23.

facts, the three conjoined appeals (against East Berkshire, Dewsbury and Oldham NHS Trusts) arose from the negligent misdiagnosis by health professionals of child abuse, causing psychiatric harm to the parent.

In the East Berkshire case, M had suffered from allergic reactions since birth. At the request of his mother, JD, M was referred by his GP to Professor Southall at the North Staffordshire Hospital for the purposes of assessing whether he could be fitted with a monitor to measure his breathing at night. Professor Southall formed the judgment that his mother was exaggerating, or fabricating, his illness, and was possibly a sufferer of 'Munchausen's syndrome by proxy'. Some two and a half years later, JD learnt of these suspicions and asked her GP to refer her to a psychiatrist who found no evidence of the syndrome. Yet, M was placed on the 'at risk register' for a period of some four months until an examination by an expert in allergic conditions confirmed that he did have severe allergies. M's mother brought an action in negligence against the NHS Trust for acute anxiety and depression resulting from the accusations made against her. In the Dewsbury case, it was held to be arguable that a duty of care was owed to nine-year-old R by the NHS Trust and local authority in respect of the psychiatric harm which she suffered as a consequence of misdiagnosis of abuse and subsequent investigation of her father who was prevented from visiting her for the ten days she remained in hospital until a diagnosis of Schamberg's disease (which causes discoloured patches on the skin) was reached. Despite the devastating result, the trauma caused to the family as a consequence of the abuse allegation which was known to the community within which they lived, policy reasons precluded a finding of a duty of care to R's father. The Oldham case concerned parents of a child who, at the age of two months, was found to have a fractured leg. A diagnosis of non-accidental injury was reached without investigation of other possible diagnoses. As a result of care proceedings, M was placed in the care of her aunt. Whilst in her care, M suffered further fractures leading to tests which revealed, some nine months later, a diagnosis of brittle bone disease – a condition which meant that she was susceptible to fractures. M was returned to the care of her parents. Her parents suffered psychiatric injury as a consequence of their separation from their daughter and the misdiagnosis of non-accidental injury.

In an action for negligence, the question was whether a duty of care was owed by the professionals to the parent and child or whether the actions should be struck out on the grounds that it was not fair, just and reasonable to impose a duty. The majority of the House of Lords upheld the decision of the Court of Appeal to strike out the claims. Central to their thinking was a perception, in this situation, of the interests of parent (to protection from unnecessary interference with their family life) and child (to protection from abuse by their own parents) as in conflict. Lord Nicholls opined that, whilst the interests of parent and child are usually 'congruent', where a parent wilfully abuses their child they act contrary to their parental responsibility and to the best interests of the child.[98] The child was the patient and a professional who suspected that a child was the victim of child abuse had to decide whether the child might have been abused, whether to communicate their concerns to other professionals and whether to investigate further. Where there was an investigation, Lord Nicholls considered that the interests of parent and child were 'diametrically opposed', it being in the interests of the child, but not the parents, for professionals to report their suspicions and for these to be investigated.[99] Whilst the disruption to family life might distinguish parents as suspects from other possible suspects (such as childminder or teacher), the conflict of interests or 'inconsistent obligations' precluded such a conclusion:[100]

> . . . readily acknowledging the legitimate grievances of these particular appellants, against whom no suspicions whatever remain, sufferers from a presumed want of professional skill and care on the part of the doctors treating their children. It is they, I acknowledge, who are paying the price of the law's denial of a duty of care. But it is a price they pay in the interests of children generally. The well-being of innumerable children up and down the land depends crucially upon doctors and social workers concerned with their safety being subjected by the law to but a single duty: that of safeguarding the child's own welfare.[101]

Lord Bingham would not have struck out the claims but would have permitted them to go to trial for judgment on the facts. He noted that the complaint by the parents was not in relation to the suspicions of the health professionals but to their carelessness in the investigation and testing of those suspicions.[102] His Lordship recognised that the separation or disruption caused by a diagnosis of child abuse without sufficient evidence was not suffered by the child alone. He explained that professionals owe a duty to the child to avoid reasonably foreseeable harm by failing to take care in

---

[98] *Ibid.*, at para. 71.   [99] *Ibid.*, at para. 88.
[100] *Ibid.*, Lord Nicholls at para. 85; Lord Rodger at para. 113.
[101] *Ibid.*, Lord Brown at para. 138.   [102] *Ibid.*, Lord Bingham at para. 39.

making a diagnosis of abuse. If they negligently fail to diagnose abuse they may be liable to the child and if they negligently misdiagnose abuse they may be liable to the child – and, his Lordship considered, to the child's parents:

> There are of course occasions when emergency action must be taken without informing the parents, and when information must for a time be withheld. But there is no reason why the occasional need for health-care professionals to act in this way should displace a general rule that they should have close regard to the interests of the parents as people with, in the ordinary way, the closest concern for the welfare of their children.[103]

Children are individuals with needs. Young children are vulnerable, although it is more usual for parents to be, as Lord Bingham observed, most closely protective of the welfare of their child than to harm them. Children are situated in relationships with their parents (which may not always be caring) and in relationships with professionals who have responsibility for intervening when they suspect the child is being harmed or is at risk of harm. Whilst children will be harmed by a failure to investigate suspicions of abuse, they will also be harmed by separation from caring parents upon negligent (careless) misdiagnosis. Parents also depend upon professionals to investigate with care their suspicions of the abuse of a child and may be harmed if they do not do so; after all, most parents will be most concerned to protect their child from harm and abuse. They will be harmed by separation from their child as a result of misdiagnosis.

Only nine-year-old R was able to pursue a claim and, in this way, hold the professionals who misdiagnosed abuse by her father to account. The baby in the Oldham case was considered to be too young to be discernibly harmed by the misdiagnosis, apart from her obvious interest in securing a proper diagnosis of brittle bone disease and the inevitable conclusion that separation from her parents even to put her in the care of a loving aunt must have had some unascertainable effect upon her. Both child and parent depend upon professionals to take care in fulfilling their duties. A presumption of individual and conflicting interests between parent and child within the constraints of legally recognised harm precludes examination of the harm of fractured relationships and the responsibility of professionals to investigate their concerns properly, thoroughly and promptly. This case

---

[103] *Ibid.*, Lord Bingham at para. 44.

provides a further example of what Joanne Conaghan has described as the limits of tort law in 'conceiving of violations of relational integrity as distinct and compensatable harms' arising from 'wrongful separation of a child from its mother'.[104] This case reveals the limits of the obligations imposed upon professionals. It demonstrates the assumptions within law of individualism and aggression as a consequence of which the vulnerable child must be protected from their parents. This will prove right in some instances but not in the majority of cases of parents presenting their child for medical attention. Parents depend upon professionals whom they consult for their professional opinion about the health and well-being of their child. The role of the law should be to foster this relationship and support professionals to work together with parents, and this means professionals having responsibilities to parents as well as to children. Rather than assume separation and aggression, the starting point should be an expectation of connection and care and obligations determined within the context of consideration of the needs of the individual child, the history of caring practices and recognition of the responsibilities of both parent and professionals to the child.

Relationships of dependency?

The legal distinctions between consent to treatment (trespass to the person), provision of information and quality of care (negligence) are merged in practice where making decisions, acceptance of information about treatment options and the quality of care provided are inseparable aspects of the experience of care. All parents depend upon healthcare professionals to provide them with information, advice and support and to use their professional knowledge and skills to meet the needs of the child. This dependency is greater where the child is gravely ill, seriously injured or has severe impairments. Where their child suffers further harm, rather than improved health, as a consequence of medical treatment to which they agreed, parents may feel let down by the professional they trusted to care for their child. Their grievances have to be articulated in terms of inadequate standard of care or a decision reached on the basis of insufficient information.

---

[104] *Supra*, n. 12, at 192–3, citing *M v Newham* [1995] 3 All ER 353, in which the House of Lords denied that the local authority owed a duty of care to a mother separated from her daughter following mistaken identity in an allegation of abuse.

In *Poynter v Hillingdon Health Authority*,[105] ten-and-a-half-year-old Matthew Poynter had, at the age of fifteen months, suffered severe brain damage due to oxygen deprivation following cardiac arrest at the start of a heart transplant operation. His parents had given their consent to the operation but brought an action in negligence on the grounds that they were not informed of the risk of brain damage occurring even with competent treatment and that had they known of this risk they would not have consented to the transplant operation. The judge, Sir Maurice Drake, found that the risk to Matthew of severe brain damage materialising during the transplant at the time (1987) and the place (Harefield Hospital), given his age and condition, 'was no more than about 1%'. Failure to inform his parents of this risk was not a breach of the duty of care owed by the doctors because, although at the time some practitioners would have informed them of the risk, 'a substantial responsible body of medical opinion' would not have done so. Matthew's parents had reluctantly agreed to the operation despite their

> strong spiritual feelings which lead them to regard heart transplantation as unnatural and wrong. They are not against conventional medicine or conventional surgery, although they both believe that alternative treatment, including homeopathy and acupuncture should also be tried, but they do both believe that the heart is not merely a pumping machine, but is of deeply spiritual significance. For this, and it may be for further reasons, they feel that heart transplantation is unnatural and wrong and they would certainly not agree to it being carried out on themselves.[106]

The doctors caring for Matthew were clearly of the opinion that a heart transplant was in his best interests. They considered his condition, cardiomyopathy, to be a life-threatening condition which presented a stark choice between a transplant operation and letting Matthew die. His parents told the court that they felt under pressure to consent – that the possibility of securing a court order had been mentioned – and of their view, with hindsight, that the risk of brain damage was not mentioned because the doctors knew that, had they been informed of the risk, they would have refused consent. In an almost opposite situation to *Poynter*, but raising the same issues, the parents of Kristian Adey considered that the advice

---

[105] *Poynter v Hillingdon Health Authority* 37 BMLR 192 (web.lexis-nexis.com/professional/).
[106] *Ibid.*, at p. 3.

that they had been given about treatment of his heart condition had been negligent. They argued that had they been properly advised, Kristian would have undergone surgery which would have given him a longer life expectancy.[107] As a matter of fact, Bennett J concluded that Kristian's parents had been provided with information about treatment enabling them to make a decision and strongly rejected the allegation that there was a policy of discriminating against children with Down's Syndrome. The objections of the children's parents had to be expressed in terms of a breach of the duty of care to provide information about the treatment of their child. What is not recognised is the nature of the relationship between parents and the professionals upon whom they depend for information and advice about the needs of their child and whom they trust to provide their child with the best possible care. In bringing an action in negligence, the parents may have been seeking damages which would have enabled them to buy goods and services to enhance their child's quality of life. They may have wanted an apology, an explanation or to ensure that, in the future, parents are provided with the information which they were not given. The existing legal principles do not permit examination of the dependency of parents upon healthcare professionals in relation to the medical treatment of their child's complex heart condition. In Matthew's case his parents had agreed to a complex and risky operation in order to enhance their son's quality of life which had ruinous consequences for his future, whilst Kristian's parents felt that they had not secured the best possible treatment for their son. Emotionally attached to their child and primarily responsible for them, focused upon meeting their needs and securing the best possible treatment for their child, parents depend upon professionals for information, advice and support in meeting the needs of their child.

Further examples of parental dependency upon healthcare professionals are the cases of *Thompson v Bradford*[108] and *Thornson v James*,[109] both concerned with the provision of information about immunisation and considered in chapter 3. Beldam LJ expressed 'the greatest sympathy' for the parents of Emma Thomson who had made the 'anxious decision' not to have their daughter immunised against measles. Emma subsequently contracted measles and was left with brain damage as a consequence. In his

---

[107] *Adey v Leeds Health Authority and another*, QBD, 1 December 2000 (web.lexis-nexis.com/ professional/).   [108] *Thompson v Bradford* [2005] EWCA Civ 1439.
[109] *Thornson v James and others*, 29 July 1997 (web.lexis-nexis.com/professional/).

conclusion, Beldam LJ acknowledged the feelings of her parents arising from their responsibilities to her and their dependence upon the healthcare professionals they had consulted but that these were not acknowledged by existing principles of law:

> Of course, any caring parent questions the decision, saying 'If only we had decided differently', but they did the best they could as caring parents. There is nothing with which they need reproach themselves, nor, in my opinion, is there any reason, on the facts of this case, to reproach the doctors who advised to the best of their ability . . .'[110]

Beyond the daily tasks of caring and the emotional consequences of seeing their child suffer, parents who feel that they have been let down by professionals may feel, in turn, that they have let their child down. As Joanne Conaghan has observed, the law of negligence 'operates within an implicit and taken-for-granted context which assumes that plaintiffs and defendants are strangers involved in random collisions, or that any prior relationship between them is strictly defined by a limited set of recognised obligations'.[111] Consequently, the question is asked whether an obligation is owed without reference to the context of the relationship between child, parent and the professional who assumed responsibility for taking care.

The parental complaint has to be expressed in terms which may fail to identify the grievance they feel. Some of the parents whose children underwent cardiac surgery at the Bristol Royal Infirmary initiated legal action searching for an explanation, an apology or compensation to assist them in meeting the needs of their child: 'The families simply want an admission of liability, a clear unconditional acknowledgement that the hospital was at fault.'[112] Jim Stewart, whose son, Ian, suffered brain damage during his operation at the age of four months, recovered compensation after the Trust admitted liability but there had been 'no investigation of Ian's case, no explanation and no apology from the NHS'.[113] Negligence law establishes minimum obligations owed, standards set according to the

---

[110] *Ibid.*, at p. 8.
[111] Joanne Conaghan, 'Tort Litigation in the Context of Intra-familial Abuse' (1998) 61 MLR 132–61, at p. 161.
[112] Lawrence Vick, solicitor for some of the families quoted in Sean O'Neill, 'Payouts in heart babies scandal could top £50m', *Daily Telegraph*, 16 July 2001.
[113] Sarah Boseley, 'We were deliberately lied to', *Guardian*, 22 October 2002.

perspective of the defendant[114] and without consideration of the needs or expectations of recipients of care. The law of negligence sets minimum standards such that care provided, if it fails to recognise the child as an individual, the nature of the responsibility of parents or their dependency upon professionals, may be experienced as inadequate, as harmful, even though, according to the law, no wrong has been committed. The responsibility of parents for their child and their dependency upon healthcare professionals can be illustrated with reference to the example of Penelope Plackett whose daughter, Sophie, suffered severe brain damage during an operation at the Bristol Royal Infirmary which successfully remedied her heart defect. She explained how she had been told that the chances of the operation being a success were 50 per cent, although this had been increased as Sophie was so well prior to the operation. She later discovered that the operation had only previously been performed four times by the surgeon, Mr Dhasmana, and all of the children had died. She explained how she 'regretted' not getting more information but 'never thought to question', 'never thought to ask him', although 'with hindsight I am acutely aware I did not ask enough questions'.[115] It was her responsibility to secure the surgical treatment her daughter required yet, in agreeing to surgery which she believed offered her daughter the only chance of life, she had subjected her daughter to a procedure which left her with brain damage.

It is asserted that the law generally premised upon patrolling the behaviours of individual aggressors must accommodate situations in which individuals are connected, by virtue of their professional, or personal, responsibilities. Determining obligations through a conceptual framework of responsibilities would, I suggest, ensure recognition of the different responsibilities of parent and professional and of the dependency of parents upon healthcare professionals as they seek to care for their child.

Obligations, responsibilities and caring

This chapter does not seek to present an alternative to the law of negligence. The overall aim of this chapter, considering civil law cases concerned with caring for children, is to highlight the responsibilities of parents and professionals and the dependencies arising out of relationships. The purpose is

[114] *Bolam v Friern Hospital Management Committee* [1957] 1 WLR 582; *Bolitho v City and Hackney HA* [1997] 4 All ER 771.
[115] BBC News, 'Travesty of brain-damaged success', 22 March 1999 (http://news.bbc.co.uk).

three-fold. First, it contrasts the enduring assumptions of abstract individualism with the reality of connections, dependency, vulnerability and needs. It is my contention that simply taking a different starting point – that parent and child are connected and parents are concerned to do the best for their child – would make a radical difference to the application of the legal principles. Secondly, it serves to highlight the responsibilities which parents do take to meet the caring needs of their children. The purpose of doing so is not to consider the familiar question of individual or collective responsibilities – tort, no-fault or welfare provision. The reason is to look behind the cases, as far as possible, to the lives of the people involved to reveal the care which parents take of their children to support the argument for a conceptual framework of relational responsibilities informed by practices of caring. Thirdly, the particular concern of parents to meet the needs of their child renders parents of sick, injured or disabled children dependent upon healthcare professionals. By consideration of these three factors, the aim has been to present an argument for determination of obligations through a conceptual framework of relational responsibilities.

7

Relational responsibilities

Introduction

As is well known, the Children Act 1989 enacted a shift in discourse from parental rights to parental responsibilities. However, as the responsibilities of parents are there restated in terms of rights, powers and duties, established assumptions, understandings and expectations are retained. It was anticipated that, having enshrined parental responsibilities within legislation, over time this would become the way of understanding the parent–child relationship.[1] As was noted in chapter 3, the Children Act 1989 further made it clear that children were the primary responsibility of their parents, limiting the state to a protectionist role in relation to children, and families, in need.[2] Whilst recent policy developments in relation to children's healthcare services may represent a change of emphasis, sending the message that all parents require support in meeting their responsibilities, what remains missing is a clear concept of parental responsibilities to children. This book has argued that, in contrast to traditional ideas about the nature of the relationships regulated by law, the parental relationship and that of professionals caring for children can be usefully conceptualised in terms of relational responsibilities. It is my contention that a conceptual framework of relational responsibilities should underpin the legal principles governing the provision of healthcare to children. Before expanding upon this, this chapter first considers a proposal for reform of the law governing children's healthcare decision-making. Consideration is then given to a proposal as to how the law can adopt an 'ethic of care' approach, using the example of Carol Smith and Bren Neale's work on post-divorce contact.

---

[1] Roger Smith, 'Parental Responsibility – and an Irresponsible State?' (1990) 71 *Childright* 7–8.
[2] *Ibid.*

Law reform

Child-centred healthcare law

In *Health Care Choices*, Priscilla Alderson and Jonathan Montgomery advocate reform of the legal framework governing decisions regarding the healthcare of children.[3] They undertake a multi-layered critique of the current law. First, they argue that an understanding of children within law as lacking maturity, rationality and competence results in the view that they lack autonomy worthy of respect and the consequent exclusion of children from participation in decisions about their treatment. Secondly, they suggest that the focus within law upon consent to treatment rather than on the process of treatment has the effect of denying children the opportunity to express their views on other aspects of their care, such as whether pain relief is administered by drug or injection or who stays with them whilst they are treated, matters of importance to the overall quality of their care. Thirdly, legal principles governing children's healthcare have been established in cases with extreme factual situations, such as children refusing consent to life-saving treatment, rather than developed from everyday, good, practice.

Priscilla Alderson and Jonathan Montgomery argue for legislation, supported by a Code of Practice, covering the whole process of children's healthcare decision-making, based upon children's experiences and informed by a process of consultation with all involved in children's healthcare provision, including children themselves.[4] In the framework which they outline, the basic principles would be set out in the legislation, with the Code of Practice providing detail, guidance and checklists identifying relevant questions to ask in difficult cases, ensuring that procedures are in place and that policies are developed to address potential problems. The Code of Practice would set standards of good practice, departure from which would be evidence of negligence requiring the professional to justify their actions in clinical terms, supported through complaints procedures and professional disciplinary action. In the framework which they propose, the court would retain the role of providing independent review, applying the legislation and Code of Practice.

---

[3] Priscilla Alderson and Jonathan Montgomery, *Health Care Choices: Making Decisions with Children*, IPPR: London, 1996.   [4] *Ibid.*, at pp. 66–71.

Central to their proposed legal framework is respect for the rights of children. Rather than autonomy, as it is currently understood, as an all-or-nothing condition which brings with it responsibility for choice and blame should it be the wrong one, they stress the importance of the participation of children in decisions about their healthcare. Participation must not, they stress, be a hollow exercise in which adults continue to determine what happens to the child, but genuine participation which requires adults to assess the extent to which the child wishes to be involved and further wants to take responsibility for the decision. They note evidence of children's involvement in their healthcare decisions which reveals a maturity of approach developed through experience of their condition and treatment, the harm caused to children by failing to inform them about treatment, side-effects and risks or by forcing treatment upon them, but also that children often wanted their parents to be involved with them in decision-making.[5] They recommend a presumption of competence from the age of five. The burden would be placed upon those disputing the competence of the child to establish otherwise. As a consequence, from that age, children would have to be involved in discussions about treatment either to secure valid consent or to establish lack of competence. They suggest that parents should continue to have the power to consent, subject to the limitation that this be exercised with the assent of the competent child. Consequently, children could give the responsibility for the decision to their parents to be exercised consistently with their views but parents could not exercise the power to give or refuse consent against the wishes of their competent child. The court would retain a role of providing independent review of children's competence. If the child is considered to be competent, the presumption should be that their decision would be respected. Where the child's refusal may lead to serious irreparable harm this may be overridden, but before doing so consideration would have to be given to the harm involved in the provision of treatment contrary to the wishes of a competent child. If the child is found to lack competence, the court should determine whether treatment, or which treatment, is in the best interests of the child.[6]

These proposals do have the merits of challenging prevailing understandings about young children and crafting a framework for children's healthcare decision-making respectful of the participation rights of children able to express their views about medical treatment. This book has

---

[5] *Ibid.*, ch. 4 considers the evidence from practice.   [6] *Ibid.*, at pp. 73–82.

focused upon the responsibilities of parents and professionals with regard to the healthcare of young and dependent children and it is not my purpose to contrast relational responsibilities with the rights-based approach of Alderson and Montgomery. Neither is it my purpose to sketch out a legal framework in the form of legislation or a Code of Practice, rather it is to identify a conceptual framework to inform the law governing the provision of healthcare to young and dependent children across decision-making, quality of care, access to treatment and supporting parents to meet their responsibilities. First, a brief consideration of how the ethic of care has been applied to the law regulating a different aspect of family life, that of post-divorce contact.

Ethic of care adjudication

In *Family Fragments?*,[7] Carol Smart and Bren Neale analyse the findings of their study in which they interviewed parents about their experiences of post-divorce parenthood. They aimed to test the assumption, central to the philosophy of the Children Act 1989, that whilst the adult relationship might have broken down, the best interests of the child of the relationship are served by maintaining contact with both parents. Carol Smart and Bren Neale identified, in the context of family life after separation or divorce, that the majority of parents were concerned for the welfare of their child and wanted their child to have good relationships with both parents. They argue that the child–parent relationship is dependent upon the parent–parent relationship which the law, framed from an ethic of justice perspective, erodes rather than supports. They reflected upon their findings to consider the difference that an ethic of care, as opposed to an ethic of justice, approach would make to the law. They suggest that '[t]o operate according to this ethic, one would have to have regard for the discharge of responsibilities, the quality of relationships, the actual situation that people find themselves in and the practice that people have been engaged in'.[8] They suggest that an ethic of care approach would involve a different process and may result in a different outcome to the ethic of justice approach:

> It would be concerned with who had held responsibility and established relationships, with the actuality of a specific family life and a

---

[7] Carol Smart and Bren Neale, *Family Fragments?* Polity Press: Cambridge, 1999.
[8] *Ibid.*, at p. .170.

specific child and with who had actively done the caring. In this formulation responsibility could be economic as well as nurturing, different children in the same family could be treated differently but *theoretical* claims about ability to care would not take precedence over, nor would they be regarded as being as significant as, *actual* past caring behaviour. The quality of the relationship between the parents and between the parents and children would also be part of the equation and the ability of parents to treat each other with dignity and respect would be considered. Whilst the ethic of justice would almost always reach the same conclusion regardless of the circumstances – namely the just outcome is always joint parenting after divorce – the ethic of care would have a range of different and individuated outcomes while also being just. What would be particularly significant about such a shift in basic moral philosophy would be that space would be given to a discourse of responsibility and not, as at present, solely to a discourse of rights or an abstract principle of welfare of children in general.[9]

Based upon the findings of their study, they advocate replacing the 'welfare principle with a hint of equality and rights reasoning' with four principles: 'the principle of actuality; the principle of care; the principle of recognition of selfhood; and the principle of recognition of loss'.[10] The first, 'actuality', would require thorough examination of the particular situation and the needs of the child. They suggest that the welfare principle should be replaced with the 'principle of care', which would result in an examination of practices of caring responsibility and consideration of the future caring needs of the child as well as recognising the needs of parents to be cared for. Family breakdown is a life-changing experience for all involved and the 'principle of recognition of selfhood' would ensure support for the development of a sense of self or identity for all in their changed circumstances. The final principle acknowledges that the law is frequently used in such circumstances to sustain broken relationships as relationships of conflict and dispute through assertion of individual rights. The 'principle of recognition of loss' would focus upon fostering relationships in their new configuration to provide the best environment, post-divorce, for the caring adults to meet the child's needs.[11]

    There are a number of observations to be made upon their proposals for an 'ethic of care' approach to post-divorce contact decisions. First, they advocate reform of legal principle – replacing the welfare principle with

---

[9] *Ibid.*, at p. 171.   [10] *Ibid.*, at p. 192.   [11] *Ibid.*, at pp. 193–6.

four principles to be applied in order to reach a decision. Secondly, the consequence of this may be a change to the process of decision-making and, in some cases, to the outcome. As a matter of process, the consequence is likely to be far greater inquiry into the past, current and possible future circumstances of the individuals involved. The outcome may generally be less predictable in the sense of removing presumptions about post-divorce parenting, but individually as predictable given the focus upon caring practices. Importantly, the result of the application of the principles would be an outcome which is informed by the concrete reality of the circumstances of the people about whom a decision is being made. This necessarily involves greater intrusion into family life than decision-making by assumptions, presumptions and the application of abstract principles. That must be the cost of informed, contextual decision-making about the lives of individuals.

With these observations in mind, the final section will consider the implications of a conceptual framework of relational responsibility for the law regulating the provision of healthcare to young and dependent children.

Legal responsibilities

This book does not seek to present a grand theory of responsibility. It examines a very specific issue centred upon the close, intimate relationship between parents and children and the professionals they consult for assistance in meeting their healthcare needs. It is already generally accepted that the particular relationship between parent and child, and that between doctor and patient, creates specific moral and legal duties beyond those generally owed to strangers. The aim of this book is to develop a conceptual framework of relational responsibilities to underpin the law regulating the roles of parents and professionals in providing healthcare to children. In this way, in the specific area of the healthcare of young and dependent children, this book seeks to contribute to the process of developing understanding of, and ways of thinking about, responsibilities in relationships and in family life.

As noted above, the parent–child relationship has been reconceptualised as one based upon parental responsibilities rather than one based upon parental rights. However, whilst this may reflect how parents think about their relationship with their child, the concept of parental responsibility or of responsibilities within the family has not been theorised. Consequently, it would appear, parental responsibility is predominantly approached as merely the correlative of rights – the responsibilities imposed upon parents as a consequence of the rights of the child. However, as discussed in chapter 1, the problems with analysis of children's rights mean that identification of parental responsibilities is not a straightforward enterprise. In the same way that legal rights are a particular form of expression (in law) of moral rights, legal responsibilities can be understood as an expression of moral responsibilities. In the same way as there has been debate about the nature of moral rights, some of which are translated into legal rights there needs to be examination of the concept of moral responsibilities underpinning legal responsibilities.

It must be emphasised that I am not rejecting the importance of rights, either moral rights or legal rights, which provide valuable protections to individuals in certain situations: in particular, universal rights to children to protection from abuse, harm and neglect. I am, like Katharine Bartlett[12] and Elizabeth Kingdom,[13] arguing that we have to be strategic in our invocation of rights. We have to select which issues are best understood, approached and resolved through rights claims. Sometimes, as in cases in which parents and professionals are seeking to do their best for the child, rights are not the most appropriate instrument for structuring relationships and resolving disputes. Rights make abstract claims when particular needs require investigation. They force the parties to express their positions in ways which polarise and position them in conflict when, in relation to children's healthcare, they share a goal.

As outlined in chapter 1, theorisation of responsibility has occurred within the context of traditional liberal thought and, more recently, in communitarian thinking. This book has adopted, as the most appropriate basis for thinking about the responsibilities of parents in relation to the healthcare of their children, a conceptualisation of responsibility based upon the feminist ethic of care. As a set of 'normative guidelines' for what parents ought to do, this provides three elements: consideration of the needs of the individual child, examination of practices of caring responsibility (including different responsibilities arising from different relationships and roles) and exploration of the wider context in which those needs are met.

---

[12] Katharine Bartlett, 'Re-Expressing Parenthood' (1988) 98 *Yale Law Journal* 293, at pp. 295–6.
[13] Elizabeth Kingdom, *What's Wrong with Rights? Problems for Feminist Politics of Law*, Edinburgh University Press, 1991.

Most fundamentally, what needs to change is the assumptions underlying the legal principles which determine disputed cases and structure the duties of parents and healthcare professionals. As outlined in chapter 1, and demonstrated in the discussion of the case law, the child is understood as dependent and thus as vulnerable and in need of protection. Assumptions of individualism mean that parents are perceived as primarily self-interested. Whilst an understanding of the individual as separate, requiring protection from aggression by others, resolving disputes through prioritisation of abstract rights or asking what is owed may be appropriate for some situations, it fails to accord with the reality of the parent–child relationship, to support parents and professionals as they seek to do their best for the child or to guide judges when asked to adjudicate. The feminist ethic of care challenges this understanding of the nature of the self. Within a feminist ethic of care, individuals are understood as primarily connected rather than primarily separate. This reflects the nature of the relationship between parent and child, and appreciation of this would have a fundamental impact upon the understanding of the roles, expertise and interests of parents in relation to their children's healthcare.

I am sure that I will be criticised for starting with the assumption that parents seek to do their best for their child. That is, that generally, parents seek to do their best for their child according to their understanding of the child's needs, to their beliefs and values, to expectations within society or their community of good parenting and according to the resources available to them. Yet, there is a lot of evidence in support of this view. 'Doing their best', an expression of acting in the best interests of their child, is a constant theme across the studies of parents caring for children, including Priscilla Alderson et al.'s study of parents with children in the neonatal intensive care ward,[14] the study by Hazel McHaffie et al. of parents of children from whom treatment was withdrawn,[15] and the studies considered in chapter 6 of parents caring for children with complex needs. Their responsibility to 'do their best' for their child is also a constant theme in the written statements provided by parents to the Bristol Inquiry and the way

---

[14] Priscilla Alderson, Joanna Hawthorn and Margaret Killen, 'The Participation Rights of Premature Babies' (2005) 13 *International Journal of Children's Rights* 31–50, considered in chapter 1.

[15] Hazel E. McHaffie in association with Peter W. Fowlie, Robert Hume, Ian A. Laing, David J. Lloyd and Andrew J. Lyon, *Crucial Decisions at the Beginning of Life: Parents' Experiences of Treatment Withdrawal from Infants*, Radcliffe Medical Press: Abingdon, 2001, considered in chapter 5.

in which parents talk about their responsibilities for their child in news-paper accounts of parents whose children have been at the centre of legal disputes. My concern that we remove the existing assumption about parents and start with the understanding that parents are seeking to do the best for their child can be supported by reference to a few examples which could be replicated numerous times over.

In the written statements provided by parents to the Bristol Inquiry, many undertake an analysis as to whether they had 'done the best they could for their child'. This emerged in parental accounts variously as confidence that they had, as certainty that events had proven that they had not, and as uncertainty as to whether they had. The children at the centre of the Bristol Royal Infirmary Inquiry were all seriously ill, requiring risky, invasive surgery for their heart condition. For most of their parents there was really little choice but to give their consent to surgery, given that without it their child would in all likelihood die in childhood, in some cases within a year, months or even days. Angela Good articulated how distress-ing it was whilst her son, Joseph, was in surgery but that she and her husband 'tried to remain positive as we felt we were doing the best for our son, that we were giving him the chance of a better quality of life'.[16] Susan Francombe's daughter, Rebecca, underwent surgery very soon after her birth for an unusual condition which the surgeon, Mr Dhasmana, had not himself previously seen. After discussing her condition with a colleague in another hospital, he told her parents that surgery was possible, that it would be 'lengthy, complex and difficult' and there was less than a 10 per cent chance of success. Without surgery, he advised them, Rebecca would only live a few days. Although Rebecca died shortly after surgery, her mother explained that they were aware of the nature and the risks of the procedure, of the limitations of Mr Dhasmana's experience and the steps which he had taken to prepare himself as fully as possible. Despite her daughter's death after surgery undertaken to remedy a complex and unusual heart condition, Susan Francombe expressed her confidence that 'We never had any doubt that everything possible that could have been done for Rebecca was.'[17] For many parents, their concern to secure the very best care for their child was expressed in the context of discovering, after

---

[16] Written statement of Angela Good with regard to the treatment of her son, Joseph, to the Bristol Royal Infirmary Inquiry, at para. 23.

[17] Written statement of Susan Francombe, with regard to the treatment of her daughter, Rebecca, to the Bristol Royal Infirmary Inquiry, at para. 31.

the event, that the care provided had been inadequate. This was clearly articulated by Lesley Smith whose daughter, Katherine, died after surgery:

> When you place your child in the hands of surgeons you want to know that these are the best. We have had that taken away and now have to live with the idea that we are to blame for her death as we did not do the best for her.[18]

For many parents, like Karen Meadows, mother of Sarah, the belief that they had done their best for their child had helped them to live with the death of their child:

> I thought that everyone had done their best. I had no guilt and did not blame anyone. Now I have lost that inner peace.[19]

The same concern is apparent in the words of Angela Stoneman, who was threatened with legal action when she refused her consent to further treatment for her four-year-old son, Daniel, who had a brain tumour. Daniel had told her that he did not want any further treatment, which offered a 30 per cent chance of recovery. She explained:

> I know that if he doesn't have the treatment he will die sooner. But my only concern is for Daniel. I don't want him to go through any more pain . . . I just know, deep down, that no matter what they do to him he isn't going to live. I can't tell you how I know this. But something within me tells me that he should not be made to suffer any more.[20]

Criticism of her decision was based in the view that she had refused consent in her own interests rather than the interests of her son. As she explained:

> They seem to think I couldn't cope with the fact that he might come out of treatment mentally retarded. But of course I could. I've already coped with a lot in my life. I'd look after him no matter what he was like if I knew he would live. I just want to do as much as I can for him.[21]

---

[18] Written statement of Lesley Smith, with regard to the treatment of her daughter, Katherine, to the Bristol Royal Infirmary Inquiry, at para. 50.

[19] Written statement of Karen Meadows, with regard to the treatment of her daughter, Sarah, to the Bristol Royal Infirmary Inquiry, at para. 39.

[20] 'Please let my son die', *Daily Mail*, 16 May 1992.

[21] *Ibid.* Daniel changed his mind and was given radiotherapy treatment. Although treatment was initially believed to have been successful, Daniel died a year later: Richard Pendlebury, 'Cancer victim who was treated with love loses his battle; A mother's dream dies with her brave little boy', *Daily Mail*, 22 July 1993.

A final example is the transplant surgery which Laura Davies underwent, pushing the boundaries of medical knowledge, about which the question was asked whether it was in her interests, the interests of her parents or the interests of the advancement of medical science.[22] Laura had been born with gastroschisis which meant that her intestines could not absorb nutrients from food and she was fed by drip until she underwent a double transplant (liver and bowel) operation in the United States at the age of four. Her condition was serious and the treatment options to prevent death from starvation limited – either she could be fed by intravenous drip, for an inevitably limited lifetime, risking infection, liver failure and metabolic disorder, or she could undergo the double transplant operation.[23] The double transplant operation could have been performed in Cambridge but, as it had not previously been performed on a child in Britain, her parents decided that their daughter was offered the best chance by undergoing the surgery where it had been performed a small number of times before. As the NHS would not fund her treatment in the United States, her parents raised £350,000 to cover the cost of the operation.[24] Although Laura recovered from the double transplant and enjoyed a few months in good health, her body rejected the transplanted organs. In September 1993, Laura underwent a seven-organ transplant, again in the United States and funded by money raised by her parents, in which she received a liver, stomach, pancreas, small and large intestines and two kidneys, believed to be the first patient to undergo an operation in which all of these organs were transplanted. Her parents knew that the chances that she would survive the transplant were small but that she would not survive without it. Laura died shortly afterwards, without having left hospital, of lymphoproliferative disease, a side-effect of the drugs used to prevent organ rejection.[25] Her treatment was not considered by a court, either on the question of whether it was in her best interests (the parents and doctors being in agreement) or on the question of the allocation of resources (her parents having raised the money for her treatment). Her case provides an example of parents and professionals working together in order to provide the best possible care for a seriously ill child. Independent assessment, at least one which examined Laura's needs and the experiences of her parents alongside the views of her

---

[22] Richard Nicholson, 'Dignity and the doctor's duty', *Guardian*, 2 September 1993.
[23] Lawrence Weaver, 'Is science exploiting Laura's suffering?' *Daily Mail*, 1 September 1993.
[24] Tony Burton, 'We've got our little girl back', *Daily Mail*, 29 October 1992.
[25] Chris Mihill, ' "Working class hero" fought for transplant girl', *Guardian*, 12 November 1993.

doctor, would have ensured that both transplant operations were in her best interests. It may have had the further consequence of silencing critics of her parents,[26] critics who felt able to condemn their decision without, it appears, seeking to learn from her parents about the burden of the responsibility of making a decision about risky, experimental treatment for a seriously ill child who was certain to die without it.

However, it is important not to replace one set of assumptions with another. There are, after all, parents who fail to do their best for their child or whose assessment of what is best is coloured more by the desire to disrupt the child's principal carer than a careful assessment of their child's needs. Hence, an understanding of parent and child as connected provides merely the starting point for full investigation of the individual child's needs, the experiences of all those involved in taking care and recognition of the external factors limiting abilities to care. I think, in this way, the law can be both child-centred and respectful of parents.

My major criticism is that current assumptions mean that insufficient attention is paid to the care provided by parents. This is not an argument for a focus upon parents, although the view that parents are particularly concerned to achieve the best for the child means that their interests are compatible rather than conflicting. This is an argument for child-centred law which is dependent upon consideration of the child as an individual, the history of caring practices which focuses upon the particular expertise gained through caring and consideration of the context in which care is provided. These are the three central features of relational responsibility which need to be examined, whether considering healthcare decisions, resource allocation, the provision of quality care or services which support parents to meet the healthcare needs of their child. There need be no expansion of these three core considerations (or 'normative guidelines') for the content of them will depend upon the particular circumstances of the child's healthcare needs which must be thoroughly investigated. Consideration of these three guidelines would ensure that decisions are made with consideration of the particular child. It would also ensure that the different experiences, perspectives and insights of all taking care of the child are understood. Furthermore, it would require acknowledgement that the limits of the ability to care for a child are not necessary limits of the

---

[26] Margaret Maxwell, 'Medical triumphs, children's tragedies', *Independent*, 3 September 1993; Melanie Phillips, 'Laura has become a surgical guinea-pig', *Observer*, 5 September 1993.

individual, but may be due to community (e.g. religious beliefs), society (such as attitudes towards the disabled) or the state (political decisions about the resources available to care).

Responsibilities arise out of relationships. The parental relationship determines the responsibilities owed by parent to child, although the exact content depends upon the needs of the child, and further is both individually determined and influenced by social and cultural factors. Children also have relationships with others, such as healthcare professionals, out of which responsibilities arise. Again the content of these responsibilities depends upon the needs of the child but also upon the area of expertise of the professional. The concern to do their best for the child, within the context of their particular role in caring for the child, is shared by healthcare professionals. This was articulated, for example, by Dr Oscar Craig, then President of the Royal College of Radiologists, in relation to the treatment of Daniel Stoneman:

> I am distressed that court action has been mentioned, but I can understand that they are acting in what they think is the best interests of the patient who can't make a decision . . . It's a distressing time for both parties. The paradox is that they both want the same thing – the best for the child.[27]

The result of a focus upon caring responsibilities would be to foster the relationship between parents and professionals and support them to work together in the shared endeavour of doing the best for the child by creating a legal framework which is centred around the child but respectful of the responsibilities of all who care. Law would cohere with best practice, promoting understanding which should minimise conflict.

It is also apparent that current legal principles do not make the job of the judiciary, providing an independent adjudication of healthcare decisions (the child's best interests), an easy one. Given the desire of both professionals and parents to do their best for the child, there is no need to change the welfare principle employed to determine the best interests of the child in healthcare decision cases. What needs to change is the approach to determination of the welfare of the child. The welfare principle needs to be liberated from the shackles of universalism, objectivity and impartiality which remain pervasive even though the enterprise is purportedly particularistic. Fact-sensitive, particularistic decisions, they are currently reached within

---

[27] Alison Gordon, 'Daniel family backs mother; "We want to end tragic boy's treatment, too"', *Mail on Sunday*, 17 May 1992.

the context of ideas about the child, understandings of parental selfishness and without confronting the unarticulated context of societal norms in relation to, for example, dominant beliefs or attitudes towards disability. To determine the welfare of the child, the best interests of the child, through application of the normative guidelines of relational responsibilities to the child might not result in different outcomes but would involve an improved decision-making process.

Chapter 2 considers the development of child-centred children's health-care services. The context revealed by the Bristol and Laming Inquires was one of long-term neglect of children's services. Insufficient attention had been given, in both national policy and local service provision, to meeting the universal needs of all children and the particular needs of vulnerable children. The predictable, but welcome, consequence is standards for children's healthcare services which are child-centred but which appreciate that children using healthcare services are, generally, situated within relationships with parents who have experience of their needs gained as they care for them. The universal support to parents in the form of making available sources of information, guidance and advice is limited intervention which may be appreciated by the majority of parents who, the evidence suggests, seek to do their best for their child according to their child's needs. Likewise, the aspirations in standards for targeted services for children with complex health needs appear to be a welcome recognition that services need to be child- and family- centred rather than structured around organisational demands. The role of the state has to be understood as different from the roles of professionals and parents taking care of and caring for children, which are close, often intimate, personal relationships. At a political level, it is necessary to explore the question of the allocation of responsibilities for caring, as between parents and institutions, and the extent to which the state should support all parents who take care of children and, more specifically, children with complex needs. Furthermore, I suggest, the role of the state is to support those engaged in the care of the child to work together in the shared endeavour of meeting the needs of the child by the creation of institutions (including laws) which foster the relationship between them.

Chapter 6 aims to highlight the practices of caring responsibility as parents seek to do their best to meet the needs of their child. The overarching question for determination in these cases of the limits of the obligations owed by healthcare professionals is determined against assumptions grounded in social expectations (that the family is primarily responsible, or will 'pick up the pieces'). The aim of this chapter is not to advocate comprehensive reform of the tort system of liability but to demonstrate the assumptions underpinning the law and the understanding to be gained by considering a different perspective. By highlighting the caring practices of parents and their consequential dependency upon healthcare professionals, this chapter seeks to advance the argument for the determination of obligations through a conceptual framework of relational responsibilities.

My aim is not, therefore, to outline legislation or a code of practice or to set out an agenda of law reform. My aim is to challenge the assumptions underlying the current law and to contribute to thinking about the meaning and content of responsibilities to children. By arguing for a conceptual framework of relational responsibilities through which to approach the law governing the healthcare of children, I hope to have contributed something to the development of a discourse of (parental and professional) responsibility. Underlying this challenge to the approach of the law and the hope that I have made a contribution to thinking about moral and legal responsibility is a more basic aim of seeking to ensure that the experiences of the people involved – the parents and, through them, their children – are recognised. Happily, most parents will not know what it is like to care for a child with a life-threatening condition or to care for a child with severe disabilities. Neither should we assume that we know what is involved in caring for any individual child. It is my contention that by developing a conceptual framework of relational responsibilities and by speaking of responsibilities, we will better appreciate what caring for a child with acute illness, chronic disease or severe disabilities involves and that the law would thereby better support parents and professionals who together take responsibility for the health of young and dependent children.

BIBLIOGRAPHY

Alderson, Priscilla, *Choosing for Children: Parents' Consent to Surgery*, Oxford University Press: Oxford, 1990

'Consent to Children's Surgery and Intensive Medical Treatment' (1990) 17 *Journal of Law and Society* 52–65

Children's Consent to Surgery, Open University Press: Buckingham, 1993

'Researching Children's Rights to Integrity' in Berry Mayall (ed.), *Children's Childhoods: Observed and Experienced*, Falmer Press: London, 1994, 45–62

Alderson, Priscilla and Jonathan Montgomery, *Health Care Choices: Making Decisions with Children*, IPPR: London, 1996

Alderson, Priscilla, Joanna Hawthorn and Margaret Killen, 'The Participation Rights of Premature Babies' (2005) 13 *International Journal of Children's Rights* 31–50

Allison, Rebecca, 'Conjoined twins with shared heart die', *Guardian*, 18 May 2002

Archard, David, 'Philosophical Perspectives on Childhood' in Julia Fionda (ed.), *Legal Concepts of Childhood*, Hart: Oxford, 2001, 43–56

Children, Family and the State, Ashgate: Hampshire, 2003

Children: Rights and Childhood, Routledge: London, 2004

Armstrong, David, 'From Clinical Gaze to Regime of Total Health' in Alan Beattie, Marjorie Gott, Linda Jones and Moyra Sidell (eds.), *Health and Wellbeing: A Reader*, Oxford University Press and Macmillan Press Ltd: Basingstoke and London, 1993, 55–67

Arneil, Barbara, 'Becoming versus Being: A Critical Analysis of the Child in Liberal Theory' in David Archard and Colin Macleod (eds.), *The Moral and Political Status of Children*, Oxford University Press: Oxford, 2002, 70–94

Aynsley-Green, Professor, Presentation, 'Practical Implications of the Emerging NSF for Children', Conference, 22 January 2003, www.dh.gov.uk

Asch, Adrienne, 'Distracted by Disability' (1998) 7 *Cambridge Quarterly of Healthcare Ethics* 77–87

Bainham, Andrew, 'Do Babies Have Rights?' (1997) 56 CLJ 48–50

'Parentage, Parenthood and Parental Responsibility: Subtle, Elusive Yet Important Distinctions' in Andrew Bainham, Shelley Day Sclater and Martin Richards (eds.), *What is a Parent? A Socio-Legal Analysis*, Hart: Oxford, 1999, 25–46

'Resolving the Unresolvable: The Case of the Conjoined Twins' (2001) 60 CLJ 49–53

'Can We Protect Children and Protect Their Rights?' (2002) 32 *Family Law* 279–89

Baker, Hannah, 'MMR: Medicine, Mothers and Rights' [2004] CLJ 49–52

Bartlett, Katharine, 'Re-Expressing Parenthood' (1988) 98 *Yale Law Journal* 293–340

Bashir, Martin, 'Living with the miracle of Gracie', *Sunday Times*, 3 August 2003

Baum, J. D. Sister F. Dominica and R. N. Woodward (eds.), *Listen. My Child Has a Lot of Living to Do: Caring for Children with Life-Threatening Conditions*, Oxford University Press: Oxford, 1990

BBC News, 'Travesty of brain-damaged success', 22 March 1999 (http://news. bbc.co.uk)

Bedford Helen and Elliman, David, 'Concerns about Immunisation' (2000) 320 BMJ 2401

Bender, Leslie, 'Frontier of Legal Thought III: Feminist (Re)Torts: Thoughts on the Liability Crisis, Mass Torts, Power and Responsibilities' (1990) *Duke Law Journal* 848–912

Beresford, Bryony, *Positively Parents: Caring for a Severely Disabled Child*, Social Policy Research Unit, HMSO: London, 1994

Expert Opinions: A National Survey of Parents Caring for a Severely Disabled Child, Policy Press: Bristol, 1995

Bloor Michael, and James McIntosh, 'Surveillance and Concealment: A Comparison of Techniques of Client Resistance in Therapeutic Communities and Health Visiting' in Sarah Cunningham-Burley and Neil P. McKeganey (eds.), *Readings in Medical Sociology*, Routledge: London, 1990

Bluebond-Langner, Myra, *The Private Worlds of Dying Children*, Princeton University Press: Princeton, 1978

Boggan, Steve, 'The girl that nobody saved', *Independent*, 6 December 1993

Boseley, Sarah, 'We were deliberately lied to', *Guardian*, 22 October 2002

Bradford, Keith, 'Not a penny', *Bristol Evening Post*, 4 July 2001

Brannen, Julia, Kathryn Dodd, Ann Oakley and Pamela Storey, *Young People, Health and Family Life*, Open University Press: Buckingham, 1994

Brazier, Margaret, 'Retained Organs: Ethics and Humanity' (2002) 22 *Legal Studies* 550–69

'An Intractable Dispute: When Parents and Professionals Disagree' (2005) 13 Med Law Rev 412–18

Brazier Margaret, and Nicola Glover, 'Does Medical Law Have a Future?' in David Hayton (ed.), *Law's Future(s): British Legal Developments in the 21st Century*, Hart: Oxford, 2000, 371–88

Bridge, Caroline, 'Religion, Culture and Conviction – the Medical Treatment of Young Children' (1999) 11 CFLQ 1–15

'Religion, Culture and the Body of the Child' in Andrew Bainham, Shelley Day Sclater and Martin Richards (eds.), *Body Lore and Laws*, Hart: Oxford, 2002, 265–87

Bridgeman, Jo, 'Because We Care? Children and Medical Treatment' in Sally Sheldon and Michael Thomson (eds.), *Feminist Perspectives on Health Care Law*, Cavendish: London, 1998, 97–114

' "Learning from Bristol": Healthcare in the 21st Century' (2002) 65 MLR 241–55

'The "Patient at the Centre": The Government Response to the Bristol Inquiry Report' (2002) 24 JSWFL 347–61

'The Child's Body' in Mary Evans and Ellie Lee (eds.), *Real Bodies: A Sociological Introduction*, Palgrave: Hampshire, 2002, 96–114

'After Bristol: The Healthcare of Young Children and the Law' (2003) 23 *Legal Studies* 229–50

'Caring for Children with Severe Disabilities: Boundaried and Relational Rights' (2005) 13 *International Journal of Children's Rights* 99–119

'When Systems Fail: Parents, Children and the Quality of Healthcare' (2005) 58 *Current Legal Problems*, Jane Holder and Colm O'Cinneide (eds.), Oxford University Press: Oxford, 2006, 183–213

British Medical Association, *The Law and Ethics of Male Circumcision: Guidance for Doctors*, 2006

Buchanan, Allen, and Dan Brock, *Deciding for Others: The Ethics of Surrogate Decision Making*, Cambridge University Press: Cambridge, 1989

Burton, Tony, 'We've got our little girl back', *Daily Mail*, 29 October 1992

Campbell, Tom D., 'The Rights of the Minor: As Person, As Child, As Juvenile, As Future Adult' in Philip Alston, Stephen Parker and John Seymour (eds.), *Children, Rights and the Law*, Clarendon Press: Oxford, 1992, 1–23

Chief Secretary to the Treasury, *Every Child Matters*, Cm 5860, London, September 2003

Choudhry, Shazia and Helen Fenwick, 'Taking the Rights of Parents and Children Seriously: Confronting the Welfare Principle under the Human Rights Act' (2005) 25 OxJLS 453–92

Clement, Grace, *Care, Autonomy and Justice: Feminism and the Ethic of Care*, Westview Press: Boulder, 1996

Conaghan, Joanne, 'Tort Litigation in the Context of Intra-familial Abuse' (1998) 61 MLR 132–61

'Tort Law and Feminist Critique' (2003) 56 *Current Legal Problems*, M. D. A. Freeman (ed.), Oxford University Press: Oxford, 2004, 175–209

Cross, David, 'Judge allows brain-injury baby to die', *The Times*, 17 April 1989

Davies, Andrew, 'Judge rules that doctors must let ill baby die', *Daily Telegraph*, 25 February 2006

Day, E., 'Do Not Resuscitate – and don't bother consulting the family', *Sunday Telegraph*, 14 March 2004

Department for Education and Skills, *Every Child Matters: Change for Children*, 2004

Department for Education and Skills, Department of Health, Home Office, *Keeping Children Safe: The Government's Response to the Victoria Climbié Inquiry Report and Joint Chief Inspectors' Report Safeguarding Children*, Cm 5861, September 2003

Department of Health, *The NHS Plan: A Plan for Investment, A Plan for Reform*, Cm 4818-I, 2000

Guide to Consent for Examination or Treatment, March 2001

Consent – What You Have a Right to Expect: A Guide for Parents, July 2001

Learning from Bristol: The Department of Health's Response to the Report of the Public Inquiry into Children's Heart Surgery at the Bristol Royal Infirmary 1984–1995, Cm 5363, January 2002

Getting the Right Start: National Service Framework for Children: Standard for Hospital Services, April 2003

Making Amends: A Consultation Paper setting out Proposals for Reforming the Approach to Clinical Negligence in the NHS, a report by the Chief Medical Officer, June 2003

National Service Framework for Children, Young People and Maternity Services, October 2004

Choosing Health: Making Healthy Choices Easier, November 2004

NHS Redress: Statement of Policy, 2005

Department for Work and Pensions, *Vaccine Damage Payments* (HB3), April 2004

Diduck, Alison, 'Justice and Childhood: Reflections on Refashioned Boundaries' in Michael King (ed.), *Moral Agendas for Children's Welfare*, Routledge: London, 1999, 120–37

'Solicitors and Legal Subjects' in Jo Bridgeman and Daniel Monk (eds.), *Feminist Perspectives on Child Law*, Cavendish: London, 2000, 251–70

Law's Families, LexisNexis UK: London, 2003

Dobson, Barbara, Sue Middleton and Alan Beardsworth, *The Impact of Childhood Disability on Family Life*, Joseph Rowntree Foundation: York, 2001

Douglas, Gillian, 'The Retreat from *Gillick*' (1992) 55 MLR 569–76

Downie, Andrew, '*Re C (HIV Test)*: The Limits of Parental Autonomy' (2000) 12 CFLQ 197–202

Duckwort, Lorna, 'Parents may face legal battle over surgery on twins who share a heart', *Independent*, 5 February 2002

Dyer, Clare, 'HIV Positive Girl made Ward of Court after Father Refuses to Allow her Treatment' (2002) 324 BMJ 1178

Eekelaar, John, 'The Emergence of Children's Rights' (1986) 6 OxJLS 161–82

'Are Parents Morally Obliged to Care for their Children?' (1991) OxJLS 340–53

'Parental Responsibility: State of Nature or Nature of the State?' (1991)13 JSWFL 37–50

'The Importance of Thinking that Children have Rights' in Philip Alston, Stephen Parker and John Seymour (eds.), *Children, Rights and the Law*, Clarendon Press: Oxford, 1992, 221–35

'Families and Children: From Welfarism to Rights', in Christopher McCrudden and Gerald Chambers (eds.), *Individual Rights and the Law in Britain*, Clarendon Press: Oxford, 1994, 301–33

'Rethinking Parental Responsibility' (2001) 31 *Family Law* 426–30

'Beyond the Welfare Principle' (2002) 14 CFLQ 237–49

Elton, Anne, Peter Honig, Arnon Bentovin, Jean Simons (1995) 310 BMJ 373–7

Evans, Ruth (Chair), *The Report of the Independent Inquiries into Paediatric Cardiac Services at the Royal Brompton Hospital and Harefield Hospital* (April 2001)

Feder, Ellen K., 'Doctor's Orders: Parents and Intersexed Children' in Eva Feder Kittay and Ellen K. Feder (eds.), *The Subject of Care: Feminist Perspectives on Dependency*, Rowman and Littlefield: Lanham, 2002, 294–320

Fennell, Phil, 'Withdrawal of Life Sustaining Treatment for a Child without Parental Consent' (2000) 8 *Medical Law Review* 125–9

'The Right of a Treatment Proxy to Challenge a Decision to Administer Diamorphine to a Patient' (2004) 12 Med Law Rev 317–22

Finch, Janet, 'The Proper Thing To Do' in John Eekelaar and Mavis Maclean (eds.), *A Reader on Family Law*, Oxford University Press: Oxford, 1994, 63–98

Finch, Janet and Jennifer Mason, *Negotiating Family Responsibilities*, Routledge: London, 1992

Fisher, Lorraine, 'Judge tells mums: give your girls MMR jabs; outrage at ruling', *Mirror*, 14 June 2003

Fortin, Jane, '*Re C (Medical Treatment)*: A Baby's Right to Die' (1998) 10 CFLQ 411–16

'Rights Brought Home for Children' (1999) 62 MLR 350–70

'The HRA's Impact on Litigation Involving Children and Their Families' (1999) 11 CFLQ 237–55

Children's Rights and the Developing Law, Reed Elsevier: London, 2003

Fox, Marie and Jean McHale, 'In Whose Best Interests?' (1997) 60 MLR 700–9

Fox, Marie and Michael Thomson, 'Short Changed? The Law and Ethics of Male Circumcision' (2005) 13 *International Journal of Children's Rights* 161–81

Freeman, Michael, 'Freedom and the Welfare State: Child-Rearing, Parental Autonomy and State Intervention' (1983) JSWL 70–91

'Taking Children's Rights More Seriously' (1992) 6 *International Journal of Law and the Family* 52–71

The Moral Status of Children: Essays on the Rights of the Child, Martinus Nijhoff: Netherlands, 1997

'The Sociology of Childhood and Children's Rights' (1998) 6 *International Journal of Children's Rights* 433–44

'Can We Leave the Best Interests of Very Sick Children to Their Parents?' in Michael Freeman (ed.), *Law and Medicine, Current Legal Issues 2000*, Oxford University Press: Oxford, 2000, 257–68

'Feminism and Child Law' in Jo Bridgeman and Daniel Monk (eds.), *Feminist Perspectives on Child Law*, Cavendish: London, 2000, 19–45

'Whose Life is it Anyway?' (2001) 9 Med Law Rev 259–80

Frey, R. G. and Christopher Morris (eds.), *Liability and Responsibility: Essays in Law and Morals*, Cambridge University Press: Cambridge, 1991

General Medical Council, *Guidance for Doctors who are Asked to Circumcise Male Children*, 1997

Seeking Patients' Consent: The Ethical Considerations, November 1998

Gillies, Val, 'Meeting Parents' Needs? Discourses of "Support" and "Inclusion" in Family Policy' (2005) 25 *Critical Social Policy* 70–90

Gilligan, Carol, *In a Different Voice: Psychological Theory and Women's Development*, Harvard University Press: Cambridge, MA, 1982

Gordon, Alison, 'Daniel family backs mother; "We want to end tragic boy's treatment, too"', *Mail on Sunday*, 17 May 1992

Gottlieb, Roger S., 'The Tasks of Embodied Love: Moral Problems in Caring for Children with Disabilities' (2002) 17 *Hypatia* 225–36

Graham, Hilary, 'Caring: A Labour of Love' in Janet Finch and Dulcie Groves (eds.), *A Labour of Love: Women, Work and Caring*, Routledge and Kegan Paul, London, 1983, 13–30

Graycar, Regina, 'The Gender of Judgments: An Introduction' in Margaret Thornton (ed.), *Public and Private: Feminist Legal Debates*, Oxford University Press: Melbourne, 1995, 262–82

Grubb, Andrew, 'Treatment Decisions: Keeping it in the Family' in Andrew Grubb (ed.), *Choices and Decisions in Health Care*, John Wiley and Sons: Chichester, 1993, 37–96

Hall, David M. B. and David Elliman (eds.), *Health for All Children*, 4th edn, Oxford University Press: Oxford, 2003, www.health-for-all-children.co.uk

Harrington, John A., 'Deciding Best Interests: Medical Progress, Clinical Judgment and the "Good Family"' [2003] 3 Web JCLI

Harris, John, *The Value of Life: An Introduction to Medical Ethics*, Routledge and Kegan Paul: London, 1985

'Human Beings, Persons and Conjoined Twins: An Ethical Analysis of the Judgment in *Re A*' (2001) 9 Med Law Rev 221–36

'Law and Regulation of Retained Organs: The Ethical Issues' (2002) 22 *Legal Studies* 527–49

Harris, Paul, 'Amazing Gracie', *Daily Mail*, 8 July 2003

'Doctors say my son is doomed. But he smiles, he cries, and he deserves to live', *Daily Mail*, 9 March 2006

Hart, H. L. A., *Punishment and Responsibility: Essays in the Philosophy of Law*, Clarendon Press: Oxford, 1968

Health and Social Care Information Centre, *NHS Immunisation Statistics England 2004–05*, 2005

Henricson, Clem, *Government and Parenting: Is there a Case for a Policy Review and a Parents' Code?*, Joseph Rowntree Foundation: York, 2003

Herring, Jonathan, 'The Welfare Principle and the Rights of Parents' in Andrew Bainham, Shelley Day Sclater and Martin Richards (eds.), *What is a Parent? A Socio-Legal Analysis*, Hart: Oxford, 1999, 89–105

'The Human Rights Act and the Welfare Principle in Family Law – Conflicting or Complementary?' (1999) 11 CFLQ 223–35

'Farewell Welfare?' (2005) 27 JSWFL 159–71

Hewson, Barbara, 'Killing Off Mary: Was the Court of Appeal Right?' (2001) 9 Med Law Rev 281–98

'When Maternal Instinct Outweighs Medical Opinion' (2004) 154 NLJ 522–3

Hickman, Martin, 'Dhasmana: Not allowed to operate on children', *Independent*, 20 June 2002

Hollander, Julia, 'Why is there no one to help us?' *Guardian*, 28 May 2003

Home Office, *Supporting Families: A Consultation Document*, 1998

Honoré, Antony, *Responsibility and Fault*, Hart: Oxford, 1999

Hughes, Judith, 'The Philosopher's Child' in Morwenna Griffiths and Margaret Whitford (eds.), *Feminist Perspectives in Philosophy*, Macmillan: Hampshire, 1988, 72–89

Huxtable, Richard, '*Re C (A Child) (Immunisation: Parental Rights)* [2003] EWCA Civ 1148' (2004) 26 JSWFL 69–77

Huxtable, Richard and Karen Forbes, 'Case Commentary – *Glass v United Kingdom*: Maternal Instinct v Medical Opinion' (2004) 16 CFLQ 339–54

James, Adrian L., and Martin P. M. Richards, 'Sociological Perspectives, Family Policy, Family Law and Children: Adult Tinkering and Sociological Tinkering' (1999) 21 JSWFL 23–39

James, Allison, and Adrian James, *Constructing Childhood: Theory, Policy and Social Practice*, Palgrave Macmillan, Basingstoke, 2004

James, Allison, Chris Jenks and Alan Prout, *Theorizing Childhood*, Polity Press: Cambridge, 1998

James, Allison and Alan Prout (eds.), *Constructing and Reconstructing Childhood: Contemporary Issues in the Sociological Study of Childhood*, Falmer Press: London, 1997

Jenks, Chris, *Childhood*, Routledge: London, 1996

'Sociological Perspectives and Media Representations of Childhood' in Julia Fionda (ed.), *Legal Concepts of Childhood*, Hart: Oxford, 2001, 19–42

Jenkins, Russell, 'Staff were right to let boy die, mother told', *The Times*, 10 May 2005

Jotangia, Dhriti et al., *Obesity Among Children under 11*, DoH in collaboration with the Health and Social Care Information Centre, April 2005

Kennedy, Ian, *Treat Me Right: Essays in Medical Law and Ethics*, Clarendon Press: Oxford, 1988

Bristol Royal Infirmary Interim Report, *Removal and Retention of Human Material*, May 2000

The Report of the Public Inquiry into Children's Heart Surgery at the Bristol Royal Infirmary 1984–1995: Learning from Bristol, CM5207(I), July 2001 (the Kennedy Report)

Keown, John, 'Restoring Intellectual Shape to the Law After *Bland*' (1997) 113 LQR 481–503

Key, Sarah, 'Huge payout "will open floodgates": 5.4m for heart-op boy who suffered brain damage', *Bristol Evening Post*, 7 December 2002

Kingdom, Elizabeth, *What's Wrong with Rights? Problems for Feminist Politics of Law*, Edinburgh University Press: Edinburgh, 1991

Kiss, Elizabeth, 'Alchemy or Fool's Gold? Assessing Feminist Doubts About Rights' in Mary Lyndon Shanley and Uma Narayan (eds.), *Reconstructing Political Theory: Feminist Perspectives*, Polity Press: Cambridge, 1997, 1–23

Kittay, Eva Feder, *Love's Labor: Essays on Women, Equality and Dependency*, Routledge: New York, 1999

'When Caring is Just and Justice is Caring: Justice and Mental Retardation' in Eva Feder Kittay and Ellen K. Feder (eds.), *The Subject of Care: Feminist Perspectives on Dependency*, Rowman and Littlefield: Lanham, 2002, 257–76

Lamb, Brian and Sarah Layzell, *Disabled in Britain: Behind Closed Doors: The Carer's Experience*, SCOPE: London, 1995

Lamb, Brian and Richard Percival, *Paying for Disability, No Fault Compensation, Panacea or Pandora's Box?* Spastics Society, London, 1992

Laming, Lord (Chair), *The Victoria Climbié Inquiry: Summary and Recommendations*, HMSO, 2003

Law Commission Working Paper No. 91, *Family Law, Review of Child Law: Guardianship* (1985)

Law Commission Consultation Paper No. 139, *Consent in the Criminal Law* (1995)

Lewis, Jane and Elaine Welsh, 'Fathering Practices in Twenty-Six Intact Families and the Implications for Child Contact' (2005) 1 *International Journal of Law in Context* 81–99

Lim, Hilary and Jeremy Roche, 'Feminism and Children's Rights' in Jo Bridgeman and Daniel Monk (eds.), *Feminist Perspectives on Child Law*, Cavendish: London, 2000, 227–49

Lupton, Deborah and Lesley Barclay, *Constructing Fatherhood: Discourses and Experiences*, Sage: London, 1997

Maclean, A. R., 'The Human Rights Act and the Individual's Right to Treatment' (2000) 4 *Medical Law International* 245–76

Maclean, Mavis, 'Letting Go . . . Parents, Professionals and the Law in the Retention of Human Material after Post Mortem' in Andrew Bainham, Shelley Day Sclater and Martin Richards (eds.), *Body Lore and Laws*, Hart: Oxford, 2002, 79–89

Maclean, Mavis and John Eekelaar, *The Parental Obligation: A Study of Parenthood Across Households*, Hart: Oxford, 1997

Maidment, Susan, 'Children and Psychiatric Damages – Parents' Duty of Care to their Children' (2001) 31 *Family* Law 440–4

Maxwell, Margaret, 'Medical triumphs, children's tragedies', *Independent*, 3 September 1993

Mayall, Berry and Marie-Claude Foster, *Child Health Care: Living with Children, Working for Children*, Heinemann Nursing: Oxford, 1989

McDermott, Laura, 'Food Promotion to Children: A Time for Action' (2004) *Childright* 14–16

McHaffie, Hazel E. and Peter W. Fowlie, *Life, Death and Decisions: Doctors and Nurses Reflect on Neonatal Practice*, Hochland and Hochland: Cheshire, 1996

McHaffie, Hazel E. in association with Peter W. Fowlie, Robert Hume, Ian A. Laing, David J. Lloyd and Andrew J. Lyon, *Crucial Decisions at the Beginning of Life: Parents' Experiences of Treatment Withdrawal from Infants*, Radcliffe Medical Press: Abingdon, 2001

McIvor, Claire, 'Expelling the Myth of the Parental Duty to Rescue' (2000) 12 CFLQ 229–37

Mencap, *No Ordinary Life*, Mencap: London, 2001

Menkel-Meadow, Carrie, 'Portia in a Different Voice: Speculating on Women's Lawyering Process' (1987) 1 Berkeley Women's LJ 39

Michalowski, Sabine, 'Is it in the Best Interests of a Child to have a Life-Saving Liver Transplantation? *Re T (Wardship: Medical Treatment)*' (1997) 9 CFLQ 179–89

  'Sanctity of Life – Are Some Lives More Sacred Than Others?' (2002) 22 *Legal Studies* 377–97

Midgley, Carol, 'She wanted to come back as a butterfly', *The Times*, 23 May 1996

Mihill, Chris, ' "Working class hero" fought for transplant girl', *Guardian*, 12 November 1993

Minow, Martha and Mary Lyndon Shanley, 'Revisioning the Family: Relational Rights and Responsibilities' in Mary Lyndon Shanley and Uma Narayan (eds.), *Reconstructing Political Theory: Feminist Perspectives*, Polity Press: Cambridge, 1997, 84–108

Montgomery, Jonathan, 'Children as Property' (1988) 51 MLR 323–42

  'Time for a Paradigm Shift? Medical Law in Transition' (2000) 53 *Current Legal Problems*, Michael Freeman (ed.), Oxford University Press: Oxford, 363–408

  Health Care Law, Oxford University Press: Oxford, 2003

Morris, Anne, 'Treating Children Properly: Law, Ethics and Practice' (1999) 15 PN 249

Morris, H. (ed.), *Freedom and Responsibility: Readings in Philosophy and Law*, Stanford University Press, 1961

Munro, Vanessa, 'Square Pegs in Round Holes: The Dilemma of Conjoined Twins and Individual Rights' (2001) 10 *Social and Legal Studies* 459–82

Naffine, Ngaire, 'Sexing the Subject (of Law)' in M. Thornton (ed.), *Public and Private: Feminist Legal Debates*, Oxford University Press: Australia, 1995, 18–39

  'Who are Law's Persons? From Cheshire Cats to Responsible Subjects' (2003) 66 MLR 346–67

Nelson, Hilde Lindemann, 'Always Connect: Towards a Parental Ethics of Divorce' in Julia E. Hanigsberg and Sara Ruddick (eds.), *Mother Troubles: Rethinking Contemporary Maternal Dilemmas*, Beacon Press: Boston, 1999, 117–35

Neustatter, Angela, 'Children: should their lives be in their own hands?', *Independent*, 3 October 1993

Newdick, Christopher, *Who Should We Treat? Rights, Rationing and Resources in the NHS*, Oxford University Press: Oxford, 2005

Nicholson, Richard, 'Dignity and the doctor's duty', *Guardian*, 2 September 1993

Oakley, Ann, 'Women and Children First and Last: Parallels and Differences between Children's and Women's Studies' in Berry Mayall (ed.), *Children's Childhoods: Observed and Experienced*, Falmer Press: London, 1994, 13–32

O'Donnell, Kath, 'Case Commentary – Re C (Welfare of Child: Immunisation) – Room to Refuse? Immunisation, Welfare and the Role of Parental Decision Making' (2004) 16 CFLQ 213–29

O'Donovan, Katherine, *Family Law Matters*, Pluto Press: London, 1993

Office for National Statistics, *The Health of Children and Young People*, March 2004

O'Neill, Onora, 'Rights, Obligations and Needs' (1985) 6 *LOGOS: Philosophic Issues in Christian Perspective* 29–47

  'Children's Rights and Children's Lives' (1988) 98 *Ethics* 445–63

O'Neill, Sean, 'Payouts in heart babies scandal could top £50m', *Daily Telegraph*, 16 July 2001

Parker, Stephen, 'The Best Interests of the Child – Principles and Problems' in P. Alston (ed.), *The Best Interests of the Child: Reconciling Culture and Human Rights*, Oxford University Press: Oxford, 1994, 26–41

Pearson Report, *The Report of the Royal Commission on Civil Liability and Compensation for Personal Injury*, Cmnd 7054, 1978

Pedain, Antje, 'Terminating Care' [2004] CLJ 306–9

  'Doctors, Parents, and the Courts: Legitimising Restrictions on the Continued Provision of Lifespan Maximising Treatments for Severely Handicapped, Non-Dying Babies' (2005) 17 CFLQ 535–44

Pendlebury, Richard, 'Cancer victim who was treated with love loses his battle; A mother's dream dies with her brave little boy', *Daily Mail*, 22 July 1993

Penna, Sue, 'The Children Act 2004: Child Protection and Social Surveillance' (2005) 27 JSWFL 143–57

Phillips, Melanie, 'Laura has become a surgical guinea-pig', *Observer*, 5 September 1993

Priaulx, Nicky, 'That's One Heck of an "Unruly Horse"! Riding Roughshod over Autonomy in Wrongful Conception' (2004) 12 *Feminist Legal Studies* 317–31

'Joy to the World! A (Healthy) Child is Born! Reconceptualizing "Harm" in Wrongful Conception' (2004) 13 *Social and Legal Studies* 5–26

Prout, Alan and Allison James, 'A New Paradigm for the Sociology of Childhood? Provenance, Promise and Problems' in Allison James and Alan Prout (eds.), *Constructing and Reconstructing Childhood: Contemporary Issues in the Sociological Study of Childhood*, Falmer Press: London, 1997

Quick, Oliver, 'Disaster at Bristol: Explanations and Implications of a Tragedy' (1999) 21 JSWFL 307–26

Read, Janet, *Disability, the Family and Society: Listening to Mothers*, Open University Press: Buckingham, 2000

Read, Janet and Luke Clements, *Disabled Children and the Law*, Jessica Kingsley: London, 2002

'Demonstrably Awful: The Right to Life and the Selective Non-Treatment of Disabled Babies and Young Children' (2004) 31 *Journal of Law and Society* 482–509

Reece, Helen, 'The Paramountcy Principle: Consensus or Construct?' (1996) 49 *Current Legal Problems*, Michael Freeman (ed.), Oxford University Press: Oxford, 267–304

Divorcing Responsibly, Hart: Oxford, 2003

'From Parental Responsibility to Parenting Responsibly' in Michael Freeman (ed.), *Law and Sociology, Current Legal Issues 2005*, Oxford University Press: Oxford, 2006, 459–83

Ribbens McCarthy, Jane, Rosalind Edwards and Val Gillies, 'Moral Tales of the Child and the Adult: Narratives of Contemporary Family Lives under Changing Circumstances' (2000) 34 *Sociology* 785–803

Ross, Lainie Friedman, *Children, Families and Health Care Decision-Making*, Clarendon Press: Oxford, 1998

Royal College of Paediatrics and Child Health, *Withholding or Withdrawing Life Sustaining Treatment in Children: A Framework for Practice*, 2 edn, 2004

Royal Society for the Prevention of Accidents, *Child Accident Statistics*, www.rospa.com/factsheets/child_accidents.pdf

Ruddick, Sara, 'The Idea of Fatherhood' in Hilde Lindemann Nelson (ed.), *Feminism and Families*, Routledge: New York, 1996, 205–20

Seton, Craig, 'Heart baby's surgery success', *The Times*, 26 November 1987

'Mother talks of "cruel fate": heart baby's death', *The Times*, 7 December 1987

'Hole in heart boy is dead', *The Times*, 15 February 1988

Sevenhuijsen, Selma, *Citizenship and the Ethics of Care: Feminist Considerations on Justice, Morality and Politics*, Routledge: London, 1998

'A Third Way? Moralities, Ethics and Families: An Approach Through the Ethic of Care' in Alan Carling, Simon Duncan and Rosalind Edwards (eds.), *Analysing Families: Morality and Rationality in Policy and Practice*, Routledge: London, 2002, 129–44

Sheldon, Sally and Stephen Wilkinson, 'Conjoined Twins: The Legality and Ethics of Sacrifice' (1997) 5 Med Law Rev 149–71

Singer, Peter, *Rethinking Life and Death: The Collapse of our Traditional Ethics*, Oxford University Press: Oxford, 1995

Smart, Carol and Bren Neale, *Family Fragments?* Polity Press: Cambridge, 1999

Smith, Roger, 'Parental Responsibility – and an Irresponsible State?' (1990) 71 *Childright* 7–8

Strong, S. I., 'Between the Baby and the Breast' (2000) 59 CLJ 259–63

Tronto, Joan, 'Women and Caring: What Can Feminists Learn about Morality from Caring?' in Alison M. Jaggar and Susan R. Bordo (eds.), *Gender/Body/ Knowledge: Feminist Reconstructions of Being and Knowing*, Rutgers University Press: New Brunswick, 1989, 172–87

Moral Boundaries: The Political Argument for an Ethic of Care, Routledge: New York, 1993

Urban Walker, Mary, *Moral Understandings: A Feminist Study in Ethics*, Routledge: New York, 1998

Weaver, Lawrence, 'Is science exploiting Laura's suffering?' *Daily Mail*, 1 September 1993

Wells, Celia, 'Whose Baby Is it?' (1988) JLS 323–41

'Patients, Consent and Criminal Law' (1994) JSWFL 65–78

West, Robin, 'Jurisprudence and Gender' (1988) 55 *University of Chicago Law Review* 1–72

Westlake, Debra and Maggie Pearson, 'Child Protection and Health Promotion: Whose Responsibility?' (1997) 19 JSWFL 139–58

Williams, Clare, *Mothers, Young People and Chronic Illness*, Ashgate: Hampshire, 2002

Williams, Kevin, 'Abusing Parents and Children: *JDv East Berkshire Community Health NHS Trust and Others*' (2005) 1 *Professional Negligence* 196–201

Wittig, Christian, 'Physical Damage in Negligence' (2002) 61 CLJ 189–208

Wolf, M. Susan 'Shifting Paradigms in Bioethics and Health Law: The Rise of a New Pragmatism' (1994) 20 Am J L and Med 395–415

Wright, Jane, 'Negligent Parenting – Can My Child Sue?' (1994) 6 *Journal of Child Law* 104–9

Young, Bridget, Mary Dixon-Woods, Kate C. Windridge and David Heney, 'Managing Communication with Young People who have a Potentially Life Threatening Chronic Illness: Qualitative Study of Patients and Parents' (2003) 326 BMJ 305

No author given, '10-hour operation to save heart boy', *The Times*, 14 January 1988
  'Please let my son die', *Daily Mail*, 16 May 1992

Websites

Bristol Royal Infirmary Inquiry, www.bristol-inquiry.org.uk (written statement of parents: Paul Bradley, Rowena Cutter, Susan Francombe, Angela Good, Andrew Hall, Karen Meadows, Jonathan Mallone, Penelope Plackett, Brenda Rex, Sandra Rundle, Lesley Smith, Mary Thorn)

Charlotte Wyatt's story is told from the perspective of her parents on the website http://charlottewyatt.blogspot.com

David Glass's story is told by his family at www.members.tripod.com/davidglass1

The EPICure study, www.nottingham.ac.uk/obgyn/EPICure/index.htm

Every Child Matters, www.everychildmatters.gov.uk

Information for parents and professionals about child health, www.health-for-all-children.co.uk

Office of the Children's Commissioner, www.childrenscommissioner.org

Routine vaccination schedule for children, www.immunisation.nhs.uk

Royal Society for the Prevention of Accidents, www.rospa.com

Scope, disability organisation supporting people with cerebral palsy, www.scope.org.uk

INDEX